DOMESTICATING THE CLERGY: THE INCEPTION OF THE REFORMATION IN STRASBOURG 1522-1524

AMERICAN ACADEMY OF RELIGION
DISSERTATION SERIES

Edited by
H. Ganse Little, Jr.

Number 17

DOMESTICATING THE CLERGY
THE INCEPTION OF THE REFORMATION IN STRASBOURG
1522-1524

by
William S. Stafford

SCHOLARS PRESS
Missoula, Montana

DOMESTICATING THE CLERGY: THE INCEPTION OF THE REFORMATION IN STRASBOURG 1522-1524

by

William S. Stafford

Published by
SCHOLARS PRESS
for
The American Academy of Religion

Distributed by

SCHOLARS PRESS
University of Montana
Missoula, Montana 59801

DOMESTICATING THE CLERGY: THE INCEPTION OF THE REFORMATION IN STRASBOURG 1522-1524

by
William S. Stafford
Brown University
Providence, Rhode Island 02912

Ph.D., 1974
Yale University

Adviser:
Steven E. Ozment

Library of Congress Cataloging in Publication Data
Stafford, William S
Domesticating the clergy.

(Dissertation series - American Academy of Religion ; no. 17)
Originally presented as the author's thesis, Yale, 1974.
Includes bibliographical references.
1. Reformation—France—Strasbourg. 2. Clergy—France—Strasbourg. 3. Strasbourg—Church history. I. Title. II. Series: American Academy of Religion. Dissertation series - American Academy of Religion ; no. 17.
BR372.S8S8 1976 274.4'3835 76-15567
ISBN 0-89130-109-7

Printed in the United States of America
Edwards Brothers, Inc.
Ann Arbor, Michigan 48104

Acknowledgments

This essay has its roots in two rather different worlds of scholarship. During a year of research in Strasbourg, many people steadied my first wobbling steps in the patient science of local history. I thank the staff of the Archives Municipaux de Strasbourg for its great help to me. M. Rudolphe Peter lent me a private copy of his thesis on Clemens Ziegler, and helped initiate me into the eccentricities of Strasbourg libraries. M. Marc Lienhard read early drafts of the chapters on Zell and Bucer. His criticisms of my text and his discussions of Zell's thought were very helpful. I extend thanks to M. Jean Rott, whose erudition and encyclopaedic recall of detail might be frightening, were they not of one substance with his gentleness and grace. M. Joseph Fuchs gave over much time to introducing me to German paleography. The profound and generous hospitality which his family extended to mine is a memory I shall not soon lose.

On the other side of the Atlantic, my warm thanks go to Prof. Miriam Chrisman. She introduced me to sources, lent me her manuscripts, wrote letters of introduction, and gave me very intelligent and highly useful advice. I have had occasion to disagree with details of her study of the Strasbourg Reformation, but never with her. Prof. Steven Ozment, my director, read the text as it was produced. His searching criticism brought it as near to maturity as it has come. I owe him very much for having taught me the craft of intellectual history over the past five years; I owe him very much as a person.

That I remained one man through it all I owe chiefly to my wife, Barbara.

"Tant que je vive mon cueur non changera
Pour nul vivant, tant soit il bon ou saige,
* * * * * *
Mon choix est fait; autre se ne fera
Tant que je vive...."

William S. Stafford
New Haven, 1974

Acknowledgments to the AAR Dissertation Series Edition

I should like to thank Prof. Ganse Little, the editor of the series, for permitting me to revise the swollen notes of the original dissertation, chiefly by translating or omitting long German and Latin quotations. I owe special thanks to Prof. Wendell Dietrich, the chairman of the Department of Religious Studies at Brown University, for his help and encouragement. Brown University granted me the funds for retyping the manuscript. Finally, I should like to acknowledge my debt to Prof. Steven Ozment, which grows at each step of my career.

William S. Stafford
Providence, 1976

Table of Contents

Introduction

When Martin Luther circulated his ninety-five theses on indulgences in the fall of 1517, he laid foundations for many different interpretations of the movement which was to follow. Some of those who later probed the avalanche which had thundered over Germany found Luther's bitter protest against Tetzel's sale of grace from streetcorners lying nearest to the surface. The medieval church was filthy with "abuses"; the Reformation had scrubbed her face. Others, probing deeper, found Luther's ideological reasons for attacking indulgences. Years of intense study of medieval soteriologies had led the young Doctor of Sacred Scripture to a radically new theory of salvation; his attack on ecclesiastical practice was secondary. Thus the Reformation was of doctrine, not of morals. A third party combined the findings of the other two. Vague theory and abusive practice had steamed and smeared the church's face beyond recognition; her children followed a stranger, thinking her to be their mother.

What has embarrassed all alike is the difficulty of accounting for the fact that the common people of Germany joined the movement. Very little evidence at all can be found to indicate that "abuses" such as clerical concubinage were graver in the sixteenth century than in the fourteenth. Still, it is clear enough that there was popular anger at the clergy's alleged derogation from its consecrated status. Yet why should that anger have led to destruction of the very standard of clerical 'holiness' on which the anger was based? It is no easier to account for the Reformation's popularity by reference to innovative doctrine. How could illiterate masses understand Luther's criticism of the principle of *facere quod in se est*? And if they had understood it, what could have torn them from the obvious common sense of saying that God will help those who try?

Also awkward is the failure of all efforts to discount the sincerity and depth of pre-Reformation piety. From all external indications, German towndwellers guarded as intense a "churchly" piety in 1520 as they had in 1450.[1] The Reformation was not the work of religiously indifferent people. It was those who were well-integrated in medieval religious values who turned against them. How could it happen that a pious people should, in the space of a few years, cast off a religion, an entire set of self-understandings and values, a whole spectrum of institutions which had defined their lives and the lives of their fathers? Why would a family which had given of its substance to provide a holy picture for the use of the faithful return to remove it from the church? Iconoclasm is not random destructive behavior. It had clear ideological content; it was a slap in the face of medieval piety. People broke statues not because they hated beauty, but because the objects had been holy to them, a holiness which had been discredited, which they had come to hate.

That is to say that accompanying the vast institutional changes of the Reformation was change in popular religious "knowledge," in the understandings by which people defined themselves and their social relations. Whatever the historical sources for change in religious culture may be, the change itself includes essentially 'cognitive' characteristics. Culture is the set of objectivated covenants, the agreed-upon norms and structures which humans invent to shape their lives. In premodern societies, religious "knowledge" had a crucial role in legitimating the rest of culture. For individuals and for groups, conferring ultimate validity on social "understandings" was extremely useful. Divine sanctions strengthened sexual morés; by offering ways to fit death into a comprehensible world, the gravest threat to the plausibility of social structure was cushioned.[2]

The complex and highly developed society of medieval Europe enjoyed a corps of experts to keep religious legitimations in good repair. Theologians and canon lawyers, men like Thomas Aquinas or Gabriel Biel, helped render sophisticated, plausible, and effective medieval society's means for dealing with the situations threatening the stability of human "understandings." As clergymen, in principle the devoted sons of established religious institutions, they had an obvious conservative bias. Yet medieval universities offered professors significant independence. Doctors of Theology were expected to discredit others' ideas, on the basis of individually developed judgments of their plausibility and social effects. Professors could develop theories significantly at variance with official religious institutions, though it was difficult to maintain them for long.

Much of medieval theological theory had not only a social but a class reference. Not only did it maintain the religious legitimations of society in general, but it functioned as the ideology of the clerical estate. Religious theory justified the existence of a social class which lived by transferring religious 'goods' from God to the people and serving God on the community's behalf. Theology both shaped and was shaped by institutions defining the nature and functions of the clergy. The entire institutional edifice within which medieval people sought salvation was predicated on the theory that men could be forgiven of guilt by the church and then restored to true worthiness through the habit of love. The grace which made both steps possible was mediated by the "work" of the secular clergy. Theory and institution were linked. Gross changes in the actual shape of the church clearly required a corresponding development of theory, and altered theory put religious institutions in question. When Luther concluded that indulgences were in conflict with a correct understanding of how humans could gain confidence in the face of death and chaos, his attack had potential implications for the finances of the diocese of Mainz, for the stone in the walls of St. Peter's in Rome, and for the orphanage in Strasbourg; not only the concept of the 'treasury of merit' was at issue.

Yet the chief question remains. To admit that an innovative theory might contradict practice does not show how the former could change the latter, especially in the face of lively defense of conservative theory. Luther's ideas had potentially revolutionary social consequences; but how could they move from the brain of the scholar to the actions of a man on the street? In Strasbourg, heretics had been seen before; once their blasphemy had been recognized, they were burned. Yet this time, the "official" values of the city appeared to adapt themselves to those of the heretics, leading to extensive reconstruction of religious institutions in the city. In 1520, no one in Strasbourg argued openly against the sanctity of the Mass; yet in 1525, the Mass was effectively abolished. How could this happen? How could pious people attack their own religion? That question itself is one version of a larger one: were elements of the old religious culture preserved or exploited in the new? In the actual political struggle to make the new ideas official, which group's interests and which ideas proved decisive? Did the changed "understandings" and changed institutions correspond to the original objectives of the reformers? Did radical religious theory significantly contribute to changing mass religious culture and the institutions which depended on it?

As a contribution to answering these questions, this essay will examine the changes in the conception of the clerical estate during the first years of the evangelical movement in Strasbourg.[3] It is a useful issue for a variety of reasons. Theories of the function of the clergy rest immediately on central theological issues such as the concept of justification and the means by which God extends his grace to the human soul. Innovation in such matters implies adjustments in the concept of the clergy. On the other hand, the concept of the clergy has immediate consequences for the entire fabric of religious institutions. If the medieval clergy's claim to mediate grace were discredited, the clerical institutions stretching along the *via salutis* would be called into question. Further, the nature of the clerical estate was an issue of primary importance during the first years of the evangelical movement in Strasbourg. The evangelical preachers' polemic against the medieval clergy was one of their most successful weapons. How did the original "insights" of the reformers require adjustments in the clergy's nature and function? In what form did the evangelical preachers 'package' those ideas for the community? In the political struggle in Strasbourg, how did the new reform program exploit reforms already underway? What interests were finally decisive? How did influential groups understand and employ the new conceptions of the clergy's status and function? And did these understandings, once rooted in Strasbourg social values, correspond to the reformers' original objectives?

To respond to these questions, we shall first analyze the form and the content of the ideas propagated in Strasbourg by the evangelical preachers. By examining tracts written for laymen, we can discern the preachers' theological motives and their intended social consequences, while discovering the precise ways in which they explained their program to laymen and tried to persuade them of its merits. Their ideas can thus be seen in their full ideological range, from decisions about the nature of grace or of religious community, to the slogans designed for political conflict. We shall then turn to the political process by which formal changes in the legal parameters governing the clergy were won. By analyzing the development of the policy of the city council (the Rat) toward the clergy during the crucial first years of the evangelical movement, we can examine in detail the constellation of interests and conceptions involved in the struggle, including their roots in late medieval Strasbourg. Further, analysis of the struggle will permit us to locate the social groups whose decisions and actions were chiefly responsible for the preachers' apparent success. In the final chapter, we will examine the development of new conceptions of the ideal character and social position of the clerical estate among the general population. Once in the people's hands, what became of the preachers' program?

In the late middle ages, religious ideas were not merely an idle amusement for the academic elite. They functioned as the ideology of social groups which had great influence on the political and social condition of late medieval towns. It was because of this that a new theory of grace and salvation could become the vehicle for profound social reform.

Chapter 1

Mathis Zell and the Medieval Clerical Estate: Human Law vs. God's Word

The sermons of Mathis Zell dominated the early years of the evangelical movement in Strasbourg. Although two priests before Zell had preached "in an evangelical manner", they were silenced immediately. It was Zell's criticism of the clergy and Zell's projects for reform that first attracted wide attention to evangelical ideas. It was his supporters, including members of the Strasbourg Rat, who established a beachhead for the new Gospel in the city. If the constellation of ideas under which the movement grew was substantially augmented by Martin Bucer and Wolfgang Capito after they arrived in the city in mid-1523, it remains true that to understand the issues which dominated Strasbourg's reformation of the medieval clerical estate, it is to Zell that we must first turn.[1]

Zell, born in Alsace in the same town as Geiler, studied at Maintz and Erfurt, finally taking a master's degree at Freiburg im Breisgau in 1505. In 1517 he was named Rector of the university in Freiburg, but in 1518 he accepted the pastorate of the Cathedral parish church of St. Laurentz in Strasbourg. He was named episcopal *penitentiarius*, for dealing with the confessions of grave sins reserved to the Bishop himself for absolution.

In 1521, Zell apparently defended Luther from the pulpit, and then began to preach in a "Lutheran" manner himself. The Bishop tried and failed to have the Cathedral chapter bring Zell's employers, the *Deputaten* (the lower chapter of the Cathedral), to dismiss or restrict him.[2] During the fall of 1522, informants gathered evidence from Zell's sermons, and on December 22, Zell was cited to appear before the episcopal Vicar to respond to charges formally presented by the Fiscal, Gervasius Sopher.[3] The charges were stated in a list of twenty-four articles, which described Zell's links to Luther, specified heretical statements he had made, and attempted to link him to a revolutionary peasant preacher.[4] The legal process dragged on after Zell protested against the legal form of the first hearing.[5] Apparently he met with some success, for on March 10, 1523, the Bishop complained to the Rat of the threatening behavior of Zell's supporters at a hearing currently in session.[6]

Later that year, Zell's first publication, the Christeliche Verantwortung (Christian Defense), appeared in Strasbourg bookshops.[7] It was obviously an outgrowth of the legal defense he had presented before the Vicar. Since Zell refers to two versions of his defense, it seems probable that the original Latin version was prepared for a formal ecclesiastical hearing.[8] It is tempting, however, to identify the Latin version with the Rechtfertigung which Zell presented to the Vicar in March, 1523.

The German version of the Christeliche Verantwortung was certainly not completed before late spring of 1523, and probably not before early summer.[9] It had become Zell's vehicle for making his case to the entire population of Strasbourg.[10] Although it kept the form of answering the twenty-four articles one by one, it went far beyond a mere legal defense. Under the pretext of answering the first three articles, Zell launched a two hundred page polemic defending Luther against the charge of heresy and describing "the imprisonment of the church", two rubrics under which he could fit whatever issues he pleased. The Christeliche Verantwortung is no legal brief. It is a polemic against the platform of Zell's local opponents, an appeal to sympathetic members of the hierarchy, a tract aimed at the lay population. The book is the first presentation of evangelical ideas printed by a Strasbourg preacher. In it, we can observe both Zell's ideological motives and the specific ways in which he made his appeal to the people of Strasbourg.

In 1524, Wolfgang Koppfel, Zell's printer, described the _Christeliche Verantwortung_ as a "weapon chest."[11] The description is apt. One finds heaped in the book all the weapons necessary to dismember the medieval church establishment. The book, Zell himself admits, is repetitious and long-winded; its frequent incoherence hurts its effect as a sustained treatise.[12] Yet it was none the less accessible to any literate Strasbourgeois, each portion a weapon for the reform-minded. Each issue that Zell treats -- the ban, marriage, penance -- presents on a small scale Zell's basic argument: that ecclesiastical institutions that do not rest on the Word of God cannot please God, and are therefore soteriologically functionless or destructive; and that they have been prostituted for the sake of the clergy's holiness-cloaked greed. The language is simple and colloquial. The examples are intended for common artisans, drawn from daily business.

The _Christeliche Verantwortung_ recapituates the sermons that touched off the reformation in Strasbourg. It reproduces long sections of sermons from 1522; throughout, it is highly sermonic in style.[13] Zell's preaching possesses the same immediacy to a lay audience, and the same lengthy detours, as Geiler's; only the ideology has changed. Unlike Geiler's reform efforts, the _Christeliche Verantwortung_ is more than a call for the moral renewal of a basically unchanged medieval church. It contains the ideas that first persuaded the population of Strasbourg that ecclesiastical institutions demanded radical reformation.

Zell's ideology is based on ideas disseminated from Wittenberg, on Luther's metamorphosis of medieval religion. Luther's radical attack on the medieval church was the product of changes in his concept of religious justification.

Years before the Indulgence Controversy, Luther's commentary on the Psalms had begun to express the theory that the human conscience gains real security only by believing God's promises, his Word. Humans have no resources that are valid before God; any attempt to develop such resources, as by learning habitually to act out of love or by stripping the soul to its divine spark, deludes the conscience and distracts it from its only sure ground.[14] The theses on indulgences of 1517 were Luther's first, conservative statement of the institutional consequences of this theory. As Luther rejected more and more of the ecclesiastical practices founded on medieval theories of salvation,[15] he came to believe that the medieval ecclesiastical system, both in doctrine and in law, was dedicated to giving consciences delusive alternatives to true faith. If the church is no more than the instrument by which God realizes his chosen means of saving souls, Luther concluded, its authentic role was limited to presenting God's Word to the conscience. Since the Word alone was effective in rescuing and governing the hearts of believers, nothing that the hierarchical, external church might invent or command independently of the Word could claim any certain validity. Once shown that the church's lawmaking had no salvific value, it was clear that the church had no right to make binding laws. Luther's effective reform treatises of 1520, _De Captivitate Babylonica Ecclesiae_ and _An den christlichen Adel_, attacked the medieval hierarchy's claims authoritatively to represent God. Scripture, as the only reliable source of God's Word, provided the sole authentically divine institutions for believers, all dedicated to fostering faith in God's promise.[16]

The logical order of these ideas, and the order of Luther's own historical development, is that change in the concept of justification should precede adjustments in the role of the church. Yet that is not the order of the Christeliche Verantwortung.[17] Zell's polemic is not against medieval concepts of salvation but against medieval church government. To defend Luther from the charge of heresy, Zell does not present issues such as sin and grace, but rather the apostolic succession. He wastes little paper on the uselessness of good works coram Deo; his target is the useless, lazy, gorging, swilling upper clergy. Systematic examination of Zell's arguments, however, shows that each one quietly rests on Luther's system of salvation. But the Christeliche Verantwortung is Zell's major statement of his ideas, addressed to an audience far exceeding his already-initiated parishioners. Why does he set cart before horse?

Zell does not work from a popular sense of the failure of the medieval system of salvation. Rather, he incites and exploits resentment against the clergy.[18] The consistent pattern of the Christeliche Verantwortung is to seize a traditional point of irritation between the laity and the clergy -- the clergy's wealth, its immunity from the troubles and burdens of lay life, its sexual instability, the overuse of the Ban -- and to trace it back to the clergy's power to make laws, which they use to maintain their luxurious status as oppressors and exploiters of the poor. Once he has shown that the root of each grievance is in the tyrannical use of religious legislative power, he then argues from exegesis of Scripture that this tyranny is a distortion of the way in which God intends himself to be represented in human society. The divine mandate of priests is no more than to proclaim the Word, to announce God's promise, to free oppressed consciences. Every man has equal access to a holy life achieved by faith. The Christeliche Verantwortung treats Luther's theory of salvation as an ideology that explains and offers an alternative to a situation in the corpus christianum which the consciousness of a divinely-sanctioned alternative has rendered intolerable. Those attracted by that ideology are gradually led to understand the relation between the individual and God in a new way. Beneath the polemic against the sacral structures of the church, Zell quietly teaches a new sort of piety, the new life of the believing man freed from the old categories of "holiness."

The Attack on the Clergy

The *Christeliche Verantwortung* is seldom free from bitter anticlerical polemic. At every turn, in every issue raised, Zell returns to the ignorant, selfish, exploitative greed of his opponents. Yet Zell is something other than a traditional rabble-rouser, whipping up anticlerical scandal on the basis of conventional moral standards. His name-calling is intended to dislodge public opinion from its passive belief in the fundamental validity of the religious establishment.

This pattern first becomes clear in the introduction to the *Christeliche Verantwortung*. Zell's first target is his accusers. He finds it wholly natural that he should be falsely charged with destroying the honor of God and the holy customs of the church; persecution is always the result of the confrontation between truth and established falsehood. Hypocritical defenders of the "establishment" always seek to preserve their own existence by using religion as a shield. For example, the manufacturers of idols at Ephesus who rioted against Paul took "the honor of Diana" as a pretext; their real intention, of course, was to keep their livelihood secure. So it is with the clergy. "Under the appearance [*Schein*] of religion, justice, the right, and the honor of God and of his saints, we also sought our own advantage and profit." Martyrs such as Stephen were killed precisely because they threatened to expose a self-serving religious establishment. Anyone who seeks "to bring things into right order, exercise, and use" can expect a like fate, since "that sort of restoration of God's rightful honor and justice can scarcely occur without pulling up the deeply rooted abuses by which some of these people make their living, of course protected by the false appearance [of religion]." The reformation of radically corrupt institutions requires that established interests be upset -- thus the truth-teller is a "destroyer." But once the "false appearance" of the clergy is exposed as a sham, there can be no argument in favor of silence:

> So, for the sake of their bellies, should we be kept in faithlessness? Because it leads to their disadvantage, should no one speak the truth? Must we carry these burdens forever on their account? So they can live softly, tranquilly, idly, splendidly, must we be always restless, always dying?[19]

This is not simply an attempt to smear his accusers. It is his first move in a campaign to discredit the clergy's "appearance," their religious pretensions, the consecrated character which for centuries had guaranteed their privileged status in medieval society.

The first step in discrediting the religious pretensions of the clergy is taken under the guise of answering the Bishop's first article by defending Luther from the charge of heresy. While searching for a standard to define heresy, Zell attacks each of the medieval institutions which claim the power to define orthodox doctrine. In the event of a profound schism, how may the correct side be identified? Papal and imperial rulings get astonishing short shrift. How can they be reliable, when such courts may be ill informed and vulnerable to deception by interested parties? Further, all doctors and fathers who have written on the Scriptures have erred. Their obvious contradictions -- the dispute between Jerome and Augustine, for example -- prove that they do not possess perfect divine authority.[20] The canon law is rotten with contradictions; it can scarcely be the work of the Holy Spirit, who never contradicts himself. Yet it is popes and councils who have produced these contradictions, sometimes so glaring that even scribes cannot reconcile them and must proclaim some canons dead letters. The books of scholastic theologians are no better. Their very method is to set opinion against opinion, quarreling over trivialities instead of proclaiming the urgent Word of Scripture.

If some portion of Zell's argument rests on the observed vulnerability of the hierarchy to sub-lunary influences, his chief weapon is the principle that the Holy Spirit cannot err or contradict himself. Whenever thereafter he observes contradiction or error in some source of religious authority, he can dismiss it.[21]

Zell's lightning campaign through the ranks of medieval religious authority seeks to destroy one of the most fundamental assumptions of the Catholic tradition, that the orthodox fathers of the church, as their views are articulated by episcopal councils and by the chair of Peter, express the only divinely authoritative interpretation of Scripture. Of course, since Zell wishes to teach in a manner that conflicts with official doctrine, it is in his interest to discredit the process by which doctrine becomes official. But Zell's target is higher. The power of the hierarchical church to define true doctrine was the cornerstone of its claim to mediate between God and man, to govern souls by God's voice, to be the visible _potentia Dei ordinata_. The church was a visible corporation capable of hierarchical government in part because it could define doctrinal articles to which the baptized had to assent and on the basis of which heretics could be identified and ejected. It had the right to do so because its head and its councils were inspired by the Holy Spirit. Zell's argument threatens both the institutional integrity of the hierarchical church, and its divinity.

Zell's intention, however, is not to leave society without a sure divine voice, but to preserve that voice from human distortion and abuse. His search for the marks that betray human origin stops at Holy Scripture, the certain Word of God, the voice of the Holy Spirit. He turns his bitterest polemic on those clerics who question the divine origin of the Bible. They are the true heretics, for heresy requires pertinancia, contumacy in error, including those who harden in error for personal advantage.[22] The great heretics at least based their errors on a few verses which they refused to interpret by clearer passages in Scripture; this lot seeks to evade Scripture's condemnation of their lives by casting Scripture itself in doubt. They are not Christians at all, rather complete skeptics. Zell rejects a total desacralization of human society. He leaves standing one visible, objective, fully divine authority: the Word of God, the Scriptures. It is above all human writers, no matter how high, holy, or learned.[23] It is the sole legitimate foundation for the institutions of the true church, the only means for determining Gods' will. Throughout the Christeliche Verantwortung Zell continues to develop his conviction that the Scriptures are a fully sufficient authority for every legitimate need of the church. They are permanent and complete, God's eternally valid and efficacious Word. They need no addition, no supplement, no adjustments. The church owes its existence and power to them, not merely historically but actually. It is only in witnessing to God's Word that the church is a divine institution.[24]

This isolation of the Word as the source of religious authority is the hinge upon which the rest of Zell's argument turns. Of course, it frees Luther from the charge of heresy; if all other human teachers err and are still not heretics, then why should Luther alone be pilloried?[25] But more importantly, it gives Zell an independent source of divine authority from which to criticize the medieval church. Scripture becomes a sword that can cut down sacred institutions while permitting its wielder to remain pious. It becomes a legal means for dissolving sacred law; one can distinguish the intention of the legislator, God, from the laws of his pretended ministers, remaining loyal to the former while disobeying the latter. One can affirm a valid and stable religious government without supporting the entire edifice of medieval theology and law. One can attack sacral divisions of society without threatening to leave it godless.

Once Scripture is established as the sole valid foundation of religious institutions, Zell presses home his attack on the clergy. Under the rubric, "Who is really the heretic?", Zell considers the central biblical "proof texts" for the papacy and the apostolic succession, comparing Luther's interpretation with the traditional exegesis. He concludes that Scripture restricts the power of the clergy to the proclamation of God's Word.[26]

Zell quickly disposes of the Matthew 16 passages, "You are Peter, and on this rock I shall build my church," and "I shall give you the keys of heaven." The meaning of the texts has been distorted so as to support ecclesiastical tyranny. Would Christ found his church on a man who can die, or fall into heresy or mortal sin, and thus leave the church without a foundation? Obviously, the gates of hell do in fact prevail against the pope and his court. Rather, the head of the church is Christ, and the "rock" of its foundation is faith in Christ. These are invincible.[27]

Again: Christ's gift of the keys has been turned into a license for the church to imitate secular princedoms, to make laws and rule subjects, with pretended divine sanction for their every act. But if Christ had wanted the church to rule the world in that manner, why did he bother with the Crucifixion? He could simply have transferred the kingdoms of the earth directly into Peter's hands. But in fact, Christ confined the church to spiritual power through preaching the Word. Luther, Zell asserts, interprets the power of the keys as the use of the Word to release consciences, or to terrify them by excommunication.[28]

Zell reserves his strongest attack for his caricature of medieval interpretations of Luke 10:16, "He who hears you hears me."

> They interpret this passage so that we are duty-bound to obey them in everything they command us to do, whether grounded in Scripture or not. And if that is so, we Christians are absolutely the most miserable people on earth. Why? Other peoples which are not Christian have nothing more than a secular government, which takes enough away from them and weighs them down well enough with laws. Outside of that, they have no further duty to anyone. We Christians are already pressed by secular government, which, however, must be borne, since the Lord teaches us that we are to obey it. But then these people come and give us one commandment on top of the other, so that they burden our souls as well. Already burdened by secular government as to our lives and belongings, these people give over our souls to the devil...If we violate [their laws], we sin mortally and go to hell, since they

> interpret this passage as forcing us to attend to them in all things.[29]

The traditional exegesis is nothing but a prop for "lazy, incompetent, tyrannical dealings." Luther's alternative, says Zell, is a clergy limited to preaching the saving Word of God.

> When we hear the servants of the Word of God preach [that Word], we ought to remember that we hear Christ himself...[Christ] sent out [the Apostles] two by two to preach the kingdom of God; whoever hears them, hears [Christ] himself. He gave them the Word and command that he received from his father, to proclaim the kingdom of God to the world...But everyone can consider for himself if preaching the kingdom of God means saying and ordering whatever we want or whatever might serve our temporal splendor, as, sadly, we have been hearing for a long time.[30]

At great length, many times throughout the Christeliche Vertantwortung, Zell reinforces the idea he introduces here. He affirms an apostolic succession, but he limits its power to the communication of a divinely received message.[31] The clergy has no right to go any further than the pure Word of God. Scripture witnesses "that we are commanded to preach only the Gospel and the word that Christ spoke to us, nothing further." If that was so for the apostles, how much more for their successors, who are all the more likely to "trouble the clear springs of God's Word"? Paul curses even angels who proclaim something else, "not to mention the Pope or the Bishop."[32]

In a long illustration, Zell describes how the

perversion of the clergy's divine commission has permitted clerical tyranny. A lord orders his servant to go to some poor prisoners and bring them a message -- the way to freedom, or at least a means of making the imprisonment glad and easy until they are wholly freed. But the servant, instead of bringing this good news, brings chains and irons and gags, refusing to permit them to eat or drink or talk unless they pay him. And, the servant tells the prisoners, when they hear him, they hear God. As proof, he shows them a sealed letter of commission [Credentzbrief], confident he can go on abusing his fellow servants with impunity since his lord is away. But if the prisoners demand to see the contents of the letter, all they find are biblical passages which give him no such rights.[33] The clergy, argues Zell, has a commission to preach the Gospel, which provides no pretext for independent lawmaking.[34] Further, the Gospel is the opposite of law. Preaching the kingdom of God means teaching how God rules in us once we have faith in Christ. That government does not rest on law; it results from the glad willingness to do good that fills the hearts of those who experience the goodness of Christ through faith.[35] The only system of law with a divine source is the law of Moses. Yet Christ came to fulfill the Mosaic law; true representatives of the New Testament, Christ's successors, are no more law-givers than he was. Their message is grace.[36]

The final text Zell examines is Christ's command to Peter to feed [i.e. pasture, "weyden"] his sheep.[37] As the last link in his argument, Zell rests his restriction of the clergy's role on the theory of justification by faith.

> The true pasture, briefly, is God's Word alone..., since by [it] alone can the soul be fed, comforted,

> and sustained in this life. No human word is capable of consoling the troubled soul, since anxiety always accompanies [human words]; all men are liars, only God truthful. Thus [we must] rely only on his Word, have faith in him alone, which faith alone feeds the poor soul, as the Lord makes sufficiently clear in the Gospel. In summary, if the Word of God is the right, true pasture with which souls should be fed on earth, and if Christ came only for the sake of souls and, caring about them, instituted shepherds, then "pasture" can mean nothing but preaching the word of God. From which it follows that whoever is told to "pasture" is not told to rule temporally or to make many laws.[38]

The primacy of the Scriptures and the restriction of the clergy to preaching the Word are radical solutions for tyrannical government. They rest, however, on the theory of the sole efficacy of the Word in the salvation of souls.

The Attack on the Medieval Religious System

Once Zell has established these principles, he pursues concrete institutions and practices which violate them. The two long polemics which follow have distinct rubrics: the first attacks the false good works by which the hierarchy sells counterfeit salvation, the second outlines how clerical tyranny has subverted the means of salvation.[39] The polemics wander far; in many places they parallel each other, and issues are scattered helter-skelter. In spite of this incoherence, Zell's intentions emerge clearly. He tries medieval religious institutions by his new standards. Authentic religious activity springs exclusively from faith, governed by God's Word. Every believer has equal access to a "common", "simple" Christian life based on the Gospel. But the medieval order maintains a separate priestly caste, while it distracts people from the Word. Zell widens his attack on the status of the clergy, and destroys parts of the medieval religious system upon which it rested. He shows that the clergy's special religious status and the burdensome imitation of clerical life imposed on the laity both proceed from the same source: the perversion of God's ordained way of salvation.

The first polemic begins with a discussion of "good works." Zell rejects the church's claim that it must supplement the New Testament's description of the holy life by prescribing additional ways to earn merit. The Scriptures are fully adequate. Paul teaches that salvation occurs only through faith; James describes the works of love that true faith produces. The believer gladly fulfills God's law. This law, however, is the law of love, not the lists of "self-invented" works that the church advertises. These "extra" works have nothing to do with faith; they are performed above and beyond what Scripture orders, for the sake of the pleasure that self-earned merit brings. The "extras" trumped up by the church for the laity -- founding churches, endowing altars, donating bells, or, above all, becoming a cleric -- distract it from what God actually does demand, feeding the poor. And, worse, the clergy has been corrupted by these endowments. Since such self-invented works have a certain appearance of righteousness and piety, (and since the clergy practices them with the greatest éclat), laymen have given great treasure to the church. Greed increasing with wealth, the clergy has broken out into pride, splendor, vice, and the lust to rule. When human reason seeks to displace God's Word, no other result can be expected.[40]

One of these "self-invented good works" is mandatory fasting, more strictly enforced than many really serious divine commands. The interdiction of certain food, whether imposed on monks all the year or on the laity during Lent, is directly opposed to Scripture. Christ says that what one eats does not corrupt the soul; Peter himself was criticized for not believing God's message that all foods are clean. "Christ says no, they say yes, but they still want to be his servants." Zell desacralizes food; what God has purified and blessed is pure on one day as well as the next, in the cloister as well as out. The real motive behind the restriction is that some people do not want to eat "common" food because they want to be regarded as "the perfect." Yet the interdiction of meat is no real burden for these gluttons, who can stuff themselves with fish. The only people hurt are the poor, who must starve themselves during the times of the year when their work is hardest. Such laws pose as aids in reaching God; in fact all they do is introduce the seductive pleasure of merit, distracting from faith, bringing damnation.[41]

This same pattern of attack is used in an issue which Zell regards as much more urgent, clerical celibacy. It is the clearest example of the way in which the medieval clergy twists or suppresses Scripture in order to establish an exceptional "holy life." Ignoring the repeated passages that recommend marriage, the hypocrites prohibit it to the priesthood, throwing a third of the Roman church into sexual promiscuity [hurerey]. If celibacy has an appearance [Schein] of serving God's honor and the salvation of souls, that still gives no one the right to forbid something the Scriptures leave open to all. How is God honored where his Word is held in contempt? "I think that one pays God the highest honor by depending strictly, in the simplest way, on his

Word, giving him the honor that he is truthful and all men liars." Once again, the real motive for celibacy is clerical exclusivity: "The true reasons for this prohibition are to have a great reputation before men, honor, the lust for honor, greed, laziness, to avoid common labor and poverty, to gain bodily pleasure, wealth, and the like."[42]

Scripture makes it clear that the holy life does not depend on celibacy. The patriarchs, several of the apostles, and the Mother of God were all married, reason enough not to forbid it. "It is only from faith that true holiness, the true pleasing of God can come...; but this faith can be the same in marriage or out." If one seeks complete chastity, one may wait for the gift within the holy state of marriage. Faith is true virginity. It makes us dependent on God in such a way that we can be married as if we were not, just as a believer may own goods as if he had nothing.[43] The married are less hindered in God's service than those constantly tortured by sexual temptation and guilt.[44] Zell tosses aside the argument that priestly sacramental activity is inconsistent with sexual congress; if "purity" is so necessary for priests, why drive them all into fornication?[45] He attacks the exclusion of a group of Christians from an institution made necessary by universal human nature, an exclusion without ground in God's Word.

Marriage is a divinely prescribed remedy for inescapable, natural sexual drive. It was made available to every man and woman, and has only been prohibited at bitter cost.[46] Obligatory celibacy has grave effects on all of society. Zell attributes to it the sexual instability which plagues Christendom. The clergy supports large numbers of loose women, giving ready protection to those who desert their families, seducing wives and daughters.[47] The clergy's example is subversive. Guilty themselves, how can they criticize others? Since it is not so bad for "spirituals" to fornicate, many laymen reason, why should it be for us?[48] Thus, in many noble families, only two or three of the men marry, the rest making do with common women or being locked up in monasteries.[49] The institution of marriage, as the sole divinely-ordained alternative to promiscuity, has fallen into general contempt. For what deeper corruption could the devil possibly hope, than that popular opinion should deprecate God's Word? "In these days, people are not as offended by a cleric who constantly exchanges one woman for another, as they are by one who, recognizing his own weakness and not receiving the grace to withstand, enters the chaste estate of marriage, marries a pious girl, with whom he commits himself to suffer both joy and trouble."[50]

The worst consequence is the torture, despair, and damnation of the trapped clergy. Zell describes the agonizing tension of the priest, sworn to live in purity but incapable of continence, never able to repent sincerely of his sins, constantly racked by desire and guilt. Zell sweeps away the bits of rationalization that make the vow seem more tolerable. It makes as much sense first to promise continence and then to pray for the gift as it does to dive into a river and then pray for salvation from drowning; or to borrow money and then pray for the means to pay off the loan. And how can such a prayer be made in true faith, when ninety-nine per cent of the clergy take the vow in order to have a soft, easy life? The comforting thoughts that the vow itself will save them even if they do not keep it, or that God will understand their difficulties and forgive them, are trampled down. Fornication violates God's law; in the Scriptures, he has provided a remedy for fornication. For those who reject that remedy, there is no excuse.[51]

Behind the false religious pretensions of celibacy crouch a rabble of evil interests.[52] It maintains the wealth of the church, since clergymen can have no legitimate family heirs.[53] The constant violations of celibacy bring in great income through ecclesiastical courts. It fills the monasteries, giving those in charge plenty of victims for their tyranny.[54] As to the nobles who send their children to monasteries -- Zell loses his temper. They do it so the family name will not suffer by children having to marry non-nobles or work for a living. By marrying only two or three of their children, and sending the others to the cloister, the family fortune can be kept intact. Yet the families hand their children over to places where they know they will be made whores and degenerates, where they will be driven to sin and finally to despair, insanity, and damnation. "O miserable nobility, o miserable citizenry, who bear their children in order to send them to hell!" They would do better to murder them in their mother's womb, or, still better, to baptize them and then drown them, once they are covered by the blood of Christ. The service of God in the cloister? A lie; "all you care about is that they never come home again."[55]

This circle of law and guilt and exploitation turns on the theory that God is pleased by clerical celibacy. At the end of a polemic against "the prohibition of marriage", Zell underlines the basic principle behind his attack:

> Why do we seek so much piety in things that God has never commanded? Why do we not keep his commandments and rest content [with that]?...They are nothing but hypocrites who, excepting themselves from the rule, take on uncommanded things and leave what is commanded unfulfilled. That is certainly not what it means to honor God. If you want to honor God, do what he has told you to do. By not

> performing what he has not told you to do, you do not dishonor him; yet it is dangerous to do what he has not ordered.[56]

Celibacy, as an essential component of the 'holiness' that separated the clerical caste from the rest of society, is dissolved, because God's Word is uniform for all members of society.

Zell's second chain of polemics against medieval religious institutions builds on the principles already expressed, but adds a new idea. From the standpoint of the canon lawyers and churchmen who had attacked Zell, one of his most dangerous threats was to reject the "liberties of the church", the immunity from secular government traditionally accorded to the church by reason of its "spiritual" nature.[57] Zell denies the charge. He has never violated the church's freedoms, merely spurned them as a Christian should spurn any form of self-interest. But what is the church's freedom, and what is the true church?

> The only church I acknowledge is the one that Christ saved with his blood, the spouse that he purified for himself and married. To the church belong all those who believe in him, wherever they come from, whoever they are, high or low, rich or poor, Jew or gentile, etc. Thus, where there is no faith in Christ...there is no church.

God hates faithless groups that call themselves the church, but the true church he loves. It is not his will that it be enslaved.[58] By defining the church as those who believe, Zell neatly turns the tables on his accusers. It is they, the hypocritical clergy, who imprison the true church. The institutions of the church should not exist merely in the interest of the clergy, but for all who believe, for the masses of the faithful.

Zell begins, naturally, with the traditional Gravamina, the complaints against the financial exploitation of Germans by the papal curia already stated by Jacob Wimpheling and reinforced by Luther.[59] Rome sells Germans licenses to use their own things; they must pay to put their children in benefices they themselves founded. Any provision for their own spiritual needs, such as the founding of a preacher's benefice, is fabulously expensive. All this money goes to foreigners; it is a wonder that there is any money left in Germany.[60]

These are the stock complaints of the long-standing movement to shelter Germany from papal exploitation in the way England and France had done centuries before. Zell's goals are more radical than this, however, and soon he dismisses the argument's importance, if not the sense of grievance he has provoked. Christians can bear robbery of the world's goods in patience. But if it is bad enough to be slaves, it is far worse to be robbed of God's Word and thereby of the soul's hope of salvation.[61] In order to support a greedy clergy cloaked by the spurious holiness of useless activities, the institutions responsible for disseminating the Word have been subverted.

Zell begins with preaching. His chief target is "incorporations." Financially pressed chapters, monasteries, and foundations could "incorporate" parishes, receiving parish incomes, and in return providing for the needs of the parish. As we have seen, Strasbourg chapters had been busy erecting this fence against inflation throughout the late middle ages; more than half of the Strasbourg parishes were incorporated. Zell attacks it as the chief institution strangling the Word of God. The income that ought to provide for preaching, goes to the "lazy, gorging, useless" members of chapters and cloisters, who make only the most contemptible provision for the needs of the parish. Instead of a true shepherd, they send a day laborer [taglöner]. Those preachers not already muzzled by the process of ordination can be kept on a short leash by the prelates who hire them. The chapters would do better to keep the money and send no one, if they would let the people choose a bishop and preacher of their own.[62] The consequence of this exploitation and censorship has been worthless preaching. All that is ever expounded from the pulpit is based on the "three virtues", pride, avarice, and ignorance: pride, the pursuit of scholastic trivialities; ignorance, the stupidity of those provided to country parishes; and especially avarice, the preacher as sales representative of the hierarchy. Busy selling his patrons' goods from the pulpit, the preacher has no time for the Word.[63] Zell repeats and amplifies his condemnation of incorporations throughout the Christeliche Verantwortung.[64] So little money is left to the parishes that no one with any ability will preach.[65] Yet the activities supported by the diverted tithes, the chant, readings, contemplation, are useless to the community, a thousand times less valuable than preaching;[66] tithes belong only to those who work in the Word.[67] Zell argues that the revenues of the church should be directed to its legitimate function, saving souls by the proclamation of the Word.

Zell turns to the sacramental structure. He defines "sacrament" as a sensory or palpable sign of the hidden grace of God; that is, signs by which God's promises are magnified to our consciences and our faith is confirmed, sure comforts against all trials.[68] Whether the rites other than baptism, penance, and the Eucharist are properly called sacraments or only mysteries [mysteria, geheymnuß] is not important.[69] The function of sacraments in the order of salvation has been destroyed by the swarm of laws and regulations that suck the poor dry and poison their consciences. Zell's heaviest condemnation falls upon the yearly cycle of penance and Eucharist to which all medieval people were subject. Referring to his own experience as the bishop's *Penitentiarius*, Zell recounts the endless trivial regulations over which the poor inevitably stumbled so they could be fleeced, the Fiscal's hunting of poor clerics like a fox after a hen.

> If some poor woman miscarries in childbed..., she is sent away to perform a heavy penance. She must weep and pay a fine for what was in no way her sin, but rather her great grief. And what is the worst, it is this way only for the poor little people. The big shots (rather, the robbers, thieves, usurers, simonists, benefice-eaters and so forth) are called gracious sir, high and worthy lord, etc.[70]

After this extortion, the people are required to go to the altar for their allotment of poison. Because their confession might have been incomplete, due to fear or poverty or forgetfulness, they fear the Eucharist as much as death itself. They get no comfort, only damnation, but, driven by the church's law, they go. Even worse is the fate of the young people forced into monasteries. Constantly driven to secret sins, afraid to make their confession for fear of harsh penalties, they finally lose hope of grace and go insane.[71] Again, avarice and the lust to rule are the real causes for these rules, nowhere grounded in Scripture, wholly useless for salvation.

> If they were to teach a common Christian life according to the Gospel, and nothing more, it would soon be said, "That sort of life and teaching is already available in the world; we have to invent some special [besondere] little works and commands, and distinctive clothing and the like, (along side of, if not against, the Gospel) over which we will be lords, and because of which we will be regarded as something better and higher, and be called worshipful, worthy, spiritual fathers and lords." Well, this is only done at the expense of the poor, suffering, imprisoned little people, who must seek the kingdom of heaven...where it is not.[72]

The sacrament of the altar ought to be free, so that it may be received with the proper desire. While not all regulations are bad, turning the sacrament into a legal obligation imprisons the conscience.[73]

Zell then turns to attack the practice of giving the laity only the bread of the sacrament. It is wholly opposed to the Gospel, where Christ instituted the Supper by raising the cup and commanding, "Drink ye all of it." There can be no excuse for contradicting Christ's will, as if the Wisdom of God were not wise enough to forsee the church's needs. "Or perhaps Christ did not erect any distinction between laymen and priests, perhaps because they [laymen] also confess Christ, which is the true ordination and priesthood." Zell, however, is not willing to violate the law unless the soul can be shown to depend on it. Although common faith demands a common administration of the sacrament, laymen should be patient. God can awaken faith without any external sacrament at all; many laymen have more faith in their one species than most of the clergy in their two.[74]

In a similar manner, Zell describes the way that the ban is used and lists of impediments to marriage enforced. In both cases, current practice perverts the original institution as the Scriptures describe it. Both are now used only to exploit the poor. The ban, misused so long that it no longer commands respect by itself, must be enforced by secular government. Yet the church has no right to use such force; its power comes only from the Word.[75]

By confining the divine voice to Scripture and the apostolic succession to those who preach the Word, Zell can effectively criticize the pretension of the medieval clergy to govern souls through religious law. In his attacks on concrete religious practices, he turns his aim to the social hierarchy of religious status. He confronts oppression with a concept of the ministry with no room for elitism. But this oppression comes to be considered as a specifically religious tyranny, an obstruction of the *via salutis*. As Zell argues about the government of the church, he also introduces a new sort of piety. Breaks are appearing in the ties of the religious life to patterns of "holy" institutions, frayed by the idea that men can only relate to God by believing a promise.

The Means of Reform

All attempts to reform the church are frustrated by a deeply intrenched system of corrupt power, which Zell must find some way to bypass. Yet his resources are narrowly limited by a conservative understanding of how governments ought to function. He does not seek to liquidate church government, or even wholly to eliminate the hierarchy, only their lawmaking. If they preach the Gospel, they carry

Christ's own authority.[76] And, as Zell insists in nearly every one of his repeated attacks on incorporations, it is a tragedy that prelates do not preach, because they are the ones the best qualified to do so, the most learned, the most highly respected.[77] Zell even accepts the principle that reform should proceed from the top down:

> [You say:] "I and other worthless people like me are not competent to attack and rebuke the big shots and prelates, rather the other way around." I hear it, and I know it full well. Things ought to proceed according to proper order. High prelates ought to rebuke those beneath them, in due order, according to God's law.[78]

But what is to be done when this chain of authority turns to defending abuses instead of reforming them? Those who have the responsibility of governing and reforming the church are precisely the people most deeply implicated in fleecing the poor and suppressing the Word of God. The pope and bishops are the very ones who founded and defend the useless offices that suck the marrow of the parishes.[79] Because the hierarchy can legislate as it will, the medieval legal system supports corruption instead of offering redress. The theologians and canonists of the church are no resource for reform, either; it was they who developed the false exegesis and wrote the glosses that permit the prelates' tyranny.[80] "We see that those who should lead, who should come to the help of the world's evils, are themselves guilty of such evils."[81] Zell confronts a closed circle of corrupt authority, perverted ideas fostering perverted institutions, with the power of excommunication protecting all.

The principle on which Zell bases his resistance is that the prelates have authority only insofar as they fulfill their proper functions. They exist for a purpose; they are established by the Word of God to pasture souls. If they abuse their position to fleece or devour the sheep and to rob them of the Word, then they ought not to be obeyed. This, for example, was why he felt free to disregard the pope's condemnation of Luther:

> I acknowledge the pope as pope, but my duty toward God is greater. If the pope is pope on the basis of divine Scripture, as he claims, then it is proper even for me to judge from Scripture if he is ruling the papacy so that his government does not lead me and others to damnation. For the same Scripture that (he claims) makes him pope, also sets standards for him [Ziel und regel/ wie er sein soll], by which we can recognize him as a pope and true shepherd. That is true for bishops and other prelates as well. Neither the papal nor the episcopal estate was instituted without any purpose, but rather for the sake of their function [Ampt], as expressed in Scripture. If they carry out their function, we are right to recognize them and pay them all honor. But if they do not do so, who will prevent me from not accepting them? For neither [the pope] nor any other prelate in Christendom was instituted to ruin and lead astray souls..."[82]

No one possesses spiritual authority merely as a result of his formal place in a hierarchy, but in virtue of the role he plays in the economy of salvation.[83]

When those normally responsible for spreading the Word are guilty of stifling it, God eventually intervenes. He sends prophets:

> God does not always rebuke [rulers] through special miraculous signs from heaven. If they do not improve their injustice and wrong-doing, but rather cling to it (as has been done until, finally, it is ruining and leading everyone to hell), there must be someone [to speak out]. Since God does not will that his creation be wholly ruined, he always raises up people through whom he rebukes the rulers.[84]

If necessary, the spirit of God will fill even the lowest and most contemptible of men with zeal for God's honor and for the good of God's people. They are driven to speak the truth, to tear the masks from the faces of the hypocrites by proclaiming the Word. God may employ those who already hold the office of the Word, such as Zell, but if these are silenced he will reach still lower, using men with no official standing at all, even laymen. It is absurd to tell such prophets to wait for a license from the hierarchy. Who ordained the prophets? Did Elijah wait for Ahab's permission? Should a dog wait to bark until the wolf tells him to?[85]

> Perhaps the time has now come for manly, fearless speaking out...Have we not lain in a heavy, hard prison of human laws for a long time, for more than a hundred years? Have these laws not been getting stricter all that time? Well, the Lord promises us in

> Genesis 15 that when the evils are fulfilled, he will free us through his Moses, me and those like me. [We] have been ordered by the lord to go to Pharaoh and to tell him to release the people, that God's people have been tyrannized enough, that God will not suffer the evils of the Amorites any longer.[86]

When the normal structures for expressing God's Word fail, eventually God will bypass the normal human institutions and commission prophets to expose the corruption.

If Zell's instrument of reform, charismatic prophets, has radical overtones, the assault on the hierarchy is kept purely verbal. Zell's weapon is the spiritual power of the Word, not any program of political organization and resistance.[87] There is no question of forced dispossession of the hierarchy, no withholding of tithes, no violence, not even disobedience of tyrannical laws unless the soul is in immediate danger.[88] Only twice does Zell sanction any overt action against religious government: people may attend sermons (though not masses or confession) in churches outside their own parish, and sexually tempted clergymen should marry.[89] In other cases, passive disobedience may be the proper response. For example, if the church annuls a marriage, violating God's Word, the couple must refuse to part.[90] The spiritual freedom proffered by the Gospel includes no right to force the reform of institutions. Individual Christians are capable only of speaking the truth, and of suffering. Further, Zell has hardly any concept of the religious power of the community. Although it seems probable that he was acquainted with Luther's 1523 treatise arguing for the community's right to choose its own pastors, only once does he even suggest that the hierarchy might give permission for such a thing.[91] The secular government receives no important role in Zell's reform. Although at the beginning of the Christeliche Verantwortung he asks the Rat to watch his case closely,[92] his most radical concrete suggestion is that the Rat punish the clergy's concubines.[93] The Rat and the whole community can hear the Word, believe it, and suffer for it, but they have no power to reform the church. Zell does not seek to erect a countervailing spiritual government. By the same principle that denies the use of force to the hierarchy, he denies any power but that of the Word to the evangelical movement.

Zell is exultantly confident of the success of the Word. No one, he says, can know what it will accomplish.[94] He does, however, speculate on the possible means by which the Word may reform the church. If he occasionally expresses the wish that corrupt prelates would simply let believers alone, his greatest hope, clearly, is that the prophetic Word will convert members of the hierarchy, that the clergy will reform itself. What if a bishop were to recognize his duty, humble himself, and begin to preach? What if the princes of the chapters were to direct their incomes toward the needs of the parishes, attracting the learned and qualified to the pulpits, instead of the choir? A precedent would be set. The shame of preaching would disappear, and the office of the Word would be restored in Christendom.[95] It is at this possibility that Zell points his concept of the prophet. He hopes that the prophet-spoken Word will reach those in the clergy who are well-disposed, appealing to all who are not wholly faithless:

> I hope that true, worthy priests and their fellows will not think ill of me because I have cried out against this useless tribe.

> Rather, [I hope] that they will support me and will protect and defend preachers like me, that they will help us scare off these wolves so that this useless class can be extinguished, the Christian church be brought back to its former worthiness and sanctity, and that they, the innocent, no longer have to pay for [the misdeeds of] these hornets. Those who oppose my preaching really ought not to think me and those like me so evil. They hear nothing from us but the truth, as their own consciences tell them. If even only a small spark of belief in Scripture remains in them, they really ought to think. Well, God has sent them prophets to rebuke their wrong-doing. If, out of the obstinancy of their hearts and blindness they refuse to acknowledge it, they should at least acknowledge that we have no right to keep silent.[96]

This is Zell's only suggestion of how God may reform the church. Behind it, though, is great pessimism. Zell repeatedly voices his suspicion that the essential resource for such a reform, a spark of faith in the Scriptures in the hearts of church leaders, has long since been extinguished. Does not their total disregard for their duties suggest that they really believe in nothing at all? Are not some of them seeking to throw the Scriptures themselves in doubt?[97] Behind Zell's technique of exposure looms the power of the Word to change the world much more radically: God may simply take his people out of the hands of the faithless shepherds.[98]

In spite of this threat, Zell's means of achieving

reform do not go far beyond Geiler's.[99] This is one example of Zell's tendency to use potentially radical principles in a conservative manner. He seeks to restore and reform a tyrannical and malfunctioning religious establishment, not to dissolve religious government altogether. Thus he permits Luther's concepts to strip the church of coercive legal power and to reshape its structure so that it serves a new theory of salvation, but he leaves standing an independent and authoritative religious government.

The Reformed Clergy

The fulcrum of Zell's religious government is the parish priest. One of the major institutional changes demanded by Zell is the increased independence and power of the local pastor. Since all clerics are equally creatures and servants of the Word, papal and episcopal monarchy cannot be maintained in its medieval form. Zell denies that the office of bishop is essentially different from the parish priest's. Both are of the same order, both are "overseers" of the people, both are consecrated to preach, absolve, and say mass. That one priest should be charged with overseeing other priests and correcting them by the Word does not argue an essential difference in class. Rather, such distinctions are based on the greater capacity and diligence of certain clerics, who are chosen to supervise without ceasing to be common pastors. Zell offers as a possible parallel the relation between the Ammeister and the other lords of the Rat. Thus, although a hierarchy of function may still exist within spiritual government, there is no essential subordination of one "overseer" to another.[100] This theoretical collegiality is translated into far greater power and status for the local pastor.[101] Zell degrades the non-preaching clergy, demands the redirection of church revenues toward the parish, argues for the right of local pastors to reject orders from the hierarchy, and confines the power of the remaining "prelates" to biblical admonition of erring local pastors.[102] While some room remains for diversity of function within the clergy, religious government comes to be identified with a largely independent local pastorate.

Yet if Zell magnifies the importance and independence of the pastor in relation to the hierarchy, he also maintains the clergy's authority over other Christians. The concept of the priesthood of all believers has little structural effect on Zell's theory of the clergy's role. Before he first introduces it, he devotes a long discussion to the distinction between "priest" and "presbyter." All Christians are priests, but only some are religious governors.[103] And Zell does not question the right of the shepherd to govern the sheep through the Word:

> A "presbyter" is an elder who, as the most learned and experienced in the law of God, is commissioned in the service of God's Word above others in the community, to teach and to rule [regieren] the community. Just as in secular government [regiment] the most experienced and clever are put in government, so it is in matters of faith.[104]

In the Christeliche Verantwortung, the way in which ministers are chosen has little to do with their authority. It is their association with the Word that is crucial. Authority descends from God to preachers of the Word. They are authenticated neither by their relation to the hierarchy nor to the community that chooses them, but by their message.[105] The sheep can distinguish the voice of Christ, but Zell does not deduce any consequent power of the sheep to control their shepherd.[106] His "community" is little more than a wholly undefined mass of individual believers, incapable of independent political organization, ruled by divinely commissioned preachers.

Zell also preserves the independence of religious government from secular government. He does not transfer any religious authority to the magistrate, and he does not attack clerical immunity. He simply does not raise the question of the clergy's obedience to the magistrate. Nowhere does he suggest that the clergy should become citizens, that they should be subject to secular legal jurisdiction, or that their incomes should be taxed or controlled by local government. The only clerical "freedom" he attacks is the alleged "freedom" to make exploitative laws. Thus it is with conviction that Zell can deny that he threatens the church's immunity. If he radically revises the means by which the clergy rules, insisting that the Word alone creates and empowers valid religious institutions, he leaves the concept of a human religious government still standing.

The effects of Zell's ideas on the status of the layman in the church are limited. He does not offer the ordinary Christian a role in the government of the church, only a government that can no longer oppress him. The primary function of the concept of the priesthood of all believers is negative, to destroy the ideology on which clerical exclusivity was built. Yet, although the layman is not turned into a clergyman, his status is enhanced. The priesthood of all believers confirms the independence of salvation from any social or religious status. All men, clergy or lay, who believe, are united with Christ in a bond of such intimacy what what is true of him becomes true of them. Union with God, perfect holiness, is as available to an artisan as it is to a monk. Christ shares his office as priest with all those who, incorporated with him, profit from his perfect sacrifice and intercession.[107] Zell does not leave this priesthood without content. He seeks forms of sacrifice and intercession which, without admitting laymen to the pastorate, will provide for concrete exercise of their priesthood. The sacrifice which all believers may offer is their bodies. By progressively killing their anti-Christian natures, they die with Christ.[108] Zell develops the office of intercession at length, especially in his surprising defense of intercession for the dead. Because all Christians are incorporated in Christ, all may properly pray for each other, whether alive or departed. Zell develops in great detail prayers for individuals to offer at requiem masses.[109] This is more than a bit of devotional conservativism; it is an effort to actualize the believer's priesthood. Zell expects the believer to engage in explicitly religious activity, to hear the Word, receive the sacraments, do penance, pray, worship, meditate, fast, give alms, and the like, all as a priest. Zell's program of ending the hierarchy of religious status, sweeping away medieval sacral patterns, and breaking the social and legal obligation to religious observance would certainly have appeared irreligious to a medieval man. Yet, clearly, Zell's intention is to leave the Christian's piety more sincere, profound, intense, and active.[110]

Implications

Zell's ecclesiology remains conservative in many respects, but it is none the less clear that the concept of justification by faith has caused him to revise his understanding of religion's place in society. The 'clerical estate" is affected the most. There is no longer any question of a ladder of status reaching from the temporal order to the eternal, one's position determined by the degree of participation in sacral institutions. Holiness comes from faith, which Zell refuses to tie to any status.[111] Religious government is treated with a gentler hand; it is still based on a modified hierarchy of authority, even if tied to the Word. Yet it could not have escaped many Catholic churchmen in Strasbourg that an institution that could not make binding laws, to which association was voluntary, which could not coerce even its own officers, and which could be judged by standards independently abstracted from Scripture, had departed rather far from the Church of Innocent III.

As the foundation both of the individual's salvation and of the institutions that govern the *via salutis*, the Word becomes the sole agent of God in the world, the sole divine resource of human society. Clearly, the role of religious institutions in society depends on how this Word is understood to function. As a wholly internal illumination directly from God, it could cut religion away from human institutions altogether. As an objective code of divine law, it could provide the ground for a theocracy. Zell follows Luther in tying the Word to objective, external institutions, to ministers who preach and celebrate the sacraments, refusing fully to implement the concept of the priesthood of all believers. He is not interested in giving individuals or communities direct access to the Holy Spirit. Yet, for Zell, the Word is subjective and internal, in the sense that it can only govern those who believe it, those who recognize Christ's voice in the minister's. Religion, therefore, is voluntary.[112] Further, since the clergy can only represent the grace of the New Testament, not the law of the Old, clerical theocracy is not possible. Yet Zell leaves other possibilities open. In a discussion of impediments to marriage, Zell launches a polemic against Roman law which suggests a wider social application of divine law:

> What does [Roman law] have to do with Christ? Should his law give way to the pagans'? Should it have to be based on the pagans' law? What has Christ to do with pagans? What similarity is there between Christ and Belial, between light and darkness? Don't you think that if we had no pagan law to govern secular affairs, we could rule the world temporally with the divine law given through Moses? The Jews ruled themselves a long time from the law; what would we lack? Indeed, I think that it is because we discarded the divine law and fell to the Roman and Greek lawbooks that we have so much error in both secular and spiritual matters.[113]

Only the ceremonial law of the Old Testament was rendered obsolete by Christ; the judicial law remains intact.

This said, it remains true that the *Christeliche Verantwortung* is directed at the reform of the church, not of all society. The only social evils that concern Zell are those caused by the clergy's tyranny and evil example. While he shows himself rather hostile to medieval secular government and the wealthy classes, and painfully conscious of the misery of the poor, his reform is limited. If he emphasizes the ethical consequences of justification, the kingdom of God in the hearts of men, he draws no general social conclusions from them. The only promise he extends to medieval men is freedom from the clerical tyranny that drains their resources and damns their souls, the end of a hierarchy of status that left laymen barely within the walls of Jerusalem.

The *Christeliche Verantwortung* cuts away the ideological justifications of a ruling class, and yet counsels the oppressed against revolt. Zell incites anticlerical resentment against a corrupt and bloated church, proffering an ideology that can shrink it into a bare instrument of the Word, but then he dams up the current with a highly traditional concept of reform. The advantage this offered to Zell in 1523 is obvious. He needed to disseminate his ideas without so alarming the religious establishment that it would overcome its internal divisions and quash the movement, and he still hoped for internal support. Yet Zell does not avoid sedition for tactical reasons alone. If he wishes to metamorphose the religious government, he also wants to leave it subject only to the Word, free of the secular magistrate, standing above the community. Zell was not so naive as to destroy the church's independence for the purpose of reformation, hoping to restore it once the process was complete. Institutional integrity could be protected only by self-reformation.

Certain strains are obvious. If Zell's concept of reform does not depart far from medieval and humanist models, his goals do. As a traditional medieval preacher newly convinced by Luther, he has no patience for the long processes of education and subtle moral reproof. The Word must be preached boldly, come what may. Yet if bitter and aggressive moral criticism was well within the traditions of medieval preaching, it was based on calling people back to standards they had acknowledged since birth. Zell preaches at the clergy on the basis of ideas that are new.[114] He found some supporting cases; two important members of the hierarchy joined the evangelical movement.[115] Yet, not surprisingly, the Bishop and most of the powerful clergy did not. The "critical mass" needed to start a process of imitative reform among the clergy was never assembled. In contrast, Zell's appeal was effective among the laity. Strasbourg citizens had little enough to lose, and Zell expressed many values that seemed evident to them, if not to the clergy. Obviously, a functional, orderly, unobstructive, less expensive, voluntary church was a much lighter load to carry. Further, Zell's caricature of clerical laziness, tyranny, and sexual instability was linked closely to a similar caricature of the nobles. To citizens whose grandfathers and fathers had struggled for a century to take power from the nobles and to limit what they perceived as their lawless behavior, the exclusively noble chapters and cloisters might well have seemed vestiges of the ancien régime.[116] Zell demanded that the clergy be honest, respectable, and hard working in the same way that citizens were expected to be honest, respectable, and hard working. He discredited what had passed as the clergy's service to the community and the concept of a special "holy" life, thus the distinctive values by which clergymen could be judged. The new standards provided by the Word -- a common pious life, marriage, service to the community, working for one's living -- could not have been very strange to common artisans in Strasbourg.

As the hope for hierarchical reform faded and the pressures from the laity increased, Zell's concept of reform was put under increasing pressure. Strasbourg citizens found it irresistable to cede more and more religious authority to the Rat, bedeviling the future attempts of Strasbourg reformers to maintain an independent religious government. With Zell's intentions and conceptual resources, it is difficult to see any other possible result. Zell strips religious institutions of coercive power, setting free a class of preachers controlled only by the Word, and making religious observance (including many forms of social control) voluntary. If the Word were to fail to provide clear and universally accepted standards of religious practice, religion would be left without any control. In an age in which religious prophets and religious ideology had a hand in almost every movement of social revolution, a powerless but wholly independent church presented the Strasbourg ruling classes with an unacceptable risk. Many among them were convinced by the polemic against the church, and were genuinely moved by a desire for reform, welcoming a pious means to cut through their deadlock with the religious power structure. The pressure from below made change in the church extremely difficult to evade, and yet socially threatening. The institutional vacuum left by reformation ideology proved an irresistable temptation. Secular government, left as the sole coercive ordering agent of medieval society, would be called on at every step of the reform to permit concrete changes, to take over administration, to repress dissent; in short, to provide religion with institutional stability. Capito, Bucer, and Zell were able to find reasons to welcome this regulation and confirmation of the reform. Yet it led to continual conflict between the Rat and the preachers. Bucer, unable to make his voice heard on the issue of church discipline, and then, he believed, sold out by the Rat's acceptance of the Interim, was finally driven to defiance and exile.

Chapter 2

Martin Bucer's Concept of the Ministry

In May, 1523, Martin Bucer arrived in Strasbourg. Excommunicated, married to a nun, and linked to the dead leader of the Knights' Revolt, Franz von Sickingen, Bucer could have expected his presence to be an embarrassment to any town in the Empire. The Rat of Strasbourg granted him physical protection when he first arrived, perhaps for the sake of his father, a citizen, but they refused to shield him from imperial and episcopal judicial process. The Nürnberg Mandate of March had barred all married clergy from holding benefices, thus attempting to cut off those who had taken this open step against church law from any possible income or position of power. Since Bucer's letters seeking a position outside of the Empire had miscarried, he was left without the means to support himself and his wife or to establish a power base from which to work for reform.[1]

The evangelicals in Strasbourg were eager to capitalize on Bucer's presence, temporary or not, as best they could. After a brief pause, Bucer began vernacular lectures on the Gospel of John in Zell's home.[2] The Rat, which was struggling to maintain an appearance of legality over against the Bishop and the collegiate chapters of Strasbourg, told Bucer to desist. Not to be frustrated, he continued his lectures in Latin, dealing with the letters to Timothy, Titus, and the Philippians. The lectures attracted wide interest, and soon Zell felt secure enough to open his parish pulpit to Bucer. He began preaching in August, alternating daily with Zell.[3] The next step was to give his ideas wider circulation through the press. In August and September, three treatises reached Strasbourg bookstalls: Das Ym Selbs (That No One Should Live for Himself), Summary seiner Predig (Summary of His Preaching), and Verantwortung (Apology).[4] These works, the printed form of the ideas which Bucer was preaching to Strasbourg citizens, present a coherent program of reform that reinforces and, in some respects, goes beyond Zell's. Bucer develops a religious theory of society that makes faith the key to achieving a just and stable order in the world. His attack on sacral status and institutions, however, is blunter than Zell's, and uncushioned by any hope in the self-reform of the current religious government. Sharpening Zell's weapons and expanding his appeal to lay values, Bucer added a radical and persuasive voice to the already aggressive evangelical party in Strasbourg.

Das Ym Selbs: Faith and the Social Order

Das Ym Selbs, Bucer's first acknowledged work, is a compact outline of his concept of social reform.[5] It is a constructive reply to those who, facing the "Gospel's" tendency to tear apart social and political groups, found in the concept of justification by faith a license for lawlessness. Bucer argues that a Lutheran concept of faith is the only means of restoring Christian society, the fabric of loving service between men that had sprung from man's original relation to God. In this treatise, intended to persuade hesitant moderates, Bucer places strict limits on his polemics. He confines them to sketches of the manner in which human egotism has corrupted the Three Estates of Christendom, with catastrophic effects on the social order. He does not attack medieval doctrine or piety as such; rather, he seeks to show that reformation ideas will not produce godlessness and chaos, but significant progress toward the kingdom of God on earth. For Bucer, true faith is the only source of human "other-directedness", and thus is the essential cement of society.

Bucer begins his treatise by outlining the origin of the human moral impulse. He creates a metaphysical basis for ethical activity which will allow him to substitute faith for love as the bond between man and God, without losing the drive to do good which springs out of union with God.

> "God created all things for his own sake," thus they all should be directed to him and be of service to him, just as anything that is made must be subject to its maker's will. Now, no creature can serve God, its creator, in his divinity, since its essence is absolutely different from God's....God in his unknown divine essence, not needing our service, since in and from himself he is, has and can do all, can not use our service. However, he shaped us and all creatures so that his goodness should be known and so that anything brought into existence by that goodness should constantly enjoy it and recognize it. Because of this, we his creatures both can and should serve him in this administration of his goodness. That is, each creature ought to serve all others with whatever God has made and given to him, so that this, his praise, increase and be attested everywhere: "The Lord is good in all things, and his mercy is over all his works."[6]

Man's status as God's creature implies a dialectic within the Man-God relation. On one hand, any creature owes service to its creator. This universal principle is apparent in daily life: the cooper quite rightly makes barrels so that he can use them to get his daily bread. Reciprocally, the proper role of the barrels is to be of use to the cooper, just because he made them for that end.[7] The same principle extends to God's creation of all things; if they play their intended role, they will be of service to him.

On the other hand, God needs nothing that man has. There is an unbridgeable gap between the wholly self-sufficient divine being and any creature. Because of this difference in the order of being, man cannot be of any possible direct service to God in himself, any more than a barrel can help a cooper in some specifically human activity like speaking or thinking.[8] Here Bucer assumes that for one being to be of "service" or "use" to another requires that the two beings have some quality in common. It is because the cooper has physical needs that the barrel, a physical thing, can be of help to him; the cooper can trade it for bread.[9] But between God and any creature, man not excepted, there can be nothing in common. Human activity cannot possibly reach God; the natural cannot appeal to the supernatural.

To show how God has prevented the frustration of the creature's natural impulse to serve him, Bucer returns to the concept of creation. God created all things so that they might enjoy and recognize his goodness. The resulting system of administration of God's goodness provides the locus for man's response to his maker: he can devote himself to other creatures' welfare. Bucer regards this service of other creatures as the only possible way to serve the infinite God; man as the "instrument of divine beneficence" can be truly, if indirectly, useful to God.

Bucer expands this pattern -- the creature's duty to the creator finding its outlet in selfless help of other creatures -- into a cosmological principle. It was precisely this order in the universe that permitted God to judge it "very good."[10] Most of the cosmos unreflectingly preserves it:

> Now all creatures are still in this godly state, except the devil and man. For [the other creatures] themselves according to their nature and order, by their good deeds serve all other creatures (not God) with all they are, have, and can do. The sky does not move and shine for itself, but for all other creatures. Even so all plants and animals: whatever they are, have, can do, or do, all is directed at the good and advancement [nutz und fürderung] of other creatures, especially man.[11]

Bucer has found the central ethical principle which will permit him to analyze the sickness of the Estates, and prescribe faith as the cure. Any creature, any man, any human institution, if it is properly related to God, will be characterized by this "other-directedness," by its active participation in God's system of beneficence.

The moral impulse is not the peculiar result of man's high standing in the order of being, nor of special qualities that make him nearer to God than the rest of creation. Rather, human reason and will merely define the specific form that the universal imperative of "other directedness" takes in the case of men.

Man does good to lower creatures by using them properly, by administering them so as to bring them to their proper end most effectively:

> Thus there is no doubt that God gave man the understanding, the ability, and the power to rule over all creatures of the

> earth, the water, and the air, to bring them to good use [ym der zu nutz und gut gebruchen].... In this it is clear how other creatures serve man's good. Man, however, serves them by using them as God has ordered it, since it is to anything's honor and benefit to be used for what it was made, as when one wears clothes, eats bread, drinks wine, takes women for childbearing, sets the wise in council, and all such things.[12]

Man's service is also distinguished from other creatures' by the fact that he is made "in God's image." Bucer never suggests that this "likeness" provides grounds for any direct appeal from man to God. Man's capacity to understand and love spiritually merely gives him the ability to seek not only the physical but the spiritual welfare of a certain class of other creatures, his fellow men:

> But since man was formed in God's image, so that, like God and the angels, he could understand and love even in a spiritual manner, God spoke: "It is not good that man be alone," that is, "does not have anyone like him. Otherwise all things are very good, for all other creatures can be of use and good to him and he to them. Certainly the benefit which he brings to other creatures in using them rightly is still only corporeal. Now, he is formed so that he can also produce spiritual good. But the other corporeal creatures are not receptive [to spiritual good]; my angels do not need it; he cannot reach us. So let us create [his] like, so that, just as we, I, God the Father, Son, and Holy Spirit, have our divine nature and beneficence in

> common, and as the angels, who have fellows of like nature and goodness, man will also have his like, whom he can serve and lead both corporeally and also spiritually, since his nature is of both sorts.[13]

Man's nature makes him potentially receptive to spiritual good and capable of helping others spiritually. On the basis of these capacities, Bucer develops a religious theory of society. The foundation of social institutions is the impulse of the godly man to do good to other creatures. Bucer first demonstrates how the institution of the family, the prime social unit, originates in man's desire, ordered by God, to serve his like. The traditional paradygm for perfect human nature, Adam before the Fall, becomes for Bucer a model for perfect human society, Adam's family before the Fall. Eve is formed precisely so that Adam will have his like, another creature fully receptive to the whole range of love and service of which Adam is capable.[14] Procreation is established for the same reason.[15] In the state of innocence, man's desire to do all possible good to others naturally expresses itself in the fundamental social institution of the family. Human vocation and society are supported by the loving service which man the creature, when rightly related to his creator, naturally extends to all.

If theories of man's ideal nature influence a thinker's prescriptions for the reform of man's actual condition, the nature of the gap between ideal and actual is at least as important. Bucer, having outlined the ideal form of man's social life, must next specify the effects of sin on it.

Man has turned away from God; as a result, he is directed to himself. Instead of seeking the good of other creatures, he seeks his own. The consequences of this egotism are catastrophic. The economy of God's goodness, from which man had profited, is reversed, turned against the rebel. The loving God rejects him, seeking his damnation; the other creatures of the cosmos that once served man now seek his ruin.[16] Man's egotism will continue to disrupt the relations between creatures until the Last Day, when God will restore all things to their proper order. Then, in the renewal of the world, all will enjoy and recognize his goodness again, except for the damned, who will have no part in it.[17] Bucer offers no hope for fully overcoming the gap between ideal and actual within the normal confines of history. Until God acts from outside of history, the millenium cannot come.

Bucer then considers egotism's terribly destructive effects on human society. Using the ethical criteria adduced from the concept of creation, Bucer diagnoses the nearly terminal illness of his own culture.

The analysis proceeds according to the framework of the Three Estates [<u>Stände</u>], priests, rulers, and workers, the social and vocational hierarchy into which medieval men normally divided themselves. Bucer treats these estates as the basic means by which men support the system of God's goodness. "The best and most perfect estate on earth, and the most blessed, is that through which one can serve his neighbor most usefully and to his greatest advancement."[18] Bucer's ethic is not directed simply at the spontaneous, incidental acts of individuals. If a creature properly acknowledges God, his entire character and way of life will be devoted to loving service of his neighbor. Thus human vocations are ranked according to the value of their service to other men. Bucer judges the conduct of each estate, its de facto effect on society, by the same standard. Is a man's way of life any 'good' to his neighbor?

Bucer's verdict is grim. He is relatively unconcerned

by the random crimes and failures of selfish men, for the corruption is far more radical. Egotism has subverted and ruined the ministry and the magistracy, the two social institutions designed precisely to deal with human corruption and malpractice. Neither religion nor law can rescue society if church and state are possessed by piratical individualism.[19] Bucer sees egotism as a corrosive too powerful for any social institution to withstand, the corruptor of the only resources for stability and justice. Society depends upon a general willingness to act for the common good, at least on the part of its leaders. Lacking that, it is robbed of its principle of cohesion, of its very foundation.[20]

Bucer begins his indictment with the ministry, the "spiritual office."

> Since spiritual service excells corporeal, and service to the whole community excells that to individuals, it follows that the Apostolic office, which does not serve various individuals but the community, and not corporeally but spiritually and by that which brings eternal salvation, is the most perfect office, calling, and service.[21]

Bucer places the spiritual office at the apex of society, a judgment which obviously relies on ideas wholly to be expected from a Dominican. He asserts the superiority of the spiritual to the corporeal, using that principle to justify a social hierarchy. Yet he bases the hierarchy of the estates on the value of the service each renders to the community. Bucer insists that it is the function of the spiritual office, the high quality of its usefulness to men, the importance of its role in the administration of God's goodness, that renders it the "most perfect." He does not permit the superiority of the spiritual to become a rationale for the high personal status and privilege of priests. To an occupant of the spiritual office, the proper conclusion from its stature should not be vanity of self-indulgent tyranny, but the most passionate and self-sacrificing service of others. Failing that, it collapses into the lowest and most evil of the estates.

The person who fills the spiritual office is commissioned by God to provide the community with God's Word. By this, he seeks to save the people, serving them in the economy of salvation. Obviously, he must be wholly devoted to the eternal welfare of others, serving at any personal cost. The minister's model is the Apostle Paul, whose devotion was so profound that he could wish to be cut off from Christ if by doing so his brothers could be saved. Those who wish to be the apostles' successors, or in Christ's place, must imitate their selflessness; they must be willing to serve their neighbor even at the cost of their own total ruin.[22]

> Therefore God ought to be asked with the greatest diligence that all those who take on the apostolic dignity and who have put themselves not only in the place of the apostles but of Christ, will not wish to be so far from the example of Christ and the apostles. If they cannot attain the perfection of love that would incline them to surrender their own salvation for the sake of their neighbors' and subordinates' salvation, let them faithfully share the Gospel...and struggle at least to approximate the apostolic temper, without seeking their own shameful profit and vain honor.[23]

But, Bucer claims, in his society the opposite is the case. He denounces the fall of the "spiritual estate" in the most savage terms. The clergy are of the "lowest, most shameful and devilish estate and entirely anti-christian nature."[24] They have completely inverted their proper role in society. Originally provided with worldly goods so that they could better serve the eternal welfare of their fellows, they now struggle to suppress the Gospel in order to keep their rich and powerful status. Abandoning their duty to the community, they seek nothing but their own interest, wholly the reverse of the true Apostolic office. "Therefore avoid their estate and character, if you may; come out of it if you can."[25]

In <u>Das Ym Selbs</u>, Bucer's attack on the medieval clergy is directed at the egotism that has corrupted the spiritual office, not at the normative medieval understanding of the office itself. Rather than accusing the clergy of teaching false doctrine or of burdening the laity with laws, he judges them by a concept of vocation applicable to all estates. Every man, every estate must be devoted to others' good. The specific way in which the clergy ought to do so, by providing for the salvation of souls, has been subverted by their selfishness. Bucer here is not arguing for the reform of an isolated institution, but is diagnosing the source of the corruption of all institutions. Yet his ideas are pregnant. The spiritual state does not exist in its own right, but for the sake of its function. It can be judged by assessing the measure in which it seeks the welfare of the community rather than its own.

When Bucer turns to the second estate, secular government, he expands his treatment considerably. He not only argues that rulers must devote themselves to the common good, but discusses means of guaranteeing that they do so. Bucer defines the office of the magistrate as the use of force to maintain peaceful order, protect the pious, and keep the impious from harming others. "Their service is directed at the whole community, to provide for its welfare with the maintenance of common peace and justice."[26] Referring to Erasmus' quotations from Aristotle and Homer, Bucer sets forth the consensus that the ruler should direct himself exclusively to the welfare of his subordinates. Again, it is crucial that a ruler be other-directed. If it is injurious for one man to neglect his neighbor, how much worse is it if the whole community suffers from a ruler's self-seeking?[27]

Bucer is quite careful to emphasize that the secular government's office is not preaching; it exists only to provide for the external well-being of the community. But Bucer's social ethics permit him to expand the magistrate's role. The magistrate must rule according to divine law, and must assist the advancement of God's Word with all his resources. Bucer leads Romans 13 in an interesting direction:

> However much it may be that temporal rule... does not consist in preaching the divine word and law, still it is proper to it to rule according to divine law and to assist the progress of God's Word with all it can do. For since "there is no power but from God, and wherever power is, it is given order by God," so it surely follows that it ought to be used according to God's order [ordnung] and will. Thus, their service should provide for the welfare of those under their power in such a manner that through it the praise of God grow and he be recognized as ruler of all rulers and king of kings. But this cannot occur (that the subject be well [nutzlich] ruled

> to the true praise of the highest king) where the secular magistrate does not rule according to God's law and is not directed at preserving it. For where God is not recognized and his obedience is not raised up before everything, peace is no peace, justice is no justice, and everything brings harm that should bring good.[28]

For Bucer, a stable and just society must be founded on the right relation of humans to God. Secular welfare cannot exist apart from religious welfare. Thus there can be no question of a truly secular state. If society depends on the ethical fruit of the God-man relation, the magistrate must foster its root. Bucer does not entertain the concept of a non-Christian magistrate who is still legitimate and useful. For Bucer, there is one kingdom of God, not two.[29]

Any attempt by the magistrate to rule independently of divine law not only brands him as a rebel against God's order, but it also provides him an open invitation to rule in his own self-interest. Bucer regards human law and attempts to rule by the use of reason with the greatest suspicion. Divine law is sufficient: "Now we must acknowledge that, just as God immeasurably exceeds human wisdom and cleverness, so must divine order and law exceed human order and law in erecting and ruling a just, honorable, peaceful, and generally effective government."[30] Thus the godly ruler constantly exercises himself in divine law, conscious that his reason is not enough to lead him to choose correctly between good and evil.[31] The ruler is a minister of God, aware that he holds his power of God and is thus careful to follow God's law.

> For anyone to rule well and not to be a tyrant, it is necessary that he be chosen from the people of God by God, that is, that he truly believe that he has not set himself up to rule, but has been called. Thus, since he recognizes himself as an under-shepherd set over, not his own, but God's sheep, he will be careful to rule them not by his own opinions, but by God's law.[32]

Magistrates, however, have generally refused to obey God. Claiming that divine law does not have any power over them, ruling by human or by pagan imperial laws, they lord it over society in contempt of God. The idea that they should punish adulterers, or enforce adequate provision of God's Word and punish those who seduce the people, only brings laughter.[33] Freed to invent their own laws, they rule in their own interest, only acting for the good of the community when it happens to coincide with their own.[34] Just as egotism has wholly corrupted spiritual leaders, "so secular leaders, who ought to be shepherds and fathers, indeed God's representatives, have become nothing but lions, bears, wolves, children, and blockheads."[35] Those who were raised up to fend off the worst consequences of human egotism have become corrupted by it themselves. Both the spiritual and magisterial offices have fallen, with terrifying consequences for the entire social order: "For while we would have all good, and would fare well both spiritually and temporally if those who led us would truly fulfill their offices, thus doubtless our total ruin will follow if they seek their own, and pull us from obedience to God to obedience to them."[36]

Bucer does not think that the lower estates, the farmers, husbandmen, and craftsmen, are working such grave damage to society. Their vocations naturally make it easy to serve others and difficult to cause harm. However, Bucer warns that "everyone" is bringing up their children to be monks and priests or merchants -- ways of life all dedicated to self-interest, leading to eternal death.[37]

The first half of Das Ym Selbs ends with a summary of Bucer's argument. Not only God's law but creation, the order God has established in the universe, makes it clear that no one ought to live for himself, but for others. The creature can work out the duty he owes to the creator by serving other creatures. Disruption of the relation with God has made man self-seeking, destroying the system of cooperation between creatures by which God means to make his goodness known and enjoyed. This egotism has catastrophic effects on society. Human selfishness is a threat to every institution that encourages peaceful, just cooperation between men.[38]

It is precisely at this threat that Bucer aims the second part of his treatise:

> How it is, however, that we can return to the sort of life in which we, as when we were first created, live not for ourselves but for the good of others and to the praise of God, is now to be said. To indicate it in short, only faith can bring about such a thing.[39]

Bucer introduces the concept of justification by faith as a medicine for society, as the sole means of reversing the destruction which self-seeking has brought about in the social order. As God created the world through Christ, so he is restoring all things to their original order through him. For creatures other than man, this restoration will be delayed until the "revealing of the children of God, that is, of the believing men," on the Last Day.[40]

> To man, however, such restoration to his proper, original character can even begin here, if still not be perfected. And this [occurs] if they believe in Christ, that is, fully trust him, that he has, through his blood, placed them again in the forgiveness and grace of the Father, and thus consequently, through his spirit, replaced them in their original order toward all creatures, that is...being useful.[41]

Bucer directs his discussion of religious justification at the consequences of faith, at specifying how faith becomes the source of a new "other-directedness" in the believing individual. Justification, from this perspective, accomplishes the restoration of men to their proper role in the original divine order of the cosmos. Faith can do so because it restores man's natural desire to serve God. Because a man believes that Christ's sacrifice replaces him in God's favor, he can be persuaded that God wills good toward him. This does not merely remind him of his duty toward his creator, it persuades him that he is God's child. Out of the love of child for father grows the "spirit of true love," the impetus to serve his father as his father wills -- by living entirely for the service of others. The original dialectic in man's relation to God reemerges, enhanced, as a result of faith.

The formal means by which this is accomplished is the possession of the Holy Spirit:

> So if we believe in [Christ's] name, he has given us the power to become children of God. For the Father has sent his spirit into our

> hearts, who cries, "Abba, beloved Father..." Since it is now clear that through faith we become the children of God and have the spirit of children, who also assures our spirit that we are children of God, from which it must come that, as we recognize and call upon God as our Father through this spirit, we therefore recognize and serve all men as our brothers.[42]

The "spirit of true love" is not merely a human psychological disposition, but the third person of the Trinity, who confirms the loving relationship with the Father and thus the impulse to do good works. Bucer suggests reinforcing psychological means by which faith permits "other directedness." Once a man is persuaded that he is God's child and heir, he becomes sure that God will provide him with all he needs. This short-cuts the perpetual struggle for the goods of life which obstructs one's desire to help others.[43] Meditation on Christ's sacrifice leads us to imitate him and to be willing to suffer anything for our brothers' sakes.[44] The increasing awareness of God's goodness makes temporal life and goods a burden, willingly given up for anyone else's profit.[45] Each of these encouragements for brotherly love depends on faith.

The fruit of this life restored by faith is eternal life. Because faith restores men to their original order, it can be said to produce "the true righteousness, in which the just man lives toward God, man, and all creatures. [The believing man] gives God honor and praise, and he is active in love toward his neighbor...and certainly from this Christian, godly life he will enter eternal life."[46] There is a qualitative continuity between the believing man's life on earth and his glorified life. Bucer holds out the hope that the first fruits of this restored order will be borne in human society.

Bucer closes Das Ym Selbs by sharpening several polemical tools. First, he explicitly and repeatedly argues for a version of the "practical syllogism": one can judge the quality of his faith by examining his life. Perfect love is the product of perfect faith. If examination shows that a person produces few or no works of love, his faith is weak or dead.[47] To Bucer, this principle is a sensible conclusion from the fact that a proper relation to God always expresses itself in a way of life dedicated to the service of others. The truly faithful man cannot help "running over" with loving activity, and that activity is visible, chiefly in his vocation. Second, Bucer insists that the works God demands of men are to help other creatures, not God -- "mercy, not sacrifice." No ceremony or work of man's devising will please him.[48] Finally, Bucer calls for pure preaching of God's Word, since it is through the Word that faith, and thus love, is born:

> But true faith certainly brings true love, from which it comes that we flow over in good works, and live for others, not ourselves, and to the praise of God. But since faith comes from the grace of God out of the hearing of God's Word, we ought to hang on to God's Word above all else, always and with all diligence hear it, read it, meditate on it, deal with it. We must not let anyone hinder this, we must set honor, life, and goods on it, whatever God has given us. For only God's Word heals and saves us, brings faith, faith, love, love the fruit of good works, from which follows the eternal inheritance and the wholly godly and blessed life, Amen.
>
> Therefore we must ask God with all

> earnestness, that in these dangerous times in which faith has foundered and love been extinguished because God's Word has not faithfully and diligently been preached, he may send us the reign of his pure, divine Word, give us grace to receive it, and turn or make an end of those who so senselessly resist it.[49]

Das Ym Selbs is Bucer's diagnosis of the sickness of his society and his prescription for its cure. In this treatise he proposes relatively little structural reform of social and political institutions, let alone foments armed revolt; if all institutions are vulnerable to egotism, no reshuffling of institutions can help society. Bucer's program of reform is rooted in the belief that society can only cohere if its members, especially its leaders, are willing to seek the good of others. If the shepherds have become wolves and the sheep have begun to prey upon each other, the flock must be scattered. The only cure is to restore man's "other-directedness." That can only be done if the source of man's impulse to service, his desire to respond to God's goodness, is restored. Thus Bucer's classic definition of faith: *persuasio bonitatis dei*.

The Summary Seiner Predig: *Religion without Religious Government*

Das Ym Selbs has an appearance of conservatism. Although Bucer advances the concept of justification by faith, he minimizes the disruptive changes in custom and law which that concept implies. Instead, he demonstrates that faith can be the source of a new social cement. He refutes those who predict that reformation ideology will ruin political order and discourage moral conduct. Rather, he argues, faith restores the proper human orientation toward God, renewing man's desire to serve his neighbor and thus re-weaving the social fabric of mutual service and responsibility. In this context, Bucer refrains from presenting the explosive effects of his concepts on medieval religious customs.

Yet Das Ym Selbs implies several fundamental changes which obviously threaten religious institutions. Faith has become the sole principle of salvation and reform. Since faith depends only on the Word, the spiritual estate has no service to render but preaching the Word. Further, the spiritual estate exists only for the good of the community. It has no right even to seek its own salvation; its only purpose is the salvation of others. Bucer intended these principles to put what he conceived to be the ideology of the medieval clerical estate in question. Salvation does not occur through priestly rites which confer sacramental grace, or through the legal enforcement of "holy", merit-earning practices. If only faith can please God, and if faith's only legitimate external manifestation is to serve others in the world, then the raison d'être of monasticism also collapses.

Bucer had no desire to disguise these implications except for the purposes of his treatise. About the same time as the publication of Das Ym Selbs, two other treatises appeared, the Summary seiner Predig and the Verantwortung. In them Bucer turns to attack medieval religion as an enemy of the principle he thinks permits both salvation and social order, faith. He sketches new religious institutions, now stripped of a clergy that, he asserts, had displaced Christ and thus corrupted the source of all human welfare for the sake of its high status and soft life.

The Summary is a lengthy description of Bucer's teaching during his recent attempt to reform the religious life of a small Alsatian city.[50] Six months before Bucer arrived in Strasbourg, it had become clear to Franz von Sickingen that his attempt to carve out a new state, based on his military power, the support of the increasingly depressed class of German knights, and Hutten's gospel, could expect serious reverses. Preparing for a bitter defensive military campaign, Sickingen dismantled his propaganda machine and lightened himself of his humanist entourage. Bucer, cut free, decided on a period of study at Wittenberg. That project was postponed when he yielded to the invitation of the evangelical pastor in Wissembourg, Heinrich Motherer, who saw in Bucer the polemical and theological gifts he needed in his struggle against the local Catholic establishment. For six months, Bucer took the movement in hand, preaching and organizing the people against the mendicant orders which dominated the town's religious government. However, no more than half of the townspeople supported the new ideas,[51] and relations with the Rat were strained. With Sickingen's downfall, the pressure of the surrounding Catholic princes on the suspect Rat grew intolerable; it was essential that they rid themselves of Sickingen's now excommunicated protegé. At the Wissembourg Rat's suggestion, Bucer and Motherer fled the town. The evangelical movement in Wissembourg was left decapitated.

The Summary is the result of Bucer's keen sense of responsibility and regret for the situation of his abandoned flock.[52] It is not only a resumé of what he taught there, but an attempt to provide the remaining believers with the resources to continue their religious life without an evangelical pastor. The situation gave Bucer a strong incentive to develop the religious powers of the laity. Yet by the time the Summary was published, Bucer was fully integrated into the reform movement in Strasbourg. The treatise obviously was aimed at his local audience as well. A clear presentation of his ideas could take the wind from the sails of the rumormongers who threatened his security in Strasbourg, and it might turn the movement towards what he probably regarded as a more fruitful concept of reform than that of Zell's Christeliche Verantwortung.[53] It could redirect and sharpen the ideology already accepted by a large number of Strasbourg citizens.

Bucer's Verantwortung, which appeared in September, 1523, shows how sharply his personal situation contrasted with Zell's. Zell had a benefice, and he was protected by a popular following sufficiently powerful to prevent his dispossession. Although the Bishop had brought action against him, he had not been excommunicated.[54] Zell was careful to refrain from concrete actions which could give his opponents a legal lever to pry him from his relatively secure position. Although he preached in favor of marriage, he was not married. While he attacked the "tyranny" of the hierarchy, he continued to hope that the hierarchy would reform itself. In contrast, Bucer had declared himself a "Martinian" -- one who had abandoned the tactics of education and compromise, seeking reform from within the church -- in 1518.[55] He had played an important role in Sickingen's diplomacy and in Hutten's campaign of violent anticlerical polemic, which had made way for the Knight's Revolt.[56] He had been one of the first reformers to marry, taking his wife from a convent. Although he had sought to maintain a veneer of legality, receiving papal dispensation from his vows as a Dominican,[57] he arrived in Strasbourg excommunicated,[58] without any sort of legal status, a refugee from the collapse of Sickingen's revolt. The Verantwortung is Bucer's attempt to show that he would not be dangerous to Strasbourg. In it, he covers himself with a cloak of legal regularity as well as he can. Yet he does not deny his radicalism; where he has found man's law in conflict with God's, he has not hesitated to obey his conscience by taking concrete action.[59]

The difference in Zell's and Bucer's personal situations is parallel to the difference in their concepts of reform. Bucer places no hope in the hierarchy. He seeks resources for reform elsewhere; he magnifies the importance of the priesthood of all believers, asserts the power of the community to select its own pastors, and proffers a certain religious authority to the secular magistrate. He carries the polemic against clerical power farther than Zell, condemning outright the concept of human religious government. Bucer argues that the fundamental tendancy of medieval clergymen is to displace Christ as the savior and ruler of souls, in order to pass themselves off as gods whose works can save men. And yet, it is precisely this turning away from God that produces the socially devastating egotism described in _Das Ym Selbs_. For Bucer, the deification of the clergy threatens not only the freedom of the Christian man, but the whole social order as well.

* * * * *

The _Summary_ begins with the struggle between the Antichrist and the Word of God. For Bucer, the Antichrist is the personification of the pretension he ascribes to the medieval clergy, the root of what he regards as its socially exploitative status: the claim that it has the right to govern souls.

> For many hundred of years, the abomination of desolation, of which Daniel wrote, has existed: the Antichrist, the man of sin and the child of perdition. In the holy

> place, he raises himself up above everything that is called God or the service of God, so that he sets himself in God's temple as a god, and claims to be God.[60]

The essential characteristic of the Antichrist is that he supplants God; he is "the power that sets itself above God and undertakes for itself the government [regiment] of souls."[61] Such counterfeit spiritual government has produced nothing but misery, care, fear, injustice, force, and trouble in the world it had dominated. It stands over against the Word. The Word Bucer preached in Wissembourg, he writes, weakened the Antichrist's kingdom by bringing peace to those who would believe.[62] The Word will be finally victorious on the Last Day:

> Although, as the Lord predicted, everything that is high and mighty in the world sets itself against him as earnestly as it can, it is no help. He drives in by force, uncovers, shames, and ridicules all that seems great and honorable to the world, and he does so, as is always his way, through what is weak and contemptible according to the flesh. I have no doubt that, as the Lord has begun...to struggle and kill the Antichrist with the spirit of his mouth, that is the powerful divine Word, so he will soon make an end [of him] through the bright appearance of his coming.[63]

Bucer does not hesitate to specify the identity of "the weak and contemptible" who can begin to overthrow the clergy's antichristian religious government. Believers can bypass the medieval religious establishment, even if they are not buttressed by an evang elical preacher. The work of the Spirit in the hearts of the faithful does not depend on priestly intermediaries, for all believers are "spiritual", all qualified to judge teaching and understand the Scriptures.

> Do not let yourselves be [turned aside], as if you were not permitted to have the Holy Spirit and thus could not read anything in the Holy Gospels and other divine writings, nor test and judge the preaching and teaching carried out for you, as some faith- and spirit-less people are trying to persuade you (blind leaders who would like to take you with them into eternal darkness). For the fact that you can see, and have gained understanding of divine matters..., means that they have less to fill their bellies and cannot exploit you with invented words so easily....What St. Paul says stands firmly: "The spiritual man judges all things." But not those alone are spiritual who are tonsured and annointed, who wear long garments and own fat benefices or are otherwise richly pastured, but those who have the spirit of Christ. He is possessed by all who are his. His are all who believe him. If you believe in Christ, you are his, you have his spirit, you are spiritual, you have all things to judge and to test.[64]

If faith is the only prerequisite for understanding spiritual matters, then the clergy cannot claim the exclusive right to define doctrine or to govern souls. Bucer goes so far as to suggest that no external qualification, even education, is of any great advantage for spiritual understanding:

> The spirit of God rests on the humble, and graciously looks after the poor who have a broken spirit and who tremble before the Word of God. Even if you are not priests or monks, know no Latin, have to work day and night, Jesus our Savior was a layman too, to the dignitaries and spirituals of the world unlearned and a carpenter. Paul too worked day and night, so as not to burden anyone. The holy patriarchs and some of the prophets were nothing better than shepherds, but still the Holy Spirit lived in them richly with his highest gifts....So sang the blessed virgin Mary from the Spirit: "The hungry he has filled with good things, and left the rich empty."[65]

Bucer does not intend to eliminate the "spiritual estate," as _Das Ym Selbs_ shows. The Spirit normally employs human preachers to pronounce the Word that brings men to faith; Bucer considers the loss of faithful preaching as the worst trial humans can bear. But if necessary, the Spirit can bypass even this institution and teach the faithful directly.[66] Bucer does not find this option comfortable, and at the end of the _Summary_ he presents another possible resolution: the Christian community has the right to call preachers of its own choosing.[67] Bucer is not interested in building a society in which each believer is taught directly by the Spirit. Rather, he means to break down the clergy's pretensions to higher religious status than other

Christians, and to end their monopoly on religious power.

Bucer stops well short of recommending spiritualism to Wissembourg believers. Possession of the Spirit is no license for individuals to cut their ties with all external standards of doctrine or life; Bucer never considers the Spirit apart from his written will, the Scriptures. The Spirit qualifies people to read the Scriptures, not to bypass them.

> How can we recognize, judge, and test [preaching and teaching] except by the Holy Scriptures? They are the single rule of teaching and preaching, certainly written by the Holy Spirit, which plentifully teach all that is good. Therefore everything that does not agree with Scripture and cannot be grounded in it, must be bad, false, and deceitful.[68]

Bucer abstracts from Scripture specific tests for preachers and their doctrine which reveal a great deal about his intentions. The most important is the "*summa summarum* of all divine writings," the kernel of the Gospel: Jesus Christ came in the flesh.

> All those who preach and teach that man can obtain grace through his own or through some other creature's work, or can earn something toward salvation, do not acknowledge that Jesus Christ came in the flesh. For the coming of Jesus Christ in the flesh is this, that he alone purifies the flesh of sin, earns, redeems, and bestows his spirit on it, so that man, who was nothing but flesh, that is, inclined to the greatest evil, is made spirit [*vergeistet*] and is

> drawn to the good. So, if one man can obtain this grace for another or for himself through his masses, brotherhoods, or good works, as sadly, the antichristian preachers lie, then Christ came in flesh in vain.[69]

This is the central thesis in Bucer's attack on clerical religious government, the test by which the Antichrist is identified. Christ alone is lord and savior of souls. Bucer denies the possibility of any human initiative or decisive contribution in salvation. Nothing men can do can reach God; only the work of the God-man, Jesus Christ, can do so. Men are inclined by their very nature to seek evil; they lack the resources to reform their lives spontaneously. Only divine intervention can reverse this.[70] Thus any institution which depends on a claim to decisive human initiative in salvation -- doing something that causes God to act -- is antichristian and faithless. Christ is the sole mediator between God and man; Bucer insists that no human intermediary usurp his place.

Bucer applies this principle by unleashing a broad attack on medieval religious institutions. Throughout the _Summary_ he argues that the traditional activities of the clergy and the entire clergy-centered system of piety violate this cental standard. The hierarchy sells indulgences, offering salvation through a human legal proclamation. Priests celebrate Mass, claiming that they thereby offer to God an efficacious sacrifice for the dead and the living. Monks claim that their prayer and devotional exercises contribute to others' salvation.[71] Laymen buy all these goods, hoping to save their souls. The cult of the saints, pilgrimages, vigils, all normative devotional exercises in medieval society, seek to bypass and displace the unique role of Christ in salvation.[72] They must be rejected by believers.

The true religious leader, then, effaces himself behind the Word. Rather than claiming the social status of "lord" or "ruler", he is Christ's and the community's servant. Christ alone is true lord over the soul:

> Concerning authority [oberkeit]: in spiritual matters, Christ has reserved it for himself, since he alone has power over the spirit. So all clergy are his servants, in all servility duty-bound to provide the divine Word to the community, and in no way to lord it over them.[73]

This Bucer opposes to the secular authorities, who are to be obeyed as God's vicars as long as they do not oppose him.[74] Although Bucer will refer to preachers as the community's spiritual leaders (vorstehern), he is very careful to avoid language which suggests any social status above the people.[75] The "spiritual estate" is defined solely in terms of service [Dienst].[76]

The isolation of Christ as mediator is important in part because Bucer's concept of social reform is related to it. To reverse human egotism, it is essential that men be aware that they receive all good from the Father through Christ. Confidence in human resources is dangerous not only because in practice human resources prove to be inadequate, but because the human being's attention is thus once again focused on himself. Only from total reliance on God can the gratitude spring up that causes men to serve their brothers.[77]

The ethical criteria developed in Das Ym Selbs provide Bucer with two other tests for preachers and their doctrine, immediately used to discredit the medieval clergy. Bucer forthrightly employs the practical syllogism: since the lives of the clergy are scandalous and useless, they cannot possess the true Spirit. For example, those who doubt the divine source of the Scriptures expose their own origin by their conduct:

> We detect nothing spiritual in them, indeed nothing in accord with natural honesty. Rather, all their thoughts and their character are directed at having people regard them as lords [with] all freedom and license [mutwill], solely on account of a little oil smeared on them by a finger, and a lock of hair cut from their heads. For this [status] they do nothing, except sell the body and blood of Christ, and mutter or shriek out the most holy Psalms without any understanding or spirit. Further, against law and right, they suck the marrow from the bones of the poor, and bring their wives and daughters into shame. In sum, all faithlessness, sin, shame, and total ruin come from them. According to the teaching of Paul in Corinthians and Thessalonians, one ought not to associate with them.[78]

Bucer then turns to discredit the papal decretals on the basis of the popes' evil lives. Such law cannot come from the Holy Spirit, if its promulgators are so wholly void of the Spirit's ethical fruits.[79]

Another test for teaching is its accord with the two great commandments, love of God and love of neighbor. Disparaging Christ's role in salvation (as do those who exalt their own) hardly promotes the love of God. And

> how does it accord with the love of neighbor

> to teach [the people] to build churches, endow masses, erect brotherhoods, buy [the clergy's] good works, burn wax, and whatever other foolishness there may be, through great outlays of money with which one should help the brothers? Since such things are not commanded by God, no one would buy them for himself if he were suffering from hunger, thirst, or cold, or was in other need. He would help himself first, have mercy on himself, which God wants (especially toward the neighbor), not sacrifice.[80]

Practices which divert charity from its proper object are condemned. Bucer immediately cites the clergy's fat life, which consumes what ought to go to the needy.[81]

Bucer intends these principles to discredit the medieval clergy, and to show that believers have the resources for religious life free of traditional religious institutions. To provide for this, he replaces medieval concepts of justification and the pious life with a system which preserves God's initiative in salvation and denies the value of human resources or mediation. He begins with a concept of faith closely parallel to Zell's:

> All truth, and the words and teaching of Christ, stand in this, that through him we have a sure faith and heartfelt trust in the Father as in a gracious god and father who gives us everything that is good for body and soul, without any of our merit, out of pure grace (but through the merit of his most beloved son, our savior, Jesus Christ), and who wills to guard us from all evil and to forgive all our sins. This is the faith by which the just live, and the righteousness

which is valid before God.[82]

Just as Bucer described in Das Ym Selbs, this faith immediately produces love and gratitude towards God, which is redirected as service to one's neighbor.[83] Toward other believers, this service can express itself as spiritual care: teaching the ignorant, comforting the weak, rebuking the errant, helping the needy, all aspects of a mutual pastorate.[84] Of course, good works no longer include support of the medieval cultus, the endowment of churches and masses; they chiefly mean meeting the concrete needs of the poor: feeding the hungry, giving drink to the thirsty, clothing the naked, housing the homeless, comforting those sick or imprisoned.[85] Bucer does not deny that the preached Word is the normal, if not indispensable, tool of the Holy Spirit in producing faith. But in all other respects, the pious life Bucer sketches can be lived very well without what he regarded as the burden and distraction of medieval ecclesiastical institutions.

Another result of faith, which Bucer develops extensively, is the killing of the flesh, the uprooting of the believer's continuing impulses toward evil. Bucer's chief example is the "contrariness" (widerwillen) that prevents the believer from being fully spontaneous in his acts of love. Those who have true faith attack this "flesh" with work, night watches, fasting, and other ascetic exercises, in order to tame it and make it obedient to the spirit. Throughout the Summary, Bucer insists on the value of freely undertaken, authentic asceticism, which he distinguishes from the law-bound, hypocritical exercises of the medieval establishment. For Bucer, the only proper stimulus for asceticism is the love produced by faith.[86]

Rather than exercises imposed by the clergy, the most

effective medicine against concupiscence is provided directly by God in the form of tribulation.

> "So that he may perfect his work, he employs an alien work." His work is to make us pious, and, as a gracious father, to do us good. But due to the evil of our tainted nature, if he always did good to us, that which is pleasing to our nature, we would laxly desert him and even presume to delight ourselves more in God's goods and gifts than in God himself. So that we can learn to recognize him and ourselves, he must take away not only his corporeal but his spiritual benefits as well, so that we may learn to find comfort [uns trösten] not in ourselves nor in the reception of God's gifts, but solely in God himself, and to hold to his bare promise, even if nothing appears from him but wrath and disfavor and we feel nothing in ourselves but sin.[87]

Having suffered himself, and writing to a threatened community, Bucer underlines the significance of tribulation. Following Luther's 1518 edition of the Theologia Deutsch, Bucer treats spiritual trial at length, occasionally using mystical language incautiously. His purpose, however, is clearly parallel to Luther's. Spiritual trial clears away false faith, trust in creatures rather than in God alone.[88] Even in such discipline, faith remains the sole principle of spiritual growth. Good moral performance directly depends on exclusive trust in God. Again, the services of a religious government are hardly indispensable.

By demonstrating that authentic piety can flourish even where there is no preacher of the Word, Bucer lays the foundation for his argument that highly "clericalized" medieval religious institutions distort and ccrrupt true religion. He compares medieval piety with the sort taught by the Spirit through Scripture; at every point, the intrusion of the medieval clergy's ideology violates the tests Bucer had earlier developed for preachers and their doctrine. The clergy usurps Christ's place in salvation. It has abandoned the community's welfare. It has imposed upon Christianity a hierarchy of religious status and a false concept of holiness that permits it to exploit religious institutions in its own interest.

He first compares monastic asceticism with the authentic attack on the flesh he has described.

> Work, watches, and fasts should not be like [those] of the hypocrites of our times, who are called monks and nuns. Their "work" is singing and muttering...; their "watch" is getting up for Matins, in order to sleep all the longer during the day; and what they consider (and sell) as a "fast" is to fill themselves up with fish once [so full] that they cannot [eat] a second time. Of them I have often said (and you know it [to be true] yourselves) that it is nothing but fraud and hypocrisy to live an idle life sustained by the poor, contrary to the clear divine command: "In the sweat of your brow shall you eat your bread." They sell their howling and muttering to the poor, and simple people are coddled by it and thus profoundly injured in their faith. In no way does it please God, since it brings no improvement [Besserung], and yet all things in the Christian community should be done for

improvement.[89]

The distinction between some days and food for which fasting is mandatory violates Christian freedom.[90] Further, buying all these works from the clergy diverts money from its proper use for needy people -- people, not God, the siants, or the dead.[91] Believers who "watch" should really do without sleep, devoting the freed time to prayer or to other useful exercises that kill the flesh and help their neighbors.[92] Believers should constantly fast, that is, live meagerly, denying the flesh.[93]

Bucer extends his polemic to many other practices. In contrast to Zell, he treats intercession for the dead as a violation of Scripture's sole religious authority. The impudent invention of purgatory by the clergy, who have not a word of authentic Scripture on their side, is contrasted to the believer's responsibility to follow Christ's voice alone, straying from that path neither to the left nor to the right.[94] Human reason and authority, long usage, and even miraculous signs should have no power to distract the elect from Scripture.[95] In fact, no good comes of prayer to or for the dead; it only reinforces the clergy's claim to save people through indulgences or masses, and diverts massive amounts of money from its proper use, helping the poor.[96] The Mass, as a sacrament strengthening faith in the unique sacrifice of Christ on Calvary, ought to be celebrated and received with the greatest possible desire and sincerity. But in current usage, it is regarded as the priest's efficacious sacrifice to God, which Bucer regards as a blasphemous usurpation of Christ's sole initiative in salvation. The Mass as a human product becomes a commodity to be sold, like any other. Bucer is keenly aware of late medieval sentiment against commercial abuse of the sacraments, and exploits it in a long polemic. The Mass salesman ought to be excluded from Christian fellowship;

they live off the community, but only those who work in the Word ought to receive support.[97] Finally, the withholding of Christ's blood from the laity is simply another prop for clerical exclusivity, in spite of the fact that the clergy ought to be servants, not lords.[98] The vigils of the religious, sung without understanding or sincerity, are the more blasphemous because they are done in the name of the whole community. Further, all such ceremonies which in theory exist for the good of the whole community, ought to be in German, so they can be understood and bear fruit.[99]

The similarity of Bucer's polemic to Zell's is evident: a false concept of holiness, used to maintain the exploitative status of the clergy, has perverted religious institutions. Bucer's insistence on Christ's exclusive role in salvation has a parallel effect to Zell's emphasis on the Word of grace, but it gives Bucer an incentive to attack religious institutions still more radically. Any form of human control over religion disparages Christ's lordship. And although Bucer makes of Scripture as clear and objective a standard as Zell, he gives the clergy no unique relation to the Word. Zell insists on the value of divinely commissioned preachers who can govern Christ's flock and insure that it does not pervert Scripture. Bucer is much more confident in the Spirit-filled laity's ability fully to understand and independently to apply what they read. Thus Bucer leaves still less ground for a hierarchy of religious status, and "democratizes" religion still more radically.

The _Summary_ was written for a community which had lost its preacher, and thus it emphasizes the independent resources of the laity far more than Zell's treatise. Yet the basic impulse for both Bucer and Zell was the same: not to create a separatist "community of the saints," but to find alternatives for the medieval church's massive institutional domination of religion and life. Further, if Bucer chastens the ministry more harshly than Zell, he does not trivialize it. The preacher is the normal means by which God extends his Word to men. Not only is the preacher an institution by which men are saved, but he is the crucial instrument through which society may be restored to an approximation of its original divine order.

The Minister in Society

Martin Bucer's treatises from 1523 are a frontal assault on medieval religious ideology. His attack carries away the institutions that rested on that ideology, not least the medieval clerical estate. Yet no revolution can rebuild society on the sole basis of its criticism of the old order; one must turn to Bucer's positive ideals in order to evaluate his resources and tendencies. Although Bucer's ideas in 1523 are cast in the form of polemics, he clearly offers an alternative to the Catholic establishment's concept of the role of the minister in society.[100]

The major social thrust of Bucer's religious criticism is to unify society by eliminating differences in the religious and ethical standards which governed various social groups. Society is bound together by a concept of justification and an ethic of service which apply to all equally. Of course Bucer does not propose an "egalitarian" community in any political sense. In spite of his tendency toward religious democratization, he retains a hierarchy of vocation, valuing the service of minister and magistrate more highly than that of the common person. But this hierarchy is not absolute; those who refuse to serve the community have no place in it. All members can be judged by common standards. The preacher is one member of human society, in which all members owe service to each other. The old sacral order, in which some persons' vocations rendered them more spiritual than others, has been dissolved. An individual's worth is no longer measured by the extent of his participation in holy institutions, but rather by the service that results from his faith in Christ.

One of Bucer's most potent tools for unifying society is to deny that the process of justification itself produces any differences between believers. Bucer's most bitter polemics against monasticism attack its elitism, the common opinion that monks' vows exalt them above common laymen:

> They say that they want to have a special crown in heaven above others, indeed they say that they alone are spiritual and in the state of perfection. And not only do they stand in this false faith, but they suppose that they and others earn heaven with such a life, which only Christ Jesus, with his bitter death, has made possible.[101]

Again and again Bucer attacks the medieval clergy for acting as lords instead of servants, due to their claim to "spiritual" status. But among believers, no distinction between "spiritual" and "secular" can be valid. All are spiritual who have Christ's spirit; that some are called to the service of the Word does not imply that they merit high personal privilege. No claim to special status based on "spiritual" capacities or a "spiritual" way of life can withstand Bucer's concept of justification. This principle is radically stated in _D. Luthers leer_:

> No distinction of persons is valid, that one person should be called spiritual and another secular among believers. Rather, all believers are spiritual and all unbelievers secular....If,

> then, all Christians are one, and neither birth nor individual characteristics nor even the distinction between sexes matters, whether one has a man's or a woman's name, then who would want to insist that one person be called spiritual, another lay, another ordained, another unordained? Whoever has a strong faith that is active in love is the spiritual person, annointed and ordained, whether (according to external doings) he is a peasant or a noble, tonsured or untonsured.[102]

All believers are equal <u>coram</u> <u>deo</u>. Whatever one is -- spiritual, ordained, priest, "sacrificer" -- all are, for all have the same righteousness in Christ.[103] Since no "external" condition can affect salvation, all external distinctions are irrelevant before God.[104] Bucer states the conclusion baldly: "If we all have salvation [<u>seligkeit</u>] from one Christ, no one is better than another."[105] Social distinctions cannot be based on differences in spiritual quality or worthiness, not because the Spirit has no connection with the external world, but because there are no distinctions in spiritual status. There is only belief or disbelief.

That is not to say that Bucer argues that religion introduces no distinctions at all into society. The spiritual office, the preacher, remains one of the Three Estates. If its pretensions to social superiority are checked, its value as the stabilizer and renewer of society through the Word is enhanced.[106] Further, Bucer clearly rejects a general dissolution of authority; the magistrate's coercive power is of God. Even tyrants must be obeyed, if their commands are not contrary to God's.[107] Bucer simply denies that justification itself is a principle of inequality, or that it releases any estate from responsibility to the community. The clergy has no grounds for considering itself intrinsically set apart from the rest of society.

The fabric of vocation, founded on differences of function, is not dissolved by Bucer's concept of justification. But all estates become subject to common standards, responsibilities, and freedoms. Since any creature properly related to God will seek the welfare of its neighbor, every individual, estate and institution must be directed to the "good" [nutz] or the "improvement" [besserung] of the community. All individuals should ready for spontaneous acts of charity, supplementing their service through vocation. Every member of the community is governed by divine law, whose freedoms and bonds are common to all: all may marry, all must obey the magistrate, whether they are lay or cleric.

Bucer does not hesitate to apply these standards to the clergy. He bitterly attacks monasticism for seeking to except itself from the requirements for common Christians. In the Verantwortung, Bucer launches a coherent attack against the three vows, obedience, poverty, and chastity, which define monastic life and buttress its claim to "perfection."[108] The vow to obey one's superior in the order not only unreasonably limits the Christian's freedom, it seeks to exempt the monk from God's commandment that all Christians obey their parents and magistrates, and, further, renders the monk unable to respond to the need of his neighbor. Even if his father is starving, the monk may not help him without permission from his superior. In contrast, Bucer insists that God's law requires universal obedience to human order [menschlichen ordenung], including proper obedience to parents and magistrate.[109] In D. Luthers leer, Bucer emphasizes this universal responsibility: "Since we are all one in Christ, and one is worth as much before God as another, the Scripture follows [that principle by declaring] that each person ought to obey secular government,...and that no one ought to exempt itself from [it]."[110] Further, contrary to the vow of poverty, "we must be ready to be serviceable and helpful to every person, in every way, and with everything that we have received, no one excepted."[111] In contrast, the monk is required to hand over his belongings to an already wealthy cloister, thus rendering himself unable to respond to the needy in the future.[112] In contrast to the obligatory chastity of the medieval clergy, Bucer argues that the decision to marry should be based simply on utility. If one has the gift of chastity, it is more useful to God and neighbor to refrain from marriage; if marriage would be more serviceable [dienstlicher] to him, then he ought to marry.[113] In *D. Luthers leer*, Bucer expresses this forcefully:

> Since it is clear...that [the clergy] are like other Christians (if they are otherwise Christians and have true faith), what God has commanded to others is also commanded to them; what is forbidden to others is also forbidden to them. For God has established marriage, blessed men and said: "Be fruitful and multiply", and that in paradise, in the state of innocence.[114]

Marriage is a "necessary, holy estate, to live honestly and usefully to the world."[115] It is obligatory for who lack the gift of chastity.

Beyond the substance of these vows, however, Bucer objects to vows themselves as illegitimate additions or subtractions from the common life of faith and love:

> Every Christian is not only duty-bound, but also inclined by the Holy Spirit, to conduct himself in all things in such a manner as most

> advances the honor of God and the welfare of his neighbor. What good are all these vows? If something you can do is to the honor of God and the benefit of your neighbor, you are obliged to perform it without [a vow]. You already vowed to do it in baptism. If it is not helpful, you are duty-bound not to do it.[116]

The clergy's so-called "perfect" way of life, which renders them immune from standards proper to the rest of society, has no other effect than to exempt them from their proper role in the divine order common to all men. Religious elitism subverts the universal administration of God's goodness. For Bucer, religious life is essentially tied to society.

It is natural for Bucer to emphasize the universal responsibility to work. True religion implies hard labor in one's vocation for the good of one's neighbor. Once Bucer has shown that the segregation of the clergy is functionless, and that its chief occupations such as masses, the chant, and prayer, are useless, he can characterize the entire caste as lazy, idle, and exploitative.[117] The responsibility of the clerical estate is to work in the Word, to study intensely and to preach daily. That is its only claim on the community's financial support.[118] Bucer links clerical exploitation to other popular economic grievances; priests, just like usurers and merchants, eat the bread of the poor and give nothing in return.[119] For Bucer, such social isolation and exploitation is essentially irreligious; the believing man lives to serve in society.

Bucer can assimilate economic and social grievances in his basic theological attack on the medieval clergy because of his concept of the faith-grounded order of cooperation between creatures. This divine order is revealed in the Scriptures, accompanied by regulations for its government. Thus Scripture becomes the most important universal standard for society, the source of all other standards. Primarily, of course, it reveals the Word of grace, all things necessary for salvation. But it also provides a rule for the organization of external life, from which no estate can escape. Any religious or social institution which wishes to play its proper role in the economy of creation must find its roots in Scripture.[120]

This principle provides Bucer with a defense for his resistance to authority and a response to the charge of provoking "uffrur," the disturbance, disunity, and rebellion that might occur if ideological unity were not forced on communities from above. Bucer argues that the blame for disturbances does not belong with those who defend the authentic divine order with the Word, but to those who continue to impose what he considers to be an exploitative and tyrannical government on the world. The right of God's Word to be heard, believed, and obeyed is prior to the claims of any human institution, since the Word reflects the God-ordained order of the universe.[121]

Scripture is also the instrument which Bucer chooses to resolve the difficult problem of the relations of one estate to another, chiefly in regard to how the clergy should be controlled. Bucer repeatedly insists that no government, secular or religious, has the power to forbid the preaching of the Gospel. In an angry reply to those who had attacked his failure to obtain permission from the Bishop to preach, Bucer writes:

> There is no authority [oberkeit] over God's Word but God himself, so that no one may forbid it or allow it. Permit a Turk to preach the Gospel for as long as you like, what he preaches

> will be a lie. Forbid it to a Christian to whom God has given it, and he will answer you as the Apostles answered the chief priests: "Man must be more obedient to God than to men." ...And if anyone wants to forbid it, he is a servant of Antichrist and no authority [<u>ober</u>], for he would like to hinder the salvation of souls, which is so much his responsibility. It is true: no one can preach the Gospel, unless he is sent. But from God![122]

This is a clear parallel to Zell's concept of the preacher's direct divine commission. It apparently conflicts with Bucer's repeated assertion that communities have the right to depose and select preachers, and that the magistrate must punish those who preach falsely. How can a human community control a divine emissary? The obvious answer is that communities can judge the authenticity of a preacher's doctrine because they possess the same Spirit and capacity to understand Scripture as he. All three estates have common access to the supreme standard of judgment, Scripture. Bucer simply assumes that Scripture is so clear that sincere believers will have no difficulty distinguishing true doctrine from false. Further, they can check their judgment by observing the quality of the preacher's life, which gives a strong indication of which spirit rules him. Again, Scripture provides the standards for judgment. Thus no conflict can arise. No true Christian community will ever silence a true preacher of the Word.

* * * * *

Just as every believer is the instrument of God's

goodness through his vocation, so the minister is God's instrument in the order of salvation. He is sent by God to announce the message of grace to a community which, recognizing God's Word, accepts him as their preacher. He is not absolutely indispensable; God can do without him. He has no power of his own; only the Spirit brings fruit.[123] But Bucer is very far from suggesting that the office of the Word, the plain preaching of the Gospel, is unimportant. God can dispense with all human institutions in unusual circumstances, but Bucer does not seek to institutionalize this divine possibility. He remains committed to preaching as the normal human component in the process of justification. Thus, the clerical estate provides the good that the community needs most: the Word of God, which saves the soul and gives rise to the loving cooperation that constitutes human community.

To protect this service from abuse, Bucer ties the minister closely to the community he serves. Only if he is subject to the same standards and freedoms as other Christians, and kept accountable to an alert community, can he be kept from spiritual pride and prevented from arrogating to himself Christ's role in the order of salvation. If he should succeed in exaggerating his status, he does more than damn the souls of those who follow him, or create a pretext for tyranny. By distracting the people from reliance on God alone as the provider of all good, he chokes off the redirected service that sustains society. An elitist clergy blocks the hope of reform, and unleashes the egotism that corrupts every social institution.

Since community and magistrate can understand the Word, they can identify and deal with evil preachers. In contrast with Zell, Bucer is willing to subject the clergy to significant social control. By doing so, he gives religion the institutional ballast that could make it viable in sixteenth century society. Yet the question of how the clergy could be forthright and independent servants of the Word, while being the servants (and subjects) of both the community and of the magistrate, is left unanswered.

Implications of Bucer's "Kingdom of Christ"

Orthodox medieval thought considered man's moral capacity to be one of his points of greatest similarity to God. The ability to love was simultaneously the source of moral activity ("good works") and one of the aspects of human nature best suited to union with God. The just man was intimate with God precisely when he was filled with love (the divine gift of the Holy Spirit) and therefore was similar to him. The sinner, fallen from friendship with God, could reattain that union "*fide caritate formata*", through faith formed by love. Sacramental grace was confirmed and actualized by learning habitually to act out of love. This habit of charity constituted a decisive likeness to God; it was the source of the deeds that, by "condign merit", resulted in eternal union with God. Thus the capacity to love did double duty; the love which produced good works also naturally appealed to God.[124] For many bands of the spectrum of medieval piety, "good works" came to mean those activities which rendered the soul like God: sacraments, ascetic exercises, prayer, contemplation, the thousand different means of imitating holy models, all of which intensified and purified love; or the pious donations which made it possible for others to pursue a "holy" life.

Bucer rejects the normative medieval account of human ethics. The foundation of the moral impulse, for him, is a relationship decisively shaped by man's essential unlikeness to God. It is the duty owed by a creature to its fundamentally dissimilar creator. Man's loving service of other men is only the specifically human form of an obligation shared by all creatures, which humans have in common with stones and cabbages. If the loving man is similar to the beneficent God, it is the feeble similarity of the tool to its user. Human ethical activity offers no resources for union with God. Its proper direction is not toward God, but toward one's neighbor.

The genesis of loving service is faith, the belief that God is a loving father, based on his Word. From this belief springs trust, peace, and gratitude. Gratitude causes the believer to wish to serve God, a desire which must be turned to other creatures. _Bucer never threatens the dependence of the ethical impulse on faith._[125] Religious activity is reformed so as to excite and purify faith; even ascetic "taming of the flesh" succeeds best by attacking false faith. That is simply to say that it is not "meritorious" activity, that it does not seek to appeal to God. Its intention is to reinforce the believer's awareness that God alone gives him all good things, that Christ's work alone appeals to God, that nothing human can stand before God. It is only when the believer is aware of his utter dependence on God that gratitude springs up and empowers him to serve others. Bucer, no less than Luther, robs humans of any resources before God.

These are Bucer's grounds for an attack on a wide spectrum of medieval concepts of "holiness." He denies not only that good works earn salvation, but also that any estate, activity, or institution is intrinsically more "holy" than any other. He follows Luther's treatise _On the Freedom of the Christian Man_ by insisting that neither "external" actions and circumstances nor any interior human disposition but faith can appeal to God.[126] The idea, implicit in much of medieval culture, that only activities proximate to sacral objects or institutions are religious, is thus overturned. Bucer's fundamental purpose is to reject the divine pretensions of all human institutions. Of course, religious activities approved by Scripture -- preaching, sacraments -- continue to be, in a certain respect, external, objective "holy" institutions, but their sole object is to foster faith. Anxious to remove every possible prop for the old "sacral" hierarchy, Bucer carries the polemic against "holy" times and places so far that he is compelled to explain why it is proper for believers to meet at a regular hour in a regular place to hear the Word.[127]

Yet other medieval institutions do not, on first look, seem to fare so badly at Bucer's hands. Several historians have commented on the apparent continuities between Bucer's ideal society and the medieval _corpus christianum_.[128] There is no separation of the religious and the secular community. Both minister and magistrate serve God's people in such a way that the administration of God's beneficence flourishes and God's praise grows. Bucer holds forward a society which approximates the world's order before the Fall, the beginning of the restoration of all things to their proper relation to God and to other creatures. Is this not a protestant version of the medieval sacral community, in which men's religious status was a function of their membership in the common body?

Bucer's ideas also seem medieval if compared to Luther's. Luther considered that God rules over the world in two separate manners simultaneously. The Word of God brought peace to consciences, reconciling them with God. Believers thus were filled with love for their neighbors, which they expressed through their vocations. Yet Luther did not think that faith was the essential principle of social existence. The fabric of vocation and authority functioned even without the force of love. To earn their living, men were compelled to serve their neighbors. Even the most evil-hearted cobbler had to provide shoes for his neighbor if he wished to eat. Structures of authority, whether familial or magisterial, functioned even when the authorities were not Christian. Even tyrants provided a minimum of order and justice, bridling the impulses of evil men to injure their neighbors, holding back chaos. The fabric of vocation was enhanced by the love that sprang from faith, but for Luther it did not depend on it. Hypocrisy was a tough social glue as well. Thus Luther accepted the possibility of irreligious social existence, a significant step away from medieval world-views.[129]

Bucer's ideas provide a clear contrast. Society depends on the other-directedness produced by faith. Bucer is not interested in searching for principles of social coherence that function in the absence of faith. Human social intercourse is a partial fulfillment of the divine order, which is essentially founded on a correct relationship to God. Where there is no faith, the divine order collapses, and Bucer sees nothing worth noting in the ruins. Egotism corrupts even the law. He has no concept of purely civic virtue; he does not find any redeeming feature in hypocrisy.[130]

Yet if this distinguishes Bucer's "Kingdom of Christ" from Luther's "Two Kingdoms", it also shows where Bucer departs radically from medieval models. His ideal society grows out of faith; the social function of religion is fulfilled exclusively through the love that springs up in the believer. Because of this, Bucer stands the ideal of the sacral community on its head. Rather than an external "holy" corporation, in which the individual is holy through his participation in the group, Bucer proposes a society that is filled with the praise of God because the men in it have faith and act in love. The renewal of the individual is prior to the renewal of society. The fabric of human intercourse comes to resemble the divine order because its members are correctly related to God, not vice versa.

For Bucer, there is no question of endowing any corporation with the resources to save men. He consistently denies any such capacity to human institutions. If men have no resources in themselves for achieving union with God, then neither does society. His whole system of social cooperation rests on men's recognition that they receive everything from God.

It is well to remember the concrete effects of the Reformation in Strasbourg on the sacral communities which had given medieval religion shape. Those which had solely religious justification -- monasteries and their lay brotherhoods; the whole spectrum of quasi-monastic communities for lay people; brotherhoods such as that of the passion play or vocation-related religious fellowships -- vanished.[131] The Rat's chapel at the Spital, the St. Erhartskapelle, fell into disuse. The city processions and mass religious festivals, the mirrors of the city's religious communion, stopped.

The movement caused profound division within other social groups. Guilds, parishes, families, freundschafften, the town itself were split into bitter factions. Almost every document in which the Rat deals with the evangelical movement mentions the "discord and division" which ruled in the city.[132] The brother of the girl who married Caspar Hedio, the evangelical preacher in the Cathedral, accused Hedio of having flagrant contempt for the Rat's laws and patriarchal authority in the family, since Hedio acted without her father's or guardian's permission. In turn, his mother, who had agreed to the betrothal, disinherited her son because he had resisted the Gospel and brought shame on her.[133] The majority of the parishioners of St. Aurelien called Bucer as their pastor; the minority, which would hear nothing of it, found a traditional priest of their own.[134] Bernhardt Wurmser begged his fellow Ratsherren not to quarrel so violently over "Lutheran matters."[135] In part, Das Ym Selbs was written to counter the spreading impression that the new divine law, the "Gospel", was seditious of all social institutions.

When this charge was cast at Zell, he had bluntly asserted the absolute power of the Word to overturn anything human.[136] Bucer replied somewhat differently. The ones causing conflict were those who sought to hinder the spreading of the Word and the emergence of God's kingdom. Thus Bucer could contemplate the actual factionalization around him, while assuring his audiences that the Gospel creates perfect social harmony.[137] Thus, although Bucer's ideas were unavailable for use in deifying the city, or any other community, he could appeal to Strasbourg citizens by promising a united, cooperating, love-filled human society, living to the glory of God, in spite of all appearances to the contrary.

Does Bucer's society essentially depend on any particular political or social unit in medieval society? It is true that although the roots of his society are in faith, he does not intend Christ's kingdom to be invisible. It reveals itself in its subjection to divine law and, above all, in the concrete, everyday cooperation of the estates for the good of all. But Bucer does not identify that society with any social or political unit. One is not born into Christ's kingdom through physical birth in a parish or in Strasbourg, but through faith. The community of true believers can exist as an isolated fragment within a hostile external corporation. Wherever individuals receive the Word, the fabric of loving service begins to be knit together. Bucer addresses both the Summary and Das Ym Selbs to Christian communities which are minorities in a political unit, subject to magistracies which he regards as indifferent or even hostile to the Gospel.[138] Of course, the full restoration of the administration of God's goodness is obviously frustrated by whatever power the regime of the Antichrist retains. Bucer naturally looks forward to a society in which the Word is as fully victorious as can be before Christ's return. Yet this hardly implies that Christ's kingdom first exists only when full victory is won, when a social unit as a whole becomes obedient. The Kingdom of Christ is not essentially dependent upon any external social or political corporation. It comes into being wherever any believer turns his gratitude towards the service of other men.

However, this community of love tends to become attached wherever possible to external corporations through its relation to the two estates, the ministry and the magistracy. Although it can exist without either institution, the lack makes its life difficult, and prevents the full flowering of divine order. As we have seen, Bucer follows Luther's argument that the Christian community may depose false teachers and choose true ones, in virtue of all Christians' Spirit-given power to recognize Christ's voice.[139] That implies the existence of some sort of visible organization. In practice, Bucer showed himself to be very flexible concerning the form of that organization. Whenever evangelicals came to dominate a traditional ecclesiastical unit, Bucer was willing to confer on it the status of a Christian community. He urged the Wissembourg evangelicals, apparently as a whole, to choose a pastor.[140] In Strasbourg, he actively organized individual parishes to demand preachers for themselves. The parishioners of St. Aurelien called him as their pastor, and he himself drafted the letter by which the parishioners of Old St. Peter announced to the Rat that they had chosen to replace their Catholic priest with an evangelical.[141] Bucer's community becomes visible as an external corporation because it normally receives the Word through preaching and sacraments, which must be supported by the institution of the ministry. The community's response to the Word, its cultivation of the means of receiving the Word, is expressed in visible actions. But all such attachments are secondary and auxiliary to the faith in the Word that brings the believing and serving community into existence.

Bucer's society also tends to become associated with a Christian secular magistrate. Thus in practice it naturally tended to fall into the normal political units of medieval society. The fact that Bucer ascribed certain religious powers to the magistrate, and insisted that he govern according to the laws of God, has started many false hares. It is beyond doubt that Bucer thought that society benefited greatly from the service of a Christian magistrate. A godly ruler could protect it from evildoers, both temporal and spiritual, and help to guide it according to divine order. Bucer certainly considered the conversion and reform of the magistrate as an important step in the advancement of Christ's kingdom in the area under that ruler's jurisdiction. No people which obeys laws other than God's is fully God's. But none of this suggests that Christ's kingdom is essentially dependent on the magistrate. The ruler is a particularly valuable servant of the community, but he does not create it. Christ's kingdom exists even where it is persecuted by authorities. The decisive principle is not attachment to any of the estates or to the social and political units which they defined, but faith, and the service it produces.

* * * * *

Bucer's ideas promise a radical change in medieval religious life. The wealth and diversity of medieval devotion and religious vocation was built upon sacral institutions and hierarchies, most of which Bucer's concept of justification simply sweeps away. Clearly, he expected laymen to greet this as a liberation. Bucer, like Zell, saw medieval religion as a game tilted against the common man. The layman worked like a slave to support the lordly monks and priests, but he himself could achieve nothing better than a feeble imitation of the holiness of those above him. Bucer pictures medieval religious vocation as elitist and essentially selfish, and therefore as irreligious. His alternative is a society in which believers all have equal status before God, in which all work to help their fellows through their vocations, where no one is capable of exploiting or lording it over another man. Any vocation that helps one's neighbor is authentically religious. Over against the heaped and tangled riches of late medieval piety, he poses a simple, strict, uniform rule: the spiritual man is a member of society, and his work is of benefit to other members. The Holy Spirit makes men good, peaceful, productive members of the renewed community, a community in which all are subject to common standards and expectations.

There is no question of emancipating society from the demands of religion. Bucer means to require intense personal religious activity of all. Faith must constantly be supported and refined, engendering a ceaseless hunger for the Word, loving discipline of the brothers, sincere asceticism, and enthusiastic use of the sacraments. Since society rests on faith, in theory there is no room for the religiously indifferent. If the religious sources of social behavior are not maintained, society will collapse into a ruinous war of self-interest. Thus the good citizen is marked both by his engagement with the Word and by his sober application to his vocation. One may observe, of course, a certain potential for formalism. The medieval man could fulfill his fellows' expectations by following the church's rules and by making a few pious donations. In the same spirit, a citizen of Strasbourg could attend the Sunday sermon and carry out his business and familial life as usual, thereby keeping his credentials as a respectable member of society. Bucer's use of the practical syllogism, judging a man's faith by his work in his vocation, might expand that possibility. Yet Bucer could hardly make clearer his conviction that social life depends on sincere and living faith. Society is rooted in universal belief, intense gratitude to God, and the selfless service that grows from it. By denying the secular roots of social behavior, he hardly means to secularize vocation. It is clear that Bucer's society no longer guards any pretense of earning God's favor, and in that sense it is no longer "sacral." But it is born of faith, and it grows toward the perfect kingdom of Christ.

Such were Bucer's intentions: a society where vocation no longer led to union with God, but rather flowed from it. This basic shift of thought offered to free sixteenth century communities of a clergy which the reformers' concept of justification made useless, to speed their internal integration, and to enhance the religious self-consciousness of laymen. Yet this "liberation" was achieved at the price of a drastic pruning of religious expression and activity. Bucer confined love's expression to concrete service of the community. He demanded a social function of every religious institution. He destroyed the guarantees of the clergy's independence. By doing so, he subverted the diversity and freedom of medieval religious life. This seemed a small price, to those who found the diversity a preposterous jungle of rival institutions and clerical freedom no more than a treadmill of obligations and oppression. Yet one liberation opened the gate to another servitude. Bucer diminished the contradictions between religious ideology and lay society by limiting religious expression to the ideals of lay communities: work, utility, cooperation, service, obedience. The way was left open for the community to make of religion its handmaiden.

Chapter 3

The Rat and the Reform: the Process of Change

During 1523, "evangelical" ideas were bandied through the markets and alleys of Strasbourg, discussed in the book-shops around the Cathedral, and talked over in guild taverns. Sermons and tracts, learned discussions and violent quarrels sowed the seed. The "Gospel" first explained how the church had fostered oppression and corruption; it then laid down new laws which offered to supercede the legal inventions of greedy priests. The clergy had been able to wallow in privileged idleness thanks to a system of salvation which justified its social status and left it theologically and legally unassailable. Yet according to the evangelical preachers, not a word of Scripture supported that system's foundation, the pretension that human (i.e. the clergy's) works could save men. In fact only Christ, not priests or monks, could do so; only God's Word, not human laws, could make the conscience secure. The preachers claimed that by fostering dependence on human resources for salvation, the medieval clergy had forced Christians to depend on it, a dependence which led to oppression of the body and damnation of the soul. Yet the Word was a sharp sword.

In 1522 Strasbourg was still a conventional Catholic city, marked by relative social tranquillity, its traditional religion whole. By 1525, the religious establishment lay in ruins. In a sudden storm, the population had jettisoned many of the religious customs of its fathers and was busy developing new patterns of religious life. The Mass was abolished, most of the cloisters were empty, and parish pulpits were occupied by Rat-appointed heretics. The traditional cult had largely been swept away. In the church of St. Aurelien, no tapers burned before saints' images. Even if some old believer had bought a candle, the pictures were gone. The Lord's Supper was celebrated and babies baptized in German, not in Latin. No more pilgrims came to the saint's tomb for healing, since the bones had been exhumed amid derision. An excommunicated runaway monk stood in the pulpit, preaching doctrines condemned by imperial decree at Worms. The legal structure supporting the medieval church had suffered too. Wilhelm von Hohnstein, Landgrave of Alsace and Bishop of Strasbourg, was still a force to be contended with, but in religious matters his writ no longer ran in Strasbourg. The clergymen who remained in the town had all become citizens, subject to the same laws, courts, and taxes as all other people in the city. The Rat alone ruled a newly integrated community. Only the princes of the Cathedral chapter chanted on, isolated exhibits of an estate now changed out of recognition.

What role did the preaching of evangelical ideas play in these changes? One is reluctant to follow the old chronicles of the "triumph of the Gospel", as if a set of purely 'religious' ideas had imposed itself upon the community, unmediated, and without reference to its 'secular' life. We have analyzed the two major expressions of evangelical ideology preached in Strasbourg, those of Zell and Bucer. In each case, new religious ideas had produced social "insight." A radically changed theory of justification, backed up by "divine law", rendered the services of a whole social class superfluous, exposing functions previously considered normal as gross perversions of the class' proper role. The clergy's "abuses", always considered as the inevitable consequences of human weakness, became symptoms of a radical dysfunction at the heart of society.[1]

By now it is no surprise to historians that in any society, religious and social thought should be intimately related. But Zell and Bucer developed their ideas in sixteenth century Europe, where political institutions were never isolated from religious institutions, and where policies were formulated by men who did not clearly separate political ideology from religious ideology. It is difficult to find a law or a custom in Strasbourg that was unaffected by the church's presence. This is not merely to say that the historian must be alert to the social influence of ecclesiastical institutions or ideas. Religious ideology was part of the cement of late medieval society, part of the construct of values and understandings that defined the places and functions of individuals and social institutions. People pursuing social change were required to do religious thinking, if only because they had to deal with the concrete expression of medieval religious ideology in law and institutions, and with their fellows' structures of meaning and values. Zell and Bucer meant to set off a major rebuilding of institutions influenced by religious ideology. Their ideas, as their world, cannot be rigidly divided into "the religious" and "the secular."

Yet in order to grasp the role of ideas in the social changes brought about during the evangelical movement, it is still not enough to understand the social intentions of ideologues. The process of change was complex, working through the tangled society and politics of Strasbourg. How did the evangelical movement relate to changes long underway, to the motives of institutions and social groups, to Strasbourg citizens' aspirations? In what forms did the people understand and employ the new ideas? It cannot simply be assumed that evangelical ideas functioned in the same way for all of the groups taking part in the movement, whether for an urban oligarchy intent on retaining power or for peasants determined to get the church's oppressive weight off their backs. Further, not all groups and institutions played identical roles in the evangelical movement. The old order was destroyed and the new ones constructed by many different hands, following projects which often conflicted. The process of change itself must be understood -- the interplay of institutions, the composition and organization of the forces pushing for change -- before one can understand how certain ideas, in certain forms, shaped a religious movement which reconstructed an entire sector of Strasbourg society.

* * * * *

In this chapter, we shall analyze the process of change from the perspective of the Rat of Strasbourg. Such a procedure no doubt invites distortion, placing a premium on the legal resolution of a long political development rather than on the development itself, exaggerating the importance of the "ruling classes" in the movement. The Rat was not the only locus of power in Strasbourg. Yet the comparative richness of sources for the Rat's activity is irresistably seductive. The Rat oversaw every step of change, if only because it answered for the peace of the city and the integrity of its laws. Every involved party, every major controversy, all the changes that affected laws had to touch the Rat at some point. If the Rat was not the Reformation's "motor", the agent chiefly responsible for overcoming the city's inertia, it was at least enormously influential. The edicts, instructions, and memoranda remaining in the archives permit us to reconstruct one example of the complex means by which the preacher's ideas pervaded Strasbourg society, moving through institutions, but chiefly into the minds of the people on whom the insituations depended.

The Rat and the Reform

The relation of the Strasbourg magistrate to the evangelical movement was ambiguous.[2] On one hand, the Rat created the legal sanctuary necessary for the growth of the young party. It abstained from enforcing the anti-Lutheran decrees of Pope and Emperor, and it actively protected the preachers from the Bishop. It had the power to stamp out the flames. It did not do so. Further, several initiatives taken by the Rat against the church during the early years of the movement seemed intimately related to the evangelical preachers' ideas. Yet on the other fronts, the Rat seemed to stand bewildered, floundering for a solution to each new crisis as it came, until the movement began to threaten its position of authority. Then it diverted the current of reform into socially safe channels.

The Rat's stance was the result of several different circumstances. Internal division over the reform movement required ambiguity. Although a cluster of active council members (*Ratsherren*) allied themselves with the movement early on, they stood over against a number of politically cautious or religiously conservative colleagues.[3] And if division had not prohibited any clear policy, political circumstances would have. The Empire and the Papacy were committed to attack any subject secular government which undertook major religious changes. The city's prosperity depended upon secure status in the Empire. Yet the population threatened to explode if reform were stifled. The Rat was caught between two fires. Further, the Reformation posed questions of religious doctrine and practice, matters which the Rat had never regarded as within its jurisdiction. If it was the Rat's accepted responsibility to watch over the city's morals, still there had never been any question of invading the central preserve of the church's authority.

Yet overt support of the preachers' Gospel would have required the Rat officially to judge doctrine and to rule on religious practices.

If the fifteenth century Rat had never sought to invade certain areas of the church's jurisdiction, however, that is not to say that Rat and church had kept all frontiers tranquil and sharply defined. The Ratsherren who presided over the evangelical movement had inherited a four hundred year old tradition of struggle against the Bishop and his clergy. While intending to leave their religion wholly intact, members had fought to restructure the relations of secular and religious government for generations. In some measure, the Rat's ambiguous policy toward the evangelical movement echoes both the harmony and dissonance between the preachers' program and the Rat's own projects for reform. Reformation ideology did not simply fulfill late medieval aspirations. It overtook and radicalized reforms already in progress, turning them in directions unforseen by their originators and, in the end, alien to medieval experience. It could claim roots in traditional religion and reform, yet the plant itself was new under the sun.

The Policy of the Late Medieval Rat

The roots of the Rat's struggle pushed up from the thirteenth century emancipation of the city from episcopal rule. The 1262 victory of the Strasbourg citizenry at Hausbergen ended the Bishop's secular government forever.[4] Yet the victory appears most decisive in hindsight; Strasbourg citizens felt far from secure. No matter how the city's constitution developed, no matter what the political circumstances, the Rat consistently maintained a policy of political resistance to the Bishop. It lost no opportunity to insure that he could not regain his lost political power. In the mid-fifteenth century, an exhausting struggle with Bishop Wilhelm von Diest ended in the Rat's complete victory. The happy coincidence of great ambition and relative incompetence in the person of the Bishop had led him to overreach himself seriously. When his projects finally collapsed, the bishopric was left strangled by debt, many of the episcopal lands mortgaged to Strasbourg citizens. His successors were left without the resources to mount campaigns against the town. The city, on the other hand, had been more modest; its wars, legal maneuvers, alliances, acquisitions, and bribery had been conducted efficiently and without grandiose ambitions. Until 1502, when Bishop Wilhelm von Hohnstein suddenly redeemed the old episcopal lands surrounding the city, Strasbourg was relatively secure from direct episcopal aggression.

Even when the city felt secure from reconquest, there were other bitter issues between it and the clergy. The most important was clerical immunity, the traditional legal independence of the church from secular government.[5] Clerical "freedoms" originally took root in early medieval society in order to protect the holy "peace" of churches and cloisters from the incursions of worldly life, and to guard the clergy from compromises with lay society that would detract from its consecrated character and its religious office. It was not right that armed struggle should disturb the cycle of prayer in a cathedral; it was not right that gifts to the church should be diverted from holy to common use. How could a layman sit in judgment on the priest who mediated between him and God, or force a man sworn to peace to kill for a town's purposes? In order to guard such values, a network of legal immunities grew, exempting clergymen and religious institutions from domination by laymen. No member of the clergy nor any religious institution paid city taxes on income, was subject to any of the town's laws or courts, or carried any part of the burden of shared defense and services. Where laymen had won independent self-government, clerical freedoms perpetuated two separate communities within one set of walls. The town's writ did not run in the zones occupied by "holy" institutions; clergymen's persons were exempt from most controls of the Rat.

Laymen occasionally seized upon clerical immunity as a focus for anticlerical feeling. It was often caricatured as a legal haven for the rich and lazy who refused to carry their end of the common load. Popular songs and pamphlets flashed hostility at a clerical caste free of the burdens of the layman's life.[6] Such cases demonstrate a certain endemic alienation of the people from the normative medieval concept of the clerical estate. Laymen naturally blurred the double standard, extending their own values to the clergy.

The Rat's objections to clerical immunities can be sketched with greater specificity.[7] It meant to make the clergy pay for its share of the expense for emergency preparations for the city's defense. It meant to keep the clergy's freedom from taxation from draining away the city's tax base. Yet the Rat attacked clerical immunities chiefly because they mocked its pretension to govern the secular lives of laymen. Legal cases involving ecclesiastical persons, property, goods, or interests were often subject to ecclesiastical courts alone. Wills, testaments, many contracts, and cases involving debt or breach of contract also frequently escaped from secular jurisdiction. The Rat was powerless over much of the litigation of its citizens, and could not enforce order in the city when the clergy was involved. Further, religious institutions had the greatest resources for speculation in grain and other commodities, the greatest capital for loans to citizens, a very large share of the land and buildings in the city, and a similarly large role in city markets and employment. Yet these religious institutions did not merely escape from taxation, but from any sort of oversight or regulation by the city government. One need not ascribe to bourgeois society any imperialistic desire to impose its way of life on the clergy in order to understand the Rat's campaign against unlimited clerical immunity.[8] The clergy's "freedoms" were permanent breaches in the power of laymen to govern even the most secular aspects of their own lives.

Throughout the fifteenth century the Rat prosecuted an unyielding, increasingly sophisticated, but largely unfruitful campaign against these weaknesses. Its principal objects were the clergy's immunity from taxation in times of emergency, its uncontrolled grasp of the levers of economic power, and its erosion of the Rat's tax base.[9] Yet even these modest goals were elusive. The clergy's "freedoms" were well protected; the Rat found itself bound both externally and internally. The edifice of medieval law and the church's power imposed limits on the Rat from without; from within, its policies were restrained by its own values. No document makes these limitations clearer than a memorandum drawn up by Sebastian Brant some time after 1490.[10] Brant was the Rat's secretary and legal consultant. He had been asked to research means by which the city could tax the clergy, or, failing that, stop the flow of taxable property into the clergy's hands and thus off the city's tax rolls.

Before Brant discusses any possible tactics, he describes at great length how weak the Rat's legal position is, how strong its opponents', and how dangerous any attempt to change the balance would be. Brant writes that he has given the matter of "burdening" the clergy as careful attention as possible; it is the most difficult, anxious, and momentous affair ever placed in his hands. Both papal and imperial law repeatedly assert the same principle: no secular government has the right to create or enforce any law or arrangement that would lay hands on the clergy's goods or hinder its free control of its possessions.[11] Brant lists relevant laws at some length, summing them up through one typical passage of imperial law. This statute declares null and void "all laws and customs introduced, established, or employed against ecclesiastical freedoms or religious persons by a city, secular power, the lords of a Rat, or any other person." Anyone involved in making such laws is subject to removal from office, imperial ban, and a thousand marks fine. There are even severe penalties against those who "counsel, aid, compose, copy, or judge according to" those laws (in which company Brant obviously feared to find himself).[12] Papal law goes further. One example is the interdict it threatens against any government forbidding its subjects to sell, buy, mill, bake, or perform any other service for the clergy.[13] The canonists have even forseen the danger of Greek gifts; laws professing to "help" the clergy are null and void as well. The commune can prejudice clerical freedom directly in one way only: by obtaining explicit papal confirmation of every provision of the law. Any vagueness will be automatically resolved in the clergy's favor.

After listing pages of obstacles, Brant finds some legal resources in medieval law for the Rat. One gap in the law which might be widened is the community's right to provide for its own citizens' welfare by governing their actions and possessions.[14] If the Rat cannot touch property already held by the clergy, it can restrict the flow of property from its subjects to the clergy. Bequests to church foundations or individual clergymen, certain sales of property, or the annuities received by churchmen from city properties might be prohibited, restricted, or conditioned.

These particular leaks in the city's tax base could even be plugged without papal confirmation. But caution intervenes: "in every way, it would be better and more lasting to do it with the good will and protection of the Pope."[15]

Brant's analysis reflects legal realities. The weight of medieval law, both secular and ecclesiastical, protected the church's immunities. Direct attack was fruitless. A town like Strasbourg simply did not dispose of the resources to permit it to violate those laws unilaterally. Any such attack would be considered as aimed at the foundations of Christendom and would receive the penalty it deserved: exclusion from Christendom. If the Rat was driven to attack clerical immunity, it could do so only in the most cautious and indirect manner, and on issues of marginal importance to the clergy.

The limits on the Rat's actions were not only external. Almost as revealing as Brant's legal analysis is his apparent anxiety about handling the matter at all. The author of the Ship of Fools was not burdened with knee-jerk respect for every ecclesiastical person and custom which surrounded him. Yet he was a faithful man, the founder of a brotherhood to promote piety in the Rat.[16] Traditional assumptions about the inviolability of the consecrated priesthood and the cloistered life were deeply embedded in his conservative lawyer's mind and in his heart. Brant's poems grow from passionate commitment to the piety of his fathers, polished, not eroded, by his humanist skills.[17] One may speculate that his reluctance to attack the church did not spring only from the fear of imperial penalties; it was also the slowness of the son to lift his hand against his mother.

The church's ideology was deeply rooted in medieval society. If alienation from traditional values permitted certain people consciously to attack the church's status, the hard expression of those values in the law rose to bar the path. Those who remained fully integrated in the medieval religious system limited their own conduct. Even glaring abuses, demanding immediate action, aroused painful ambivalence. How could one remain pious while assaulting God's representative? It is essential to understand that in some respects, the Rat's campaign against clerical immunity was highly conservative. The Ratsherren were by and large pious men.[18] They were struggling to protect themselves, to gain a more favorable division of financial burdens, and to promote the economic and legal integrity of the city, but they did not intend to impeach the clergy's religious offices. It was no part of their program to disrupt monks' cloistered lives, or to obstruct the secular clergy's provision for the community's salvation. There is no evidence that the Rat ever systematically resisted the enforcement of canon law in matters clearly related to the cure of souls. When adulterers were punished, marriages annulled, fast-breakers fined, or tithe-withholders excommunicated, the parties involved no doubt resented the church, and the Rat occasionally used its influence on behalf of a citizen tangled in ecclesiastical courts. Yet it was at least as likely to help the church enforce its judgments.[19] During the half century that preceded the Reformation, the Rat repeatedly tested its limits. Gradually but stubbornly, it attempted to abridge certain of the clergy's "freedoms." In no case did it display any desire to judge doctrine or to govern religious life; it merely intended to assert its control over the clergy's role in secular aspects of the city's life. The Rat showed itself to be alienated from only one element of the ideology of the medieval clerical estate: the assumption that complete clerical immunity was an essential condition of the clergy's religious function.

During the 15th century, the Rat made almost no progress at all in the matter of criminal jurisdiction over clergymen. Although it occasionally claimed that the "Rachtung" of Speyer, a compromise pact with Wilhelm von Diest, had granted it power over clerics committing flagrant criminal acts, that claim was never upheld.[20] In practice, it was seldom made. The Rat was impotent. This fact was brilliantly illustrated by a series of incidents on the eve of the Reformation.[21] A canon of the renowned collegiate chapter of St. Thomas, Johann Hepp, seduced a young woman who, unhappily, fell ill while in her lover's house. He had her taken to Hagenau where she died shortly later. Strasbourg citizens were goaded to fury by rumors that the girl had died because Hepp had violently abused her. The Rat arrested Hepp, but then it promptly transferred him to the Bishop for judgment. Hepp was successful in persuading the Bishop that he was innocent of the girl's death, and he was given a light penance and released. He was not satisfied. He went to Rome, where he sued the Rat for having arrested him in violation of his immunity. The Rat defended itself at great expense, but lost the case. This was not a sufficient slap to the Rat's pretensions. On the pretext of avenging their bullied confrère, two canons of the chapter of Young St. Peter in Strasbourg kidnapped and abused the daughter of Johann Murner, the lawyer who had defended the city in Rome. They then complained to the Rat of a threatened ambush by the lawyer and his friends. There was nothing that could be done. Under pressure from the Rat, the chapter paid Murner an amend of 500 florins, but he resigned his Bürgerrecht and left Strasbourg. No doubt this incident further polluted a sky already black with hatred. Yet it served also to fling the Rat's impotence in its face. Often the Rat could use its influence to good effect, but it had no coercive powers over the conduct of the hundreds of clergymen within its walls. The clergy swore no oath of fidelity and obedience to Master and Rat; they were subject only to the tangled jurisdictions of church courts. It was an immunity that hamstrung the Rat's attempts to maintain peace within the walls and to protect the interests of its citizens.

Slightly greater progress was made on taxation. The clergy agreed to pay the normal city tax on the purchase of wood, the sale of grain, and the milling of flour, and it eventually consented to the tax on wine. On one occasion, it helped to pay the cost of preparing the city for defense against an invasion. Yet during two succeeding invasions, it refused, once after it had agreed in advance to pay.[22] So far from being able to sustain a permanent claim on clerical incomes, the Rat was never able to demand voluntary contributions for the mutual defense.

Finding the way straight forward blocked, the Rat tried a detour. It could tie the clergy to the town through voluntary contracts. During the fifteenth century, the Rat offered individual priests a modified form of the _Bürgerrecht_.[23] The priest who purchased it gained most of the rights of citizenship, especially legal aid and protection. In return, he became subject to city taxes, laws, and courts just like any other citizen. Yet not all conditions were the same. Clerics were not required to swear the oath of loyalty; they could substitute a solemn promise, taken "by their priestly office." This left the priest room to argue that he had not traduced his estate or evaded his superiors' jurisdiction through his bond to the town, since his ordination vows still defined his primary obedience, unchallenged.[24] The town profited from this modification as well. Those who did not actually swear the oath could not sit on the Rat or its courts, or hold city office; clerical _Bürgerrecht_ would not put priests back into town government.[25] Besides the mitigation of the oath, there were other modifications:

clergymen could hire substitutes for duties such as defense, police, or travel. The sum of these modifications was not trivial. They represented a deliberate effort to protect the clergyman citizen's priestly character. He need not violate his vows or turn any of his time away from his sacred office. Owning the Bürgerrecht did not force him to live like a layman; it merely offered him the protections and privileges of citizenship in return for the surrender of the immunities obnoxious to the Rat.[26]

For many priests, the advantages outweighed the costs and the dangers. Well over a hundred purchased the Bürgerrecht during the fifteenth century.[27] Yet it would seem likely that in most of these cases, unusual circumstances rendered the Rat's offer of protection irresistable. This flow of priests in trouble did little to change the relations between the city and the clergy as a whole. In the 1460's, however, the Rat found a formula which could appeal even to the powerful collegiate chapters. The Rat offered to take the chapters under its Schirm in exchange for the right to emergency taxation, a small annual payment, the yearly recitation of a Mass on the city's behalf, and a formal promise of fidelity to the city. From the chapters' point of view, it was a seductive offer. The Schirm offered them the city's full physical and legal protection. Since they had a perpetual feud with the Bishop and were enmeshed in endless litigation, the Rat's influence and political power offered very useful support. Just making peace with the Rat itself would have great advantages. Further, the Schirm would guarantee them the best possible protection of their property and persons against the townsfolk. The chapters refused the Rat's first offer, but once the condition of emergency taxation was dropped, they acquiesced. Between 1462 and 1464, all four chapters, Strasbourg's most powerful religious institutions, entered the Schirm.[28]

In some respects, it was a significant victory for

the Rat. The fee hardly constituted taxation; it paid for services rendered. But the cornerstone of the Strasbourg religious establishment promised fidelity to the town, a formal bond which, if only morally and in principle, limited the clergy's independence. Further, the Schirm gave the Rat official footing in the struggle between the Bishop and the chapters. This promised to increase its influence in the church, to give it official allies among the clergy in its own struggle against the Bishop, and to expand its means of exploiting division in the clergy.

It was only a crack in the wall, but as time passed its importance grew. As the heat of popular anticlericalism increased, the chapters began to find the Schirm a necessity rather than a luxury. A formal bond with the Rat became an esential condition of secure and stable existence in Strasbourg. The Rat had gained a powerful lever. Yet this lever had to be used with circumspection. Any basic threat to clerical privileges might panic the clergy into unity, and rob the city even of the limited power it had.

Yet in spite of the promise of this step, the Rat's grant of the Schirm to the chapters was in itself a poor compromise. The goods of the chapters were not taxed. The city gained neither criminal nor civil jurisdiction over their members; the promise of loyalty did not include any promise of obedience. Further, the Schirm was expensive for the city; the Rat was continually called in to ward off the effects of quarrels. After Strasbourg cloisters publicly boasted of using prints of Ulrich Hutten's portrait as toilet paper, Hutten declared a private war against several Strasbourg religious institutions, his right as a knight. Both Bishop and Rat worked to resolve the dispute, at great length and expense. The chapters later paid the Bishop two hundred florins for his expenses, but because they were under the city's Schirm, they paid the Rat nothing.[29] It would seem likely that the city's extra expenses often outweighed the chapters' payments by a considerable margin.

The only fully successful measures taken by the city against clerical privileges were those which exploited the breaches suggested by Brant's memorandum. If the clergy could not be taxed, their accumulation of property within the city could be curtailed drastically. The Rat prohibited new ecclesiastical foundations in Strasbourg, although it was unnecessary; there is no evidence that anyone considered founding anything during the entire fifteenth century. More effectively, the Rat limited bequests to the church to one percent of the donor's family's holdings. The loud protest by the clergy indicated the effectiveness of the measure; the Rat did not budge. One by one, other cracks through which the tax base was draining were found and plugged. The children of Strasbourg families who were placed in convents could inherit goods and properties from their families, and often left them to the church at their own deaths. In 1471, the Rat resolved that all future inheritances by nuns would only last during their lives. Upon the nun's death, the property would revert to her family. Further, a guardian was to be appointed for each case, responsible to pay full taxes on the property and to see that the statute was not circumvented. This measure also provoked long and bitter criticism, including Geiler's celebrated sermon in which he referred to the Rat as satanic. The Rat talked to Geiler, but it did not move.[30]

In 1489, the Rat took a more radical step. A substantial amount of property was flowing to the clergy because of defaults on loans made to laymen, or in consequence of litigation in ecclesiastical courts. The Rat attempted to control this flow by declaring itself the sole competent judge of all legal cases involving land or houses in the city, regardless of the status of the persons involved.[31] About the same time, projects began to be formulated for meeting another apparent threat. The annuities to clergymen from the incomes of certain properties occasionally grew so heavy that the buildings fell into disuse and payments were defaulted; the properties then could be bought or seized by members of the clergy. Brant's memorandum reveals the first sketch of a regulation permitting laymen to buy back annuities by payment of a lump sum.[32] This stopgap, however, was not passed until 1523, when it was accompanied by other measures of greater danger to the clergy.

The 1523 Attack

Through the eve of the Reformation, the Strasbourg Rat struggled against the clergy's immunities. Its goals were limited: to preserve itself from military conquest, to protect its sources of revenue, and to govern Strasbourg's "citizenly" life as coherently as possible. To succeed, it believed it necessary to gain some sort of control of those areas of the city's life where the clergy's "citizenly" conduct intersected with the laity's. The desire to tax the clergy was not simply a greedy hunger for the chapters' riches; it also grew from the need to protect the town's tax base and thus lay self-government itself. At the core was the problem of jurisdiction; without some form of legal control of the clergy, laymen could not govern their own affairs. Yet none of these goals was understood by the Rat as being subversive of the clergy's religious office. "*Bürgerlich*" life could be distinguished from "*geistlich*" life.

In 1502, the Rat's strategic position in the bishopric suddenly changed. Bishop Wilhelm von Hohnstein suddenly redeemed all episcopal lands, including the ones surrounding Strasbourg, from the debts that had protected the city for decades. The Rat's immediate response was to buy every yard of land it could around Strasbourg and along the normal routes of invasion.[33] One may infer that this wholesale campaign to buy a buffer zone drained a substantial portion of the Rat's financial resources. The expense caused by fear of military reconquest by the Bishop reinforced the resentment against the clergy's immunity from taxation, which the Rat feared would drain the tax rolls. According to evidence recently discovered by Francis Rapp, several sessions of the city council on the eve of the Reformation were filled with shouted fears that the clergy meant to reconquer the city bloodlessly through financial subversion. When the clergy had all the property and no more taxes went to the _Pfennigturm_, the bankrupt Rat would not be able to refuse the rich priests anything. The key word in the chorus against the clergy was not "greed", but "the lust to rule."[34]

Whether the _Ratsherren_ were in earnest or merely speaking in the exaggerated voice of council-room debate, in 1523 they decisively moved against the clergy. In the spring and summer the Rat suspended the chapters' _Schirm_, passed an ordinance permitting the repurchase of annuities paid to members of the clergy from city properties, and launched a new program of poor relief.[35] Supported by the rising storm of anticlericalism called up by the evangelical preachers, the Rat forced the chapters to acquiesce in clear invasions of their rights, by threatening them with still graver ones.

Analysis of the Rat's initiatives shows that they bore no necessary connection to the preachers' ideas. They were, in the main, traditional attacks on the clergy's immunities, still designed not to threaten its religious activity. Yet the preachers rapidly assimilated the Rat's program; the force of events and the rapid acquisition of many _Ratsherren_ by the evangelical movement changed both the ideological and political context of the Rat's measures. Projects which had grown up in Geiler of Keysersberg's world were transformed into weapons turned against the medieval clerical estate itself, its religious office at its heart.

That the original intentions of the Rat were wholly traditional is clearest in the new regulation of annuities. It had been proposed by Sebastian Brant before Luther's name had ever been mentioned in Strasbourg; it was no more than an attempt to free Strasbourg properties from an irreversable drain of income to the clergy. The reform of poor relief is a more ambiguous case.[36] There has been a sharp debate over the new order's inspiration. In October, 1522, Daniel Mieg, a prominent member of the Rat, returned from diplomatic work in Nürnberg, carrying with him a copy of Nürnberg's new plan to rid itself of beggars and to provide for the worthy poor in a decent manner. This plan was rapidly printed and circulated in Strasbourg, and Mieg submitted a revised version of his own to the Rat. Public welfare systems were not unknown in the late middle ages. The Nürnberg plan, however, departed from its forerunners by absolutely prohibiting all begging and by establishing a Rat-governed system to care for all deserving needy people in the city. The plan was to be financed from the revenues of old pious benefactions for the poor and all the alms collected publicly in Strasbourg. The Rat negotiated with Strasbourg religious institutions for the release of these incomes, and in August, 1523, it proclaimed the new ordinance.

In itself, the new system did not presuppose allegiance to evangelical ideas.[37] If Luther had pronounced himself in favor of care for the poor through rationally organized public administration, so had Geiler von Keyersberg twenty years before. The August proclamation itself gives pride of place to curing the 'plague of beggars' which diverted alms from the worthy poor; it does on to say that the Rat has established the system "in consideration of brotherly love, which is most highly commanded by God and which is the best and most fruitful means for men to obtain [erlangen] divine grace and salvation."[38] Zell gave brotherly love high priority, but he hardly would have agreed that it was a means of "obtaining" grace.[39] If the new system discouraged spontaneous acts of charity, that was as much a source of concern to the evangelicals as to the Catholics.[40] It may be argued that such measures sapped the traditional direct involvement of the church in meritorious acts of charity by individuals, but such an attack was oblique. There is no evidence of such a programmatic connection between Zell's sermons and the new system. Further, the Rat did not displace any coherent church administration, it did not forcibly seize ecclesiastical revenues or employ them for its own use, and it did not invade the church's jurisdiction.

It remains true, however, that the political context gave this late medieval program an evangelical appearance. While the plan was circulating among Ratsherren at the end of 1522, the plan to protect Zell's preaching of the "Gospel" was also considered and then carried out.[41] It is quite possible that Mieg, later one of evangelical movement's strongest supporters, was already a partisan of Zell's. Lukas Hackfurt, an avowed evangelical, was chosen to administer the plan, and already in 1524 the program was being heralded as an example of the moral improvements the Gosepl brought in its train.[42] If evangelicals had not invented the plan, it agreed well with their attack on the clergy's self-insertion in the community's religious life and with their calls for social cooperation and brotherly love.[43] It could be assimilated into their program.

The Rat's other measure, suspending the Schirm, exhibits a similar pattern. In themselves, the Rat's actions and proclamations were in full continuity with its fifteenth century policies. The evangelical movement, however, assimilated and radicalized them.

In April of 1523, the Rat refused to accept the chapters' payment for the Schirm. It announced that the old conditions were henceforth unacceptable, and any clerics who wished continued protection would have to appear before the Rat as individuals.[44] Making good use of the rising winds of anticlerical feeling, the Rat stripped the chapters of their chief shield in order to squeeze new concessions in taxation and jurisdiction from them. Its original bargaining proposal went quite far: to obtain the Schirm, a priest had to purchase the modified Bürgerrecht. In the summer of 1523, the Rat published the conditions:

> The priests who purchase the Bürgerrecht or who receive it from their parents should, in place of an oath, give their faith, solemnly pledge, and promise to be loyal [treu und holt] to the City of Strasbourg, to seek its good [nutz und frummen] and to warn of and prevent harm to it as far as possible, to keep their best houses here in the city of Strasbourg, to obey all commands of the Meister and Rat, and to keep [the oath] that is sworn yearly before the Cathedral. If he is in a lord's service, who calls upon him within a year's time, he will be permitted to go. If he has some preceding war, no one should either help or counsel him....He should join a guild like any other citizen, and this vow will bind him as long as he is a citizen...They shall carry all citizenly burdens, although, of course, they are to be free of voyages [on the city's behalf] and their cares [?], and may pay an amend for their duty on night

watch...[45]

These conditions are parallel to those applying to lay citizens. They subject the clergy to the Rat and the burdens of citizenship in precisely the same measure as laymen. Yet the modifications which during the fifteenth century had permitted clergyman citizens to retain their priestly character are retained here. From one perspective, the modifications represent the minimum concessions the Rat had to make if it hoped for acceptance by the clergy. Yet they clearly insure that the priest's "geistlich" life will be unmoved and unimpeded by secular government, while tying his "bürgerlich" life to the Rat.[46] It is essential to note that the Rat had no intention at all of treating 'priestcraft' as a craft like any other. The opening salvo in the Rat's attack on unlimited clerical immunity remained faithful to the campaign's old limitations.

The chapters, too, were faithful to their old policy. This basic attack on their economic and political immunities was a far graver matter than the other issues in 1523, such as annuities or benefactions for the poor, on which they were willing to make concessions. During the year which followed, the chapters marshalled powerful sources of support outside of Strasbourg, going so far as to ally with the Bishop.[47] During that time, however, the context and the implications of the Rat's campaign changed sharply.

The Evangelical Preachers' Assimilation of the Rat's Program

We have seen that the Rat's attack on clerical immunities in 1523 did not depend on the ideas of evangelical preachers. Its roots were in a fully traditional policy. Further, Mathis Zell, the only evangelical preacher in Strasbourg when the Rat suspended the Schirm, studiously avoided the question of clerical immunity, at least in print.[48] His basic thesis, the illegitimacy of human law in religious matters, finds no echo in the Rat's projects. The Rat did not directly attack the clergy's religious status; Zell did not directly attack its political status. Yet as the evangelical movement accelerated, the preachers adopted the issue of clerical citizenship as a major plank in their platform, giving it an ideological context much more radical than the Rat had done.

Prior to the fall of 1523, there is little evidence that the evangelical preachers treated the issue at all. Zell's Christeliche Verantwortung does not mention clerical obedience to secular government, taxation, jurisdiction, the sharing of citizens' burdens, or the Bürgerrecht. If these were wise tactics for a tract directed in part at the upper clergy, they also agreed with Zell's insistence on the independence of the preacher of the Word. Yet Zell had other resources. The bitter polemic against clerical self-seeking, against the luxurious, idle, careless life style of the clergy, at one point erupts into an ironic reference to the clergy's "freedoms" as carnal freedom to seek personal advantage in the name of religion.[49] There are indications that Zell may have developed the issue of clerical immunity, as an example of the clergy's self-seeking, more fully in his sermons.[50]

During the summer of 1523, Bucer developed this theme further. The clergy's refusal to submit to the secular magistrate is one more technique of evading standards which apply to all Christians, in order to keep a luxurious style of life for themselves. God has ordered every person to submit to the magistrate.[51] In the defense which Bucer submitted to the Rat in June, 1523 to counter the Bishop's accusations against him, he expressed his own submission to the Rat's commands, on the grounds of its divine authority. Appealing from the Nürnberg Reichstag's decision that married priests be barred from church office and stripped of their immunities, Bucer makes a suggestive contrast between clerical freedom and the "common" freedom he claims:

> I do not desire any freedom above other Christians and laymen. I want to acknowledge the secular authority in all respects like a layman, pay it whatever obedience is possible, whether it concerns honor, body or goods, just as I and every person is bound to do by divine law....Only let me serve my neighbor with that which God has given me, and thereby earn my living, since that is forbidden to no one.[52]

Bucer suggests that he be treated by the same standards applying to laymen. He had strong ideological reasons for that. As we have seen, Bucer's ideas tended to dissolve religion-created distinctions in social status. His concept of justification by faith and his ethic of service assailed clerical exclusivity, subjecting all social classes to common standards. His insistence on subjection to the magistrate explicitly includes taxation; he wants none of the traditional immunities. Although he does not mention the Rat's demand that clerics purchase the Bürgerrecht, made less than a week before his appearance, he would seem to allude to the issue throughout. Yet clerical citizenship had not yet become the central symbol of the evangelical polemic against clerical exclusivity that it shortly would.[53]

Zell's and Bucer's ideas shared another affinity with the Rat's programs. Each side (though in different measures) could contemplate stripping the religious government of certain of its political and economic institutional foundations. Yet the connection had not yet been rendered explicit.

Zell's and Bucer's attacks on religious government *per se* were far more radical than the Rat's; on the other hand, they had not yet considered the concrete issue of citizenship.

The evangelical leader who moved most rapidly to assimilate the Rat's goals was Wolfgang Capito.[54] Capito arrived in Strasbourg in June, 1523, to assume an enormously rich and powerful benefice as provost of the chapter of St. Thomas. For several months he worked to achieve a compromise between the evangelicals and the conservatives. As provost of St. Thomas, he was immediately caught up in the negotiations following the revocation of the *Schirm*; although he urged compromise on the canons, it seems that he also defended the chapter's interests.[55] In an attempt to quiet the city and to begin to allay anticlerical feeling, he took the Bishop's part in a compromise effort to get rid of Zell.[56] During a climactic interview, he told Zell to leave town for the sake of peace. Zell's explosive reply, flaunting the power of the Word against Capito's 'weak' human reforms, ultimately drove the latter from his position, but he continued attempts to mediate between the evangelicals and the old believers until August. On July 9, 1523, however, he purchased the *Bürgerrecht*.[57] It seems unlikely that he did so for ideological reasons; he later mentioned that special circumstances in the Chapter of St. Thomas drove him to take the step sooner than he might naturally have done.[58] By November, however, when Capito published the *Entschuldigung*, an open letter to the Bishop defending his conduct, he had developed a strong link between the "evangelical" ethic of brotherly love and popular anticlericalism, which he explicitly expressed in the demand that the clergy take the *Bürgerrecht*. According to Capito, the Gospel justified the demand that clerics carry the same burdens as citizens. The Rat's requirement that the clergy purchase the *Bürgerrecht* is supported by explicit divine commands, the universal duty of brotherly love, and natural decency.

> [The clergy ought] not to use its freedom so insolently against the common good, but, along with others, be willing to carry citizenly and common burdens....We are supposed to be subject to every authority for conscience's sake. We are enclosed in the city by gate and nail, guarded and protected; we have all the advantages of citizenship. Why then do we insist on being free of, exalted above, citizens' burdens?[59]

God orders everyone to submit to temporal authority. Love and natural decency require that everyone be willing to help carry the common load. Further, clerical citizenship would buffer the popular resentment of the clergy. It would lubricate points of friction, and the citizen-preacher would have a favorable position from which to work for peace and unity. Yet Capito is careful to emphasize that taking the Bürgerrecht has not voided his legal character as priest. He has not withdrawn himself from his ecclesiastical superiors' jurisdiction. Rather, he obeys both the Bishop and the Rat, each according to his proper jurisdiction.[60]

In this defense of his purchase of citizenship, Capito's ideas do not appear to threaten the clergy's religious status more radically than the Rat's demands. Being a citizen merely means that one formally recognizes his duty to share common burdens and to seek the common good. It does not mean abolition of the Bishop's jurisdiction in religious matters. Later in the tract, Capito attempts to bridge this conservative acceptance of episcopal authority and Zell and Bucer's absolute rejection of human law in divine matters. For Capito in 1523, hierarchical church government was a legitimate masquerade, permissible for the sake of order, peace, and unity, but without any absolute divine justification:

> 'We should be passive subjects, like sheep.' That is true. But sheep that can think, sheep of the eternal shepherd, whose voice we submissively worship in our prelates when they take his word in their mouths. When not, we regard them as other lords, not as shepherds; we obey, tolerate, and suffer them, as long as they do not try to force us against God....[Christians] accept the word of admonition from their leaders, as long as it agrees with Scripture, but [they accept] commandments and grace from God alone, through Christ Jesus our Lord. The Christian willingly tolerates external regulation [ordnung], if it is necessary for maintaining peace and unity on account of our sinfulness -- as long as it remains merely the regulation of external community [beywonung], and not compulsory law for the internal soul.[61]

In medieval and reformation thought, it was a matter of course to justify secular government by the need to preserve the external welfare of the community. But Capito uses the same rationale to justify religious government. The church (which Capito here considers as an external community) from time to time requires that peace and unity be imposed on it through human laws, promulgated by a human hierarchy. At some length Capito examines the record of the ancient councils, all of which made temporary laws for the sake of order and unity. The apostles reconciled Jewish and Gentile converts by forbidding the eating of blood; when the law was no longer needed, they abolished it. By the same principle, it was proper for the Archbishop of Rome to make of "tu es Petrus" a pretext for authority over the other patriarchs; it was the only way to impose order on the quarreling Greeks.[62]

These laws are temporary and human, not eternal or divine. The pope and his bishops are no longer worshipped as gods, and their administration is no longer believed to have roots in Scripture. Yet still, they need not be so defensive:

> Our human laws, order, authorities, lordships, jurisdictions, pomp, power, and force are unknown to Scripture and to the teaching of the Gospel. Yet they are necessary, due to our urgent need...just as the temporal sword is necessary and has been retained among Christians. We all live here together, good and evil [alike], and, like monkeys, we are easily moved to imitation by an external example. Yet the temporal sword has Scripture for it; the [religious] order among us, as it exists currently, does not have a single letter. It seems to me, gracious Prince and Lord, that this concedes the clerical estate a great deal, and could be a vehicle of reconciliation. But it is impossible to maintain it with rigor, since it is undeniable that the Spirit of God neither will nor can bear law or order.[63]

Capito grants a fragile pretext to the medieval religious hierarchy: imitation of the Scripture-confirmed secular government, a temporary expedient for maintaining order in the church. This permits him to argue for the obsolescence of some church laws, and for the mutability of all laws, the essential ideological conditions for relatively conservative reform. Yet it permits Capito to promise the Bishop that the hierarchy would still function.

The Entschuldigung illustrates a step in the process by which the Rat's program, originally rooted in anticlerical feeling but also limited by conservative religious and institutional principles, could be assimilated by evangelical ideology. Capito reproduces the old idea of the coexistence of two jurisdictions, one religious, one secular, to which both priests and laymen should be subject. But he goes further; he relativizes the religious government's claim to divine sanction for its laws. Capito's hope that this formula could bring about a compromise between the warring parties proved vain, of course. Zell and Bucer could not accept any diminution of the absolute opposition between human law and divine Word; and Capito's proposal rested precisely on the possibility that laws created by the church hierarchy could be binding if intended to further peace and unity, even at the price of distorting Scripture. Both Zell and Bucer fundamentally rejected the concept of religious government through the legal administration of an ecclesiastical hierarchy.[64] Capito later joined them, dedication to the sole efficacy of the Word overcoming his sensitivity to the concrete institutional nature of the church.[65]

In the end, practical political circumstances dictated that the "Gospel" could survive only by abrogating the Bishop's jurisdiction at every turn. The preachers' marriages, an example which Capito followed in the summer of 1524, exploded any remaining hope for compromise with the Bishop. The magistrate was left as the sole coercive authority in society, alone responsible for enforcing peace and unity in the community. The preachers retained only the power of the Word.

Capito, however, brought the issue of clerical citizenship itself into great prominence as an evangelical issue. Not only could the *Bürgerrecht* provide a practical refuge when the Bishop threatened the preachers, but it presented them with a keen and highly popular polemical weapon against the medieval clergy. Bucer petitioned the Rat for the full *Bürgerrecht* very shortly after the publication of the *Entschuldigung*, and the other evangelical leaders who had not already done so soon followed suit.[66] Clerical citizenship became an essential plank in the preachers' platform, one element of the dissolution of medieval religious government.[67] It was in that radical form that the preachers presented it to the people of Strasbourg.

The End of Immunity

As the evangelical preachers assimilated the issue of clerical citizenship and as the city of Strasbourg plunged into basic changes in the ministry and its functions in the spring of 1524, the negotiations between the Rat and the chapters on the *Schirm* made no progress. As we shall see below, during this time the Rat's bargaining position was complicated by a stream of petitions from the members of parishes under chapter control, demanding evangelical preachers of their own choosing and eventual dissolution of the bond with the chapters.[68] Under great pressure from the people, threatened by the Bishop and the constellation of powerful supporters the chapters had summoned, in July the Rat offered a compromise to the chapters, perhaps in hope of gaining cooperation in the matter of the parish pulpits. The Rat began by demanding that clerics purchase the full *Bürgerrecht*, but it immediately followed the demand with conditions for those who refused. As before, the canons would have to promise loyalty to the city, but the actual content of that promise was specified as abstention from citing citizens before courts outside the city and from attacking the city's freedoms. The fee for each chapter was raised slightly. The only other change from the old Schirm conditions was the assessment of a substantial fee for each member of the chapter, according to a scale based on his office. The city reserved the right to suspend the Schirm if the chapters violated its conditions before the new ten year term was completed.[69]

The chapters were slow to reply, and in the interim the population neared the bursting point. Rumors were flying that canons from Young St. Peter had paid ruffians to start fires or seize the city in order to "punish the Lutherans," rumors backed up by depositions the Rat received from outside the city.[70] The parishioners of Young St. Peter had already shown themselves to be aggressive on the matter of incorporation; the combination of their frustration with the rumors led to a near-riot on August 20. The canons of Young St. Peter gathered their valuables and fled from the city, soon followed by part of the treasure of St. Thomas.[71] This first flight of part of the canons of Strasbourg chapters changed the situation. It excited a broad range of citizens with evangelical inclinations. On the twenty-second or twenty-third, the Rat received a petition from the parishioners of five major churches, demanding that evangelical preachers be appointed to all pulpits. The Rat immediately decided to send that matter to the Schöffen.[72] Then, recorded in the same document, it changed its position on the Schirm.[73] The flight of the canons was a grave danger signal for its old policy; if the chapters could not remain in peace, Strasbourg would be publicly exposed as an enemy of medieval religion and law. Thus the Rat sought to protect the chapters' rights against their parishioners, if only to permit them to negotiate the release of the pulpit rights to the Rat. But the population and the Rat's own sentiments left little further room for compromise on the Schirm.

> Since the canons are withdrawing from the city, one should send to the canons and monks [pfaffen und geistlichen] in all chapters, cloisters, and churches, and question them as to what my lords and the citizenry are supposed to have done wrong. Those who wish to remain in this city should all swear (except for the counts [=the Cathedral chapter]) to be faithful and loyal to the City of Strasbourg, to its citizens and associates, to advance its good and turn away its harm, etc. One should order [them to pay] the wine tax and customs duties; no household goods are to be let out of the city without the knowledge of my lords.[74]

The Rat, moved both by the allegations against the chapters and by the pressure of the population, imposed these temporary measures on the canons in order to tie them to the city until the issues were resolved.

The growth of the population's tension did not slow. In September the riots of the Treger affair broke out. Treger, the Provincial of the Augustinians, was imprisoned by a mob, and several cloisters were invaded and pillaged. On September 10, 1524, the guilds, speaking officially, demanded that "priests and others who have been free up until now should carry citizens' burdens."[75]

In this context, perhaps thinking it necessary to

face danger boldly, the chapters made counterproposals to the Rat. On September 24, they announced that they were willing to promise loyalty to the city, as long as that loyalty did not conflict with previously contracted duties. They agreed to continue paying the standard taxes on wine, the milling of grain, etc., and they conceded to the demand to join guilds. Yet they firmly rejected any abridgement of their independence from secular legal jurisdiction, and they offered to pay only a tiny fraction of the individual fees that the Rat had proposed in July.[76]

As we shall see, by the middle of October the Rat was ready openly to declare itself in favor of a large part of the evangelical movement's achievements. Its mind made up by the citizenry, it was no longer willing to compromise on the Schirm.[77] On November 15, the Rat's delegation to the chapter of St. Thomas bluntly laid out what the "common man" wanted:

> The commons [gemeine] has indicated to the Rat that the reason for the tension and discord between the clergy and the commons of the City of Strasbourg is that the commons is burdened with taxes [sull (=zoll), zellen, ungelt und stubgelt], but up until now the clergy has been freed from them all, much to the common man's damage and lack since the more he pays in taxes, the more he needs to support his wife and children [?]. The common man further complains that he has had to suffer much disgrace, mockery, and shame in regard to his children and women who have cared for [?] the clergy, and he refuses to stand for it any longer. [The common people] will not be satisfied unless clergymen carry citizens' burdens as they do, and become citizens.[78]

According to the delegation, the general population demanded that priests pay the same taxes as everyone else, and that their behavior be subject to the Rat's discipline as citizens. By saying that, the Rat indicated that it would not give ground on the two points which the chapters' counter-proposals had rejected: full taxation, and subjection to secular legal jurisdiction. Its concrete proposal to St. Thomas specified a heavy schedule of taxes on property and income, and full submission to the strict *Bürgerrecht* conditions of June, 1523.[79]

The chapters made one last search outside the city for pressure which could move the Rat. After the Bishop's renewed efforts to mediate the issue broke down, the chapters reached mutual agreement: rather than accept the Rat's conditions, they would go into exile.[80] Their reasons are not far to seek. The increase in anticlerical violence made further stay in the city, unprotected by the *Schirm*, unacceptable. Things had reached a breaking point. The Rat would not yield, and yet to acquiesce to its demands would mean surrendering a legal status it had enjoyed with full moral confidence for generations. Further, it would leave them sworn to obey a magistrate which had supported gross violations of law and illegitimate changes in basic religious institutions, in support of a heresy.

On December 1, 1524, the canons made a last effort at compromise. They offered to concede full taxation -- in fact, to carry burdens heavier than the citizens' -- if the Rat would withdraw its demand for citizenship. The Rat, answering, reminded them that it did not require an oath, warmaking, or travel. It was not enough. On December 6, most of the canons who had not already deserted the city quickly rode out of the city gates, carrying their remaining treasure with them. The Rat, surprised and infuriated, captured a few returning canons and set about finding out what had become of the treasures. The last incentive to compromise gone, on January 16, 1525 the Rat ordered all resident clerics to assume the Bürgerrecht, on pain of expulsion from the city.[81]

* * * * *

The Rat launched its attack on clerical immunity as Zell's movement was rapidly gaining strength in Strasbourg. Yet the Rat's policy was hardly inspired by Zell's ideas. Its roots were in a policy which the Rat had pursued for generations. Residents had grown accustomed to the idea that their "bürgerlich" conduct could be distinguished from their "geistlich" conduct; they thought it normal to be subject to two governments simultaneously, secular and religious. The Rat meant no more than to apply this distinction to the clergy. By making clergymen citizens, it would end the century-long disruptions that clerical immunity had caused in the Rat's authority over the secular affairs of its own citizens. It meant to keep the clergy's essential religious character intact. It modified those provisions of the oath of citizenship which tended to derogate from the priestly office, providing for its primary obedience to spiritual jurisdiction, its unwillingness to take oaths to secular governments, its pacifism, and its duty to devote all of its time to religious pursuits.

During the two years of struggle over the Schirm, the form of these provisions did not change. Yet the significance of the issue did. In one sense, when the canons left the city it signalled the victory of the Rat. Clerical immunity could threaten secular government no longer. Yet if the religious context had remained unchanged, the desertion would have indicated a major failure of the Rat's policy. The Rat's original goal was not to hound clergymen out of the city, but to bind them to it. The canons gone, their perpetual chant and prayer stopped, the holy places empty: it would have been unbearable for a pious people.[82] But the city's religious life had changed, and the canons were not missed.[83] The medieval religious government had been abolished; the forms of piety which it has supported were being dismantled. The attempt to govern the clergy while leaving their religious office intact had failed. The members of the Rat had changed their values; the city as a whole had turned its back on the old understanding of the clergy's religious office. The citizen preacher was part of the new understanding.

The Rat's Policy Toward the Evangelical Movement

The issue of clerical citizenship illustrates the complex process of change during the evangelical movement. We have seen how the movement radicalized the Rat's campaign against clerical immunity, turning a program rooted in the fifteenth century into a plank in the Reformation's platform. The preachers themselves were not conscious of the issue until the Rat's attack was well underway; rapidly extending some of their basic ethical principles, they assimilated it and quickly moved to exploit it as a popular, visible change, distinguishing the old clergy from the new. The Rat's program and the preachers' interacted, leaving neither the same.

Different complexities emerge from the Rat's policy toward the evangelical movement itself. From 1522 to 1524, the Rat took actions which changed the character of the clerical estate irreversably. In rapid series, it was confronted by evangelical preachers seeking asylum, first because of their sermons, and then because of their marriages; by parishioners who seized pulpits and installed ministers to their liking; and by citizens who threatened to overturn the religious government violently and thereby to destroy the legal order on which the Rat's foundation was built. How did the Rat react? How did evangelical ideas make themselves felt? When the Rat finally established religious changes, how did it tailor them, how were conflicting interests resolved? The Rat's policy toward religious change, which from 1522 to 1524 chiefly involved the social and religious character of the ministry, is a particularly illuminating example of the ways in which evangelical ideas influenced social and political institutions.

* * * * *

Throughout the first years of the movement, the Rat shrouded itself in ambiguity.[84] It would not permit evangelical preachers to be persecuted, but it gave them no overt help in spreading their ideas. It temporized when it could, and when the population would not wait any longer, it struggled to keep its own actions legal. It tried to maintain a legally regular position in the Empire, while keeping its increasingly evangelical population quiet. The effect of this delicate balancing act was to create conditions under which basic religious change could occur with as little effect as possible on the city's social, economic, and political position.

The ambiguity of the Rat's policy did not please either party. Nikolaus Wurmser, the bitterly anti-Lutheran dean of the chapter of St. Thomas, was infuriated by the Rat's pronouncement of January, 1523, that all preachers should preach the Gospel without fear. That "stupid" decision, wrote Wurmser, showed that "the Rat is on the side of Luther and his teaching."[85] For Martin Bucer, however, the Strasbourg Rat was hardly on Luther's side. After the Rat had denied him permission to lecture in June of 1523, he wrote to Zwingli:

> The brothers have twice tried to open the door for me to preach the word of God, assembling for me to lecture in German on some books of the New Testament. But the Rat (of which a considerable part has, up to now, little favored the Gospel), observing the large number of citizens that heard me, forbade me to lecture on anything. It seems that they feared that under the pretext of hearing me lecture, an assembly of citizens would contrive something against [the Rat], or would be less heedful of what the Rat told them. Thus, everywhere, [rulers] fear to lose their kingdoms to Christ, though his kingdom is not of this world.[86]

The Rat protected Strasbourg's religious ferment from outside interference, and kept the peace. In this period, it never unilaterally imposed religious changes on its citizens. When opinion was divided in the city, the Rat allowed its citizens to follow their convictions, protecting each party from the other and preventing disorder. When politically active citizens finally reached a consensus, changing the city's balance decisively, the Rat institutionalized certain reforms in a socially conservative manner. The Rat was not the "motor" of the Strasbourg reformation, but it actively maintained the conditions under which change could occur.

The Defense of the Preachers

The Rat first confronted the evangelical movement in Strasbourg during the series of legal attacks on evangelical preachers which began in 1521, not ceasing until 1524. The dismissal of Peter Rumpsberger from Old St. Peter on grounds of his evangelical ideas occurred in 1520, but it left almost no trace.[87] Not until December 28, 1521 was the Rat's attention drawn to such a case. On that date, it received a petition from Tylman von Lyn, a lector at the local Carmelite monastery. The letter was a blistering demand for the protection of the Word of God against those who sought to suppress it. The Bishop's Fiscal and Notary had called upon Tylman and his prior and had forbidden him to preach or confess, presenting him with a list of six theses from his sermons. To the Rat, Tylman denied having preached those doctrines, but then he offered to defend them in a public disputation. He attacked papal absolutism, the hierarchical government of the church, human religious laws, monasticism, celibacy, and the withholding of sacramental wine from the laity. The last thesis boldly asserted the priesthood of all believers. After sketching his case with some violence and with very little explanation, Tylman petitioned the Rat for support. Ratsherren, he wrote, possess the sword in order to defend the good; they are duty-bound to defend justice and truth to the death. In this case that means to defend him as a preacher; no man can come to the truth if the truth is not proclaimed.[88]

There is no record of any response from the Rat, and during the summer of 1522, Tylman was removed from his office permanently and sank from sight.[89] Although Tylman may well have had grounds to hope that he could persuade certain Ratsherren with leanings toward church reform to defend him, the only result was that evangelical ideas gained publicity, and the Rat's role was publicly brought into question.

During the spring of 1522, Zell's sermons were beginning to attract large crowds and increasing loyalty from citizens in his parish. Several petitions were sent to the Rat, asking it to provide Zell with a pulpit in the Cathedral nave itself, since the adjoining parish chapel had become too crowded and the Cathedral chapter had refused to open Geiler's old pulpit to Zell. The Rat complied on June 21.[90] The next issue of serious legal implications did not arise until July 9, when the deputy of the episcopal vicar appeared. He opened his presentation with two assertions: the Edict of Worms had condemned Lutheran teaching, and further, Basel had expelled a popular preacher even though three hundred citizens had pleaded for him. Then he turned to the case at hand. A peasant had begun to preach against the sacraments, the papacy, and celibacy in Strasbourg. He demanded that this man, known as Karsthans, be imprisoned or handed over to the Bishop, a necessary measure to prevent the spread of heresy.[91]

The deputy's statement about the events in Basel is interesting; it seems to imply that Karsthans preaching had a following in Strasbourg, and that the deputy thought the Rat might be inclined not to enforce the law against anyone supported by a substantial group of its citizens. The Rat's response is no less interesting. It had Karsthans interviewed. He denied that he had been "preaching", since he had only answered questions, and he denied that he was a heretic: he was willing to be corrected by Scripture. After much discussion, the Rat cited the deputy's admitted lack of personal knowledge of the facts of the case as grounds for refusing to imprison the peasant. It made no public effort to find other witnesses. It did, however, require the peasant to abstain from further preaching.[92] Not until September 6 did the Rat take further action. Karsthans was accused of preaching again, this time including the use of provocative language and (according to some sources) extending his attacks to the Rat. On this occasion, the Rat imprisoned and exiled him without delay. It is clear, however, that the Rat had not been willing to permit him to be attacked solely on the grounds that he had engaged in evangelical agitation. In spite of the fact that Karsthans had no legal status in the city, the Rat protected him for two months.

This reluctance did not go unnoticed by the Bishop. On August 2, before Karsthans exile, the Bishop sent a delegation to the Rat in order to clarify its attitude toward a prospective campaign led by his officials against heresy.[93] After reviewing the papal and imperial condemnations of Luther's teaching, he noted that many within his diocese were paying no heed to the law. He, however, meant to prevent the division and injury that the dissemination of condemned ideas would inevitably produce. He requested the Rat not to hinder him if he took legal steps against people under the Rat's jurisdiction. Further, he requested that if any people should attempt to evade punishment by purchasing the Bürgerrecht, that the Rat would refuse to protect them.

It seems likely that the Bishop's message was occasioned by the Rat's still-continuing refusal to deal with Karsthans. Shortly to begin gathering evidence against Zell, the Bishop was concerned that the Rat not interfere with his jurisdiction over priests in the city. The Rat's reply, made after long discussion, shows that the Bishop's worries were justified. To be sure, it first stated that it was not inclined to hinder the Bishop's exercise of his rightful authroity if he acted against the clergy. Yet he should remain faithful to the Rachtung of Speyer: that is, work solely through his Official and Fiscal in Strasbourg, not citing anyone to courts outside the city, nor employing force. But if a priest had friends or relatives who wished to support him against the Bishop, there was nothing that the Rat could do about it. The Bishop should be careful not to prosecute any citizens in reprisal for complaints against clergymen. Finally, the Rat turned to the Bishop's own administration: he should provide the parishes with learned, pious priests, who would explicate the "Holy Gospel and the teaching of God and the Apostles," and no longer speak for their own greed and profit. The Rat verbally protested its respect for the Bishop's jurisdiction, while in fact raising conditions which would render his execution of any concrete programs difficult. It is a technique we shall find in use again, as the Rat tried to keep its footing during the evangelical movement.

Although neither the Bishop's letter nor the Rat's reply mentioned Zell by name, he was the logical target of any anti-Lutheran campaign. After Tylman's final removal in the summer of 1522, Zell was the only remaining evangelical preacher in Strasbourg. By that time, he had gathered a good deal of popular support, recognized by the Rat when it granted him a pulpit in the Cathedral. In November, the Rat again had occasion to deal with Zell.[94] A quarrel had flared up between him and Dr. Peter Wickram, the incumbant of Geiler's former _Predikatur_. The Rat sent emmissaries both to Zell and to Wickram, ordering them ("Dr. Peter _very firmly_") to stop attacking each other from the pulpit, and to preach exclusively from the Gospel, Paul, and Acts. This action already implied several components of the Rat's future policy toward preachers. The Rat believed that it had the authority to prevent behavior by the clergy which might threaten public order. By confining the preachers to the explication of certain New Testament books, provocative side issues might be avoided, perhaps in the expectation that the Gospel itself was non-controversial. Both measures were taken in order to limit the divisive effects of preaching on the lay population.[95]

As the year drew to an end, the Bishop finally gave his Fiscal the formal order to punish priests who had publicly expressed their opposition to papal and imperial mandates and to the "existing Christian order." In December, the Fiscal cited Zell to appear before the Vicar on the twenty-second of that month. Two angry and threatening placards were nailed to the Vicar's door by residents; on the twentieth the Bishop wrote in protest, demanding that the Rat protect his officials.[96]

On January 4, 1523, a council meeting was held in which the Rat took a momentous stand. The Bishop had explicitly justified his anti-Lutheran campaign by his desire to prevent the disunity and the breakdown of cleric-lay relations that the spread of Lutheran ideas would cause. The Rat agreed that it wanted its citizens, and all clerical and secular residents, to be able to live together peaceably. But it drew a sharply different conclusion. As far as it was concerned, the minutes read, Zell had preached nothing but "God's Word and the Holy Scriptures"; he had repeatedly offered to prove so to anyone who thought the contrary. Thus, the Rat determined itself to defend him in his expression of God's Word.[97] It decided to take immediate concrete steps. Delegations were to be sent to four relevant parties. First, the Cathedral Chapter was asked to get the lower chapter, the Deputaten, Zell's employers, to retain him as the pastor of St. Lawrence, and to insure that he "could speak the Word of God without fear to his parishioners and to others who hear his sermons, for the Rat intends to protect and guard him [in the employment of] the Word of God and the truth." In return, the Rat would persuade Zell to abstain from any irrelevant nonsense or slander.[98] Second, the Deputaten themselves were to be told that if they meant to keep the Rat's <u>Schirm</u>, they had to protect the city from discord between the clergy and the townsfolk, in this case by retaining Zell and by not obstructing attendance at his sermons. The Rat's delegation was to instruct Zell in his turn to preach nothing but the

Word of God and the teachings and writings of the Apostles, and to abstain from "other unnecessary, provocative polemics [tandmeeren]". But he should then be admonished, in the Rat's name, to preach the Word of God and the Scriptures boldly and without fear, for the Rat would guard, protect, and take care of him.[99] Fourth, all preachers in all Strasbourg's ecclesiastical institutions were to be instructed to refrain from slander and other worthless or provocative talk from the pulpit. They should preach whatever was "in accord with the Holy Gospel and divine Scripture, and of service to peace and unity."[100] On January 8, the Rat's delegation carried out their commissions.[101]

The chief reason that the Rat gave for defending Zell was that he preached nothing but the Scriptures and God's Word. Because of that, it felt justified morally and legally in obstructing attacks on him. Contrary to the Bishop's contention that Zell represented the teaching of the Lutheran party and thus was a violator of the papal and imperial mandates, the Rat regarded him as a simple expositor of God's Word, to be defended from attack. On at least one level, the Rat showed itself to accept the sola scriptura principle. Since Zell confined himself to God's Word, on that ground alone he was acceptable to the Rat and worthy of defense. Further, the Rat rejected the Bishop's argument that peace in the city depended on suppression of evangelical preaching. It told the Deputaten that in this case, peace would be maintained if the clergy gave way to the laity; it clearly thought that the Bishop was demanding that the common folk pay the price of peace by sacrificing a popular preacher. It is difficult to resist the impression that a number of Ratsherren regarded Zell at least as their champion against clerical arrogance.

The Rat's affirmation of this form of the Scripture principle no doubt helped the evangelical preachers gain popular acceptance. Yet it is not necessary to conclude that the Rat's decision implied conscious allegiance to Lutheran ideas.[102] The decision was not understood to attack the town's still-faithful Catholic preachers. There is no means of distinguishing the Ratsherren who understood the radical bases of Zell's sermons from those who merely accepted him as a preacher against abuses in Geiler's mold. Clearly, the January decision was more than an attempt to restrict preachers to non-controversial issues by limiting them to the Gospel; Zell's reliance on Scripture was advanced by the Rat as a prima facie case for his acceptability, sufficient to justify resisting the Bishop. But for many members, it need not have been more than a naively accepted minimum standard for compliance with customary limits, showing that a popular preacher was worthy of defense against a clergy many saw as power-hungry and self-seeking.

There can be no misunderstanding the legal content of the Rat's decision. The promise to protect Zell was a direct rejection of the Bishop's request that the Rat refuse to protect priests being prosecuted.[103] The Rat cut off Zell's sermons from the Bishop's jurisdiction. Yet it did so by legal means, chiefly by pressure on Zell's patrons and on the Cathedral chapter. It did not forcibly suppress the Vicar's proceedings against Zell;[104] it simply obstructed the process of dismissing him from his offices. The two poles of the Rat's policy are apparent: it avoided open and conspicuous contempt of the law, and yet it refused to acquiesce in the suppression of the Gospel.

Several political factors cooperated in bringing the Rat to Zell's defense. He clearly had earnest support among certain groups of citizens. The placards nailed to the Vicar's door were aggressive in tone, and the Bishop certainly interpreted them as a threat of violence. Yet the spontaneity and directness of the Rat's action do not suggest that it was coerced by the threat of riot. They rather witness to the influence of Zell's upper class supporters and to his general popularity in the city. At least a minority of Ratsherren was determined that he not be removed, with the rest of the Rat unwilling to contravene its fellows. The reasons which the Rat proffered indicate that, at the very least, ideas were current in the council chamber upon which the preachers could easily build.

The Rat actively worked on Zell's behalf through the spring of 1523, splitting the Bishop and the chapters with the help of evangelical sympathizers in the church establishment, with the lever of the Schirm, and by impressing upon the Bishop the threat of anticlerical riot if Zell were not retained. A succession of replacement preachers selected by the Deputaten began to preach evangelically in their turn. Finally, the Bishop agreed to retain Zell for another year. Until his excommunication for marriage in 1524, Zell was left alone.[105]

The limits of the Rat's willingness to defend evangelical preachers were sharply expanded by its dealings with Martin Bucer and Anton Firn. In virtue of his father's citizenship, Bucer was granted official protection from force [Gewalt] when he arrived in Strasbourg in late spring of 1523, but he was refused legal protection. It was not the first occasion that the Rat had heard of Bucer. On January 11, 1523, only days after active defense of Zell had begun, two deputies from the Rat of Wissembourg asked the Strasbourg Rat for advice regarding Bucer, then active in Wissembourg. According to the visitors, he was preaching "the evangelical truth from the book of Matthew", but the Bishop of Speyer, identifying him as a member of Luther's party, had ordered them to exile or imprison him. The Strasbourg Rat's response was to describe the tactics it had just developed for protecting Zell's proclamation of the Gospel.[106]

In June, however, the Rat treated Bucer with a good deal of reserve. As we have seen, his personal situation was very different from Zell's. He had no benefice giving him a solid legal foundation in Strasbourg. He had been excommunicated in the diocese of Speyer. He was married and thus ineligible for ecclesiastical office, according to the just-issued mandate of the Nürnberg Reichstag. Finally, he was closely associated with the rebel knight Franz von Sickingen.[107] The Rat was under suspicion of having supported the Knight's Revolt, and fully accepting Bucer would have lent credence to those accusations.[108] Granting Bucer complete Schirm, or winking at his preaching and public lectures, would have openly committed the Rat to support his gross legal irregularities, of which it had been officially notified by the Bishop of Strasbourg.[109] They could keep him safe, but they would not support him.

After the initial refusal to permit Bucer to preach, however, public support for him grew. Through the summer he demonstrated his docility and moderation; when Zell opened his pulpit to Bucer in August, the Rat agreed.[110] Yet it refused Bucer's petition for full Bürgerrecht in November, 1523, and did not finally grant it to him until 1524, after all the other evangelical preachers had also married and been excommunicated.

There are certain respects in which Bucer's pessimistic assessment of the Rat's refusal to permit him to preach, quoted above, was justified.[111] The Rat's protection of Zell meant much less than a blanket commitment to Bucer's own version of evangelical ideology or program of institutional change. Zell's program was less radical than Bucer's, and his personal status offended no sensibilities. Defending Zell did not mean to defend illegal changes in the institution of the ministry as gross as marriage. The Rat could still protect itself behind an ambiguous duty to defend the "divine

Gospel and truth."

Many of the ambiguities were dissolved when Anton Firn married. He was the preacher at St. Thomas, the parish church of the chapter of St. Thomas. On October 18, 1523, he announced from the pulpit that he had married his former housekeeper and mistress, and that he would bring her to church the following Sunday.[112] The Nürnberg Mandate made the chapter's duty quite clear; married priests were to be stripped of their benefices and incomes. In practice, it had proven difficult to enforce the Edict of Worms or any other anti-Lutheran standard based only on doctrinal judgments; evangelical preachers early learned to shroud traditional doctrinal standards in a fog of rationalization. Marriage, however, was an open and unequivocal violation of papal and imperial law, obvious to any observer. If the Rat was to continue to protect a "Gospel" which was constantly evolving in a more radical direction, it would have to do so sailing against the wind of the Empire's law. Firn's marriage and subsequent refusal to compromise forced the Rat to develop means of protecting illegal conditions within its walls without threatening its own position by openly violating the law. The Firn affair was crucial for the preachers as well. For the first time, they employed the tactic which came to characterize the movement in Strasbourg. After preaching had spread the rationale for an illegal innovation and a core of supporters had been formed, the preachers blatantly abrogated the law. This forced the Rat and the slower elements of the population, already loosely allied to some more moderate conception of the "Gospel", to adopt the new conception, or to turn to reaction and repression.

After Firn's announcement on October 18, the Bishop wrote to the chapter and the Rat, again demanding help or at least no interference in his compliance with the Nürnberg

Mandate by prosecuting Firn. The chapter hesitated. Firn was a citizen, and he had assembled a group of strong and potentially violent supporters among his parishioners. The chapter thus made the politic decision to ask the Rat's permission in advance.[113]

The Rat was divided. At least a minority of Ratsherren publicly supported Firn. The wives of Frederich Ingold and Jakob Spender, both prominent Ratsherren, accompanied Firn's bride to the altar at the wedding ceremony.[114] Hoping to evade the issue, the Rat did not answer the Bishop's letter. To the chapter it replied that the matter of firing Firn was outside of its own competence. It would, however, assure the chapter of protection against force. The next week, however, when Firn refused to be fired, the Rat was forced to act. On November 15 Firn ascended his pulpit as usual, chasing away the priest whom the chapter had hired to take over the services. Seeking to support the chapter's rights, and to avoid any violent clash with Firn, the Rat sent him a delegation, offering to obtain his full year's salary if he would step down voluntarily. Firn followed the lead of Zell and Capito; going over the Rat's head, he appealed for a public hearing and final judgment by the community, "to which, by the command of the Holy Spirit, it belongs to judge." The Ratsherren then gave him notice that the Rat would not defend him against the ecclesiastical system and the Nürnberg Mandate.[115]

The Rat was pushed into a painful choice between acting in contempt of the entire body of medieval law and custom by protecting Firn, and alienating Firn's supporters by appearing to aid the suppression of the "Gospel." It first attempted to ward off the danger of provocative confrontations by telling the chapter that Firn should not be pressed further, since he had appealed for legal judgment. The chapter refused, reconfirming the dismissal on November

29 and again on December 7.[116]

On December 3, Zell himself publicly married.[117] Firn could no longer be isolated, and Zell's public support was far too great to be crushed. Thus, on December 7, the Rat sent a delegation to the Bishop, carrying with it instructions which were remarkable in several respects. The Rat chose this occasion not only to discuss the matter of clerical marriage, but also to forward the chapters' request that the *faits accomplis* of the new welfare system and the regulation of annuities be ratified, and to notify the Bishop of the status of the negotiations on the *Schirm*.[118] It is possible that the Rat intended this juxtaposition of issues to cause the Bishop to give ground on these relatively harmless issues by offering him hope of gaining cooperation on the essential ones. And in fact, the instructions offered a compromise on clerical marriage, outlining circumstances under which the Rat could afford to support the Bishop's prosecution of the married clerics. Yet behind this formal offer of compliance, the interests of the *Ratsherren* who supported Zell and Firn were well served. The instructions hid a coherent defense of the principle of clerical marriage; only the cutting edge of the preacher's absolute distinction between divine and human law was dulled. Further, the compromise itself required that the Bishop undertake something which neither he nor his predecessors had ever successfully executed: stopping the illicit sexual activity of the clergy.

> The Rat regards [both] such innovations [i.e. clerical marriage] and other of the clergy's disorderly and scandalous ways of life, which have been practiced in the City of Strasbourg for a long time, not with little but with great offense and displeasure. The Rat could

well abide that His Princely Grace, as the authority competent to punish [such offenders], act against them legally in all such crimes, [as is] both godly and just. The Rat will not hinder His Princely Grace [from so doing].

However, at the same time His Princely Grace is to be reminded that through the various publications which have been appearing for several years and through the preachers, the common people throughout the city and the countryside have been taught and made aware of divine and also of human statutes more than has been [the case] in the community for long years. Now if one wishes to proceed harshly with the penalties of canon law against the priests who marry (according to the command of God, as they publicly claim from the pulpit), and at the same time not to inflict equivalent punishment...on other priests and clergymen who openly and scandalously live in violation of divine and human statutes and all decency, [proffering] an evil example, what will be said by the common man, and by all who are inclined towards honor? Certainly nothing other than that a person who, according to the permission of divine Scripture, marries and longs to live honorably, is dispossessed, driven out, and excluded from his benefice, all freedoms, and priestly office, and another person, who lives in public licentiousness, vice, and dishonor...is tolerated and permitted to remain. For it is not hidden, rather clear before the eyes of His Princely Grace, that even though the estate of holy matrimony is not forbidden to anyone by God, but only (perhaps by good intention) forbidden by the fathers of the church to priests and those in the orders, and, decreed as religious criminal law [_strefflich gesatz_], both the canon law and His Imperial Majesty's law appoint and lay down equivalent penalties for all clergymen who marry and for those who live offensively with concubines and frivolous women. [_Crossed out_:] For a long time many of the clergy have remained unhindered, tranquilly carrying on their injurious conduct and offensive lust in violation both of divine decrees and human statutes, and now that someone else is acting in accord with the command of God, they dare to drive him out. [_End of cross out_.] Thus, where equivalent punishment is not applied in both cases, in accord with the _Racht_ [the Rachtung of Speyer?], then more reluctance and discord than peace and unity will spring up in the community, as His Princely Grace...can assess for himself.

On this account, it is the Rat's humble plea that His Princely Grace take this extremely troubling burden, which involves not only the temporal but also the eternal and the salvation of souls, into gracious consideration, and reflect on whether, in order to avoid this situation [?], His Papal Holiness, His Imperial Majesty, and the Common Estates might undertake a paternal, gracious, and Christian inquiry at the planned Reichstag, so that such discord can be allayed and a God-pleasing Christian unity established.

Item: also request...that His Princely Grace appoint understanding men learned in the Holy Scripture to pay heed to the preachers and if they preach something other than what is in accord

> with the Holy Scripture, or something that cannot be proven from Holy Scripture, reject it, so that the laity and the common people are not thereby led into error and the perdition of their souls.[119]

We have quoted this document at length in order to illustrate the complexity of the Rat's response to radical religious change during the year which followed. The compromise offered to the Bishop -- far more subtle than appears on the surface -- was designed to serve the interests of all parties involved. It stayed well within the limits of the law, yet it covertly defended clerical marriage. It did not challenge the Bishop's jurisdiction over his priests, yet it introduced conditions rendering episcopal prosecution very difficult, and offered the Bishop graceful and secure legal grounds to withhold action. The Rat agreed that the law on the books should be respected as the law, but at the same time it argued that in itself the law was of doubtful merit and was extremely dangerous to enforce.

On one level, the bald legal content of the instructions is to acquiesce in the Bishop's request not to hinder the prosecution. That is, the Rat agrees not to obstruct the Bishop from doing what unquestionably it was his right to do. It avoids open conflict with the central, best defended core of the Bishop's customary authority: his disciplinary jurisdiction over the secular clergy. Further, the Rat does not assert its approval of the preachers' actions. The instructions open with clear disapproval of clerical marriage, and there is no reason to doubt that at least a minority of _Ratsherren_ were shocked, if not by the unchastity itself, then by its bold illegality.[120] But above all, the Rat's equation of clerical marriage with other forms of sexual irregularity permitted it to retain a posture of legal orthodoxy in the eyes of the Empire;

clerical marriage was agreed to be illicit before the law, as custom demanded.

Throughout the evangelical movement, the major source of the Rat's resistance to the preachers' program was the Rat's natural respect for law. Whatever contrast appears between divine and human law in its documents is very softly stated; divine law does not give reformists the right unilaterally to abrogate the customs and laws of generations.[121] Dependent on the structures of medieval law for both existence and essence, the Rat could not treat law in a cavalier fashion. It feared isolation and illegality.

Yet on the other hand, the Rat also thought that it could not support the Bishop's campaign against evangelicals. The threat posed by the Gospel's disorderly supporters, in this case by Firn's bellicose parishioners, was considerable. The influence of "respectable" citizens sympathetic to the preachers and hostile to the traditional clergy grew daily. Above all, support for clerical marriage had gained substantial ground within the Rat itself. Even the most conservative members were sensitive to the dangers involved; means had to be found to impede the Bishop, without open resistance.

The Rat's position did so. By insisting that clerical marriage be treated as the equivalent of concubinage and other sexual "abuses", the Rat enormously complicated the Bishop's task. Concubinage had been winked at or treated lightly for generations. Wilhelm von Hohnstein had issued decrees against cohabitation, but they had been of no effect at all on the upper clergy.[122] He himself admitted that the "abuse" was so deeply ingrained that many had thought that any campaign to root it out would do more harm than good.[123] By equating the legal status of concubinage and marriage, the Rat demanded that the Bishop treat both with equal rigor -- long believed futile -- or with equal leniency. Further, the preachers thus could not simply be isolated and excommunicated as individuals; it could only be done as one element of a general attack on clerical immorality. It may have occurred to Zell's defenders on the Rat that many of the same problems of enforcement could be expected to frustrate such a campaign as all its predecessors.

The instructions offer legal alternatives to a prosecution. For both Rat and Bishop, non-compliance with the Nürnberg Mandate could be justified by the clear and present danger of a popular uprising. Maintenance of public order was the Rat's central responsibility. It gave the Rat a legally sustainable interest in requesting the Bishop's abeyance; it gave the Bishop solid grounds to acquiesce. And a supplementary argument could justify indefinite non-enforcement of the Mandate: the appeal for a council or Reichstag. The Rat's instructions argue that the law against clerical marriage is itself of doubtful merit, that the population will respond violently to one-sided repression, that the issue is moot in many other places in the Empire, and that it is therefore essential that the matter be reexamined by the relevant authorities and a universal solution found.[124]

The Rat's instructions for the delegation to the Bishop, then, amount to an explication of how the Nürnberg Mandate might not be enforced and yet not be held in contempt. The Rat's legal orthodoxy could be protected by a vocal adherence to the law on marriage. For Zell's and Firn's sympathizers, the equation of concubinage and marriage would render the Bishop's prosecution difficult if he accepted it, and provide grounds for the Rat's opposition if he did not. The Bishop was given means legally to justify postponing or dropping the prosecution. For all parties, the appeal for a council permitted those who valued legal regularity to seek reform without unilateral, illegal "innovation."

In explaining why the Bishop's intention to prosecute

only the married priests is ill-conceived, however, the Rat's instructions reveal the beginnings of ideas a good deal more radical. In the document's opening lines, to be sure, the Rat's equation of clerical marriage with other licentious ways of life tends to reinforce the old distinction between the character of the priest and that of the layman. Different ethical standards ought to apply to each group; marriage can still be forbidden to the consecrated. But later in the instructions, this division shrinks into an artificially created human distinction, decreed not by God but by the Fathers, "perhaps with good intention." The Rat explicitly asserts that no divine command or passage of Scripture forbids marriage to anyone. Further, the Rat's language suggests a growing reluctance to distinguish between one sort of sexual respectability proper to the clergy and another lower one proper to laymen. A priest might well marry out of "an inclination to honor"; precisely the same desire for sexual order and respectability ("honor") is seen as rendering the common man unwilling to see married clerics punished and profligates go free. For the layman, any decent man will shun promiscuity and marry; the Rat observes that that is exactly what the priests, claiming to obey the command of Scripture, have done. However, this is not to say that the Rat grants divine law absolute priority, justifying the preachers' violation of human law. What the Rat does imply is that the issue, _on its merits_, deserves careful review by all relevant authorities in the Empire.

This guarded tendency to extend lay sexual values to the clergy is closely related to Zell's and Bucer's program. The preachers used the egalitarian principle of justification by faith and the legal weapon of the unique divine status of Scripture to attack the clergy's special social and ethical position. The idea of the clergy's unique sacral status once refuted, marriage could be made available to all.[125] Those ideas were clearly winning support in the Rat.

In the last clause of the instructions, the Rat turned from Firn's marriage to preaching in general. To understand the significance of the Rat's request that sermons be overseen, we must return to a decree it issued a week earlier, on December 1. On that date, the Rat had ordered all preachers to preach nothing but the Gospel, and to avoid all other irrelevant, provocative, or seditious talk.[126] The decree reasserted the Rat's decision of a year earlier to defend Zell and limit preaching to the Gospel. An intervening event, however, increased the significance of the new decree. The Nürnberg Mandate of early 1523 had ruled that preaching must be restricted to the Gospel interpreted according to "writings approved and received by the Church." In the new decree, the Rat had diluted this already watery clause still further: the demand for traditional exegesis became a mere prohibition of "worthless talk inconsistent with the Christian faith."[127]

The final clause in the Rat's instructions on December 7 clarifies the December 1 decree. The Rat requests that the Bishop create a special commission for the doctrinal review of sermons. As such, the suggestion hardly subverts the Bishop's authority; it is the standards of judgment which the Rat proposes which are radical. The learned judges should not simply examine sermons for "accord" with Scripture, which might mean no more than non-contradiction, allowing great scope for ecclesiastical initiative, but for availability of scriptural _proof_. This step unequivocally puts forward the _sola scriptura_ principle as the only measure of doctrinal acceptability, one which the Rat regards as essential for salvation. Those teachings which cannot be proven from Scripture must be rejected so that the people "are not led into error and the perdition of their souls." The Scriptures are not yet understood as the sole repository of rules and regulations for the church, but for the Rat they are already the only guarantee of true doctrine.

The Bishop's response to this extraordinary set of proposals came on December 14. He first agreed to cooperate in having the new welfare system and the regulation of annuities confirmed. As to the Rat's compromise: desiring to avoid discord, he would punish profligates as well as the married, but he would not abandon his prosecution. He had heard before, and consistently rejected, the argument that sexually irregular priests should be left alone in order to avoid worse evil. Answerable to God, Emperor, and Pope, he was constrained by his office to pursue lawbreakers. On the other hand, he wrote, he firmly intended to avoid giving anyone grounds for unrest, and he promised to support any project at the coming Reichstag which would lead to peace and unity. Finally, he had no objection to oversight of the pastors, since he himself had never ceased doing so. The latest example was his prosecution of Zell![128] The Bishop thus accepted the Rat's formal requests, but rejected their object, the postponement of the campaign.

In the meantime, the Rat had Firn to deal with. He had continued to mount the pulpit in spite of notice of his dismissal. Around December 13, two delegations called on the Rat which, in the clearest possible manner, contrasted two understandings of the nature of the Rat's obligation to uphold law. A group of Firn's parishioners appeared, carrying a petition which Firn had helped them compose and later to publish. Firn also submitted a petition of his own. The parishioners told the Rat that its duty to defend law began with the law of God. The Rat had defended their fields and pastures in the past; it should also protect their souls, assuring that God's name was kept holy among them. Yet the canons' sexual lives were a dishonor to God; clerical marriage could end it. Further, the Rat had just ordered that only the Gospel be preached. Firn was seeking to live according to Gospel. Divine law could not be displaced, even by ancient custom or the Imperial Mandate. The Rat's duty, therefore, the petitioners wrote, was to protect Firn. Firn's own petition was even blunter: he would obey God rather than any human authority, whether religious or secular.[129]

The canons of St. Thomas waited on the Rat in their turn. They demanded their rights according to the customary understanding of the Rat's duty to protect order and the rights of all. Armed citizens had appeared in their cloister, and canon's lives had been threatened because of their dismissal of Firn. Yet the Rat had just promised to protect them from violent coercion.[130] The issue could scarcely have been more clearly joined. Could the Rat permit the Gospel to cause the violent disruption of residents' customary rights?

After receiving the petitions, the Rat issued a temporary injunction permitting Firn to continue to preach, while it took the matter under advisement.[131] During the following week, the Rat decided to maintain customary law, in this case both the law of the Empire and the ancient rights of the canons. On the advice of a special commission, it ordered Peter Butz, its secretary, to draw up a presentation to the _Schöffen_, the 300-member assembly of guild representatives normally asked to confirm decisions of major importance.[132] Both in the instructions given to Butz and in his final text for the presentation, the Rat spelled out the grounds for refusing to help Firn keep his benefice and for urging towndwellers not to take sides. Butz planned to begin by reading aloud the text of the Nürnberg Mandate and then to narrate the whole controversy at length, showing how the Rat had acted to keep the peace, obey Imperial law, and yet achieve a fair compromise. Butz was then to warn the _Schöffen_ in detail of the imperial penalties which threatened the city if it were to contravene the Nürnberg Mandate. The _Schöffen_ should urge their fellow citizens and guild brothers to leave this priests' quarrel to the priests and stay calm, leaving the negotiations in the Rat's hands. In return, the Rat promised to seek relief from higher authorities in the Empire. "It should not be concluded that we want to drive out and suppress the evangelical truth."[133]

At the same time, the Rat decided on a compromise in the Firn affair, to be executed should the Schöffen grant it full powers to act. The chapter would be requested to grant the Rat the power (without setting any precedent) to appoint a pious and learned priest who had neither wife nor concubine to the pastorate, until the Reichstag met "or the shouting changes somewhat." The Rat expected this formula to permit the chapter to guard its legal regularity and yet to appease moderate residents.[134]

The Bishop had taken the Rat at its word, agreeing to prosecute all sexual offenders. By reinforcing citizens' consciousness of what was at stake in obeying imperial law, and by setting a precedent for replacing an irregular priest with a universally acceptable one, the Rat hoped to prepare its citizens for the impending prosecution.

It is not known if the presentation was ever in fact made to the Schöffen; there is no evidence that the Rat offered its compromise to the chapter.[135] By the end of the week, the situation had changed radically. On the sixteenth, the chapter acceded to the Rat's request that Firn be allowed freely to enter the pulpit and sacristy, in order to avoid violence. On December 19, the Rat reversed the position outlined in its instructions to Butz. It publicly ordered that Firn retain his position at St. Thomas. It is unknown whether the decisive factor was the danger of riot, Firn's refusal to accept any compromise whatsoever, a collapse in the chapter's resistance, or an internal victory by the Rat's evangelical members. After December 19, however, the Rat refused to be party to the dispossession of married priests. The position it expressed to its emmissaries to the Nürnberg Reichstag early in January, 1524, returned to the arguments earlier rejected by the Bishop. The old condemnations of clerical marriage were dubious. No council had been held in a long time, and in the interim the people had become acquainted with Scripture. Further, inequitably harsh punishment of married priests could result in a rebellion. The whole matter ought to be reconsidered. The Rat instructed its delegates to appeal for a free council to settle the matter.[136]

The lines were drawn. The Rat would not help enforce the Mandate, especially if the married clergy was singled out for prosecution; the Bishop was intent on doing his duty, remaining faithful to medieval ideals of clerical character. On January 20, 1524, he ordered that the six married priests be cited to appear at his court in Zabern to be stripped of their benefices. The six immediately appealed to the Rat for protection as citizens. They were less concerned with the citizen's right not to be cited to courts outside the city walls than they were with the form of the hearing itself. They demanded the opportunity to attack the law against clerical marriage in a formal hearing; the Bishop seemed likely to confine them to bare responses to the facts of the case.[137]

The Rat did not respond to the Bishop's action until February 10, but it clearly considered that the Bishop had broken a mutual understanding that he would not pursue the inequitable prosecution against which it had warned him. In a new set of instructions for a delegation, the Rat again told the Bishop that it did not intend to interfere in his jurisdiction, but that his one-sided repression threatened to provoke a riot. If he singled out the married priests (who had so plausible a case), and did not proceed with equal harshness against the profligates who had held high ecclesiastical office in the town for so long (which he clearly had the legal powers to do), then it was likely that the common people would rebel. On the other hand, if he should decide to delay for the sake of peace, he could answer charges of disobedience by citing the fear of riot. Thus the Rat retained its earlier insistence that all sexually irregular priests be equally treated for the sake of the city's peace. Yet it clearly pointed away from any prosecution at all, even one based on that principle. It explicitly mentioned those holding high office, men against whom the Bishop had no practical power at all; and at length it urged him to temporize on the entire matter until the Empire as a whole had decided the issue.[138]

The Bishop answered the Rat in two ways. He first agreed to postpone the deadline of the citations until March 14.[139] Then, on the nineteenth of February, he undercut the Rat's formal case for further delay by issuing a decree ordering all clergymen to expel women from their dwellings, on pain of privation of their benefices.[140] On the fourteenth of March, he excommunicated the married priests. The letter of excommunication was posted in Strasbourg on April 3;[141] on April 10, the preachers published a joint appeal to a future council, alleging numerous irregularities in the Bishop's action.[142]

The Bishop's attack on concubinage went unenforced, but it succeeded in blowing away the smokescreen of the Rat's insistence on equal enforcement. To protect the preachers, the Rat was now forced to take open action. It sent a delegation to the Cathedral chapter, requesting that it prevent the Bishop from taking any further steps against the priests, and it sent a final appeal to the Bishop in their behalf on March 18. There the matter died. The Bishop took no more steps, and the preachers worked on in their positions, protected by the Rat.[143]

The chief effect of the preachers' marriages on the political status of the evangelical movement was to clarify the positions of all parties involved. Although the preachers continued to spread legal fog, several of the radical legal implications of their ideas had become clear to all. The Bishop had ended all hope (or fear) that he would collaborate with the movement. The Rat had sought to maintain a certain ambiguity, preventing the prosecution of the married priests without openly holding the Nürnberg Mandate in contempt. By grounding its protests in the increasingly real threat of riot and in alleged legal inequities in the Bishop's campaign, it could protect itself against blatant exposure in the Empire and rupture with its own conservative wing. But even beneath the offers of compromise, the Rat gave clear evidence of sympathy with the preachers. Not only did it in fact protect them once its maneuvers were overturned by the Bishop, but it publicly represented their arguments as having merit. Scripture was the rule of doctrine, requiring reexamination of human law that conflicted. If the Rat did not approve of the preachers' lawbreaking, it remained true that in Strasbourg, excommunicated preachers could not only proclaim the Gospel, but they could incite others to abrogate Imperial law without forfeiting the Rat's protection.[144]

The Seizure of the Pastorates

By the beginning of spring in 1524, the Rat's long chain of ad hoc decisions to frustrate episcopal repression had in effect created a legally neutral religious environment in Strasbourg. The Rat had isolated the preachers from the oversight or control of the Bishop. Finding itself unwilling to permit Zell's removal, it had, in effect, removed the content of sermons from the Bishop's oversight. The only standards enforced were the Rat's own: rootage of sermons in the text of Scripture, and abstinence from provocative language. Within those limits, preachers could express a wide variety of religious ideas from the pulpit. When, at the next crisis, the Rat prevented the enforcement of the Nürnberg Mandate's penalties for clerical marriage, it thereby gave sanctuary to institutional innovation. Even blatantly illegal religious changes were possible, as long as preachers could present a plausible justification for them in 'divine law' and if they were supported by a significant proportion of the population. By 1524, much of what the preachers understood Scripture to enjoin was not yet generally accepted in Strasbourg, but, if only on a naive level, the principle of _sola scriptura_ was.

It would seem reasonable to conclude that a significant number of _Ratsherren_ were personally attached to evangelical preachers and their ideas, the new religious alienation from the medieval clerical estate reinforcing their old political quarrel. Still more clearly than this, the documents present a picture of the Rat believing that by defending the preachers it was following the wishes of the "common man", wishes which the threat of rebellion rendered it dangerous to flout. To defend Firn and Zell was to protect the values of a significant group of its citizens. Thus when groups of citizens took the initiative of change into their own hand, it was entirely to be expected that the Rat would pay close heed to their requests.

During the spring of 1524, the preachers began to break new ground. Rapidly turning the focus of polemic against the cultus of the medieval church, they abrogated the Lenten fast, and on February 16 the Eucharist was distributed in both species.[145] On February 28, the Rat ordered that no new innovations were to be undertaken, judging its situation to be precarious enough.[146] On the nineteenth of April, however, the Mass was read and Baptism performed in German.[147] The change in the preachers' focus left the practical initiative for further change in the status of the clerical estate in the hands of laymen. In the earlier battles concerning the preaching of evangelical ideas and marriage, the preachers themselves were the logical ones to initiate change by open abrogation of the law. In contrast, it was the laymen who paid tithes and who, according to the preachers, had the right to appoint their own ministers. And, more importantly, those issues were directly related to several of the Strasbourg lower classes' most substantial grievances against the clergy. The gardeners, the poorest and most volatile group of Strasbourg citizens, paid tithes which were often bitterly resented,[148] not for the support of their parish priests but to the chapters which had "incorporated" the parish churches, and which therefore both controlled the appointment of the pastor and kept for their own uses a substantial proportion of the tithes.[149] By demanding the right to choose their own pastors, and by then demanding renegotiation of financial arrangements or even complete disincorporation of the parish, many citizens of Strasbourg launched their first direct attacks on the domination of their religious lives by the upper clergy.

On January 28, 1524, the parishioners of the church of St. Aurelien requested the Rat to permit them to call Martin Bucer as a preacher to supplement their Catholic priest. The chapter of St. Thomas, to which the church was incorporated, immediately served notice that the appointment of pastors was their affair alone. The Rat, after hearing the parishioners' case, proposed that the chapter draw up a list of several prospective pastors among whom the parishioners could choose. This was clearly an attempt to give the petitioners a measure of freedom, while leaving the chapter its control of the ideological orientation of its pastor. The parishioners immediately understood this, and clarified their intentions. They would only accept a pastor "who preaches like the others in the city"; if the chapter would only give them someone "sawing on the same old fiddle", they would prefer permission to hire a preacher of their own choice at their own expense.[150]

The Rat had good reasons for being slow to grant the parishioners' request. It had no legal right to interfere with the chapter's free disposition of the pastorate, and in the past it had studiously avoided open violation of the law. Matters were not helped by the fact that the Nürnberg Mandate expressly provided that married clerics, such as Bucer, should not have benefices.[151] As late as January 4, the Rat had actively kept its distance from Bucer.[152] To pass from the protection of priests legally possessing benefices to publicly approving the illegal installation of an audacious laybreaker like Bucer in an incorporated parish was a very large step. It was eased somewhat by the fact that the parishioners did not request that the Catholic pastor be deposed, or demand that the chapter pay Bucer's salary. Finally, the parishioners refusing to compromise, the Rat acceded. The chapter protested, but to no effect. On February 21, Bucer preached his inaugural sermon.[153]

The continued tenure of the old minister and the parishioners' independent support of Bucer left a protective ambiguity for both the chapters and Rat. That stage lasted less than two weeks. On March 2, the parishioners of Young St. Peter, in the parish incorporated to the chapter of the same name, cooly sent a message to the Provost and two canons of the chapter, announcing the appointment of Capito as pastor and the deposition of the old priest. A parallel message to the Rat met with an immediate order to cease and desist. The Rat told the parish that it was willing to try to obtain the right to appoint pastors from the chapter, but that it would not tolerate unilateral invasions of others' legal rights, undertaken without its agreement. After lengthy delays, a noisy mass of people ("more than one hundred") met before Ammeister Mieg's house to press for speed. Since a large proportion of the parishioners of Young St. Peter were gardeners, the focus of long-growing fears of anticlerical riot, the Rat may well have concluded that the danger of serious disturbances was acute. Within two weeks, Capito entered the pulpit with the Rat's permission.[154] The chapter, however, apparently refused to recognize the decision, and the dispute continued. Very shortly thereafter, the parishioners of St. Aurelien returned with another petition. Since their Catholic pastor had resigned, due to illness, they had chosen Bucer as full pastor of the parish. After temporizing, the chapter had stated that any pastor the Rat would accept would be accepted by it as well, this time. The parishioners came to the Rat for confirmation. On April 4, the Rat assented.[155]

Shortly thereafter, the parishioners of Old St. Peter presented a petition introducing a new issue, the reorganization of parish finances. The manuscript itself is as revealing as the content of the text. Although it purported to express the desires of the parishioners, the hand in which the document was written is Bucer's. The rhetorically and theologically sophisticated language indicates that Bucer not only acted as scribe but as author. It is the first solid evidence that evangelical pastors covertly organized the parishes. Nikolaus Wurmser's personal diary accused Capito of inciting the parishioners at St. Aurelien to name Bucer as pastor.[156] Capito had become Wurmser's bête noire, however, and there is no clear evidence to support the claim.[157] This case, however, is clear. Although it is possible that Bucer merely composed the petition at the request of and according to the basic ideas of the parishioners, it seems more likely that a somewhat covert program of popular organization and education supplemented the preachers' activity in the pulpits.[158] It is interesting to note how this program differed from that of subversive groups in the peasantry.[159] The preachers organized the population according to institutions with pre-existent legal status (the parishes), and persuaded them to initiate changes and then submit this action to the scrutiny of public authority.

The petition itself bluntly announced that the parishioners had chosen Theobald Schwartz, assistant to Zell, as their pastor after the Rat had delayed answering earlier requests. Then it turned to the parish's incorporation to the chapter. By right, the pastor's stipend, the churchyard, and all parish revenues, cheated from them, belonged to the parish. As governor of all temporal matters, the Rat ought to force the chapter to return them. Out of Christian meekness, however, the parishioners were willing to make do with an adequate salary for the pastor.[160]

The Rat confirmed the choice of Schwartz on June 11, but there is no record of an adjustment of the parish's financial relations with the chapter. During the summer of 1524, the issue of disincorporation became tense. On May 30, the St. Aurelien parishioners had demanded severance from the chapter, and throughout the summer the parishioners of Young St. Peter petitioned, lobbied, and threatened for financial reforms.[161] A large group of gardeners in St. Aurelien, spurred by a bad harvest, refused to pay their tithes.[162] The Rat undertook to negotiate the issues with the chapters. Formal negotiations on the _Schirm_ had reopened on April 20, and at the end of July the Rat offered a compromise which, although giving ground on the issue of jurisdiction, would have imposed heavy taxes on the chapters. The canons were not inclined to accept the further financial loss implied by disincorporation of the parishes, a step which no medieval law required.[163]

During the summer of 1524, the Rat tried to achieve modest, legal compromises, protecting the essential interests of all parties. It had agreed to present parishioners' requests for the right to choose their own pastors to the chapters, and it had enforced those demands with firmness. Although they were illegal, so long as financial arrangements were left alone the chapters' protest could be muffled. Severance of parishes from the chapters, however, was another matter. It threatened the chapters' economic viability, and the Rat was not willing to press the matter.

Two events brought matters to a head. On August 17, the Bishop formally protested to the Imperial administration, the Reichsgericht, against the Rat's invasion of his jurisdiction and its appointment of excommunicated, married priests to pulpits over which it had no legal right.[164] On August 21, unbearably pressed by its parishioners' pressure on one hand and the Rat's exactions on the other, and under suspicion of subversion,[165] the canons of Young St. Peter took their treasure and deserted Strasbourg. The next day, St. Thomas sent away their treasure as well. It may well have reminded citizens of the nobles' desertion a century before, which had confirmed their alienation from an artisans' government; or of earlier mass exits of clergymen, flung as a rebuke in the citizens' faces.[166] It gravely threatened the Rat's policy. If Strasbourg were publicly exposed as a town where those who observed the religion of their fathers could not live in peace, the Rat's carefully cultivated ambiguities would be burned away. As that blow fell, on August 20 Conrad Treger, the Provincial of the Augustinians, published a pamphlet decrying the "Bohemian heresy" (Hussitism) into which the evangelical preachers had seduced the people of Strasbourg. Treger had already achieved local notoriety by (according to the evangelicals) promising to debate the preachers, asking only safe-conduct, and then when the Rat sought to arrange a debate, backing out. His new pamphlet gradually became known, tension exploding into a mushroom cloud of anger by the middle of September.[167]

In this context of barely restrained fury, a petition was presented to the Rat which forced a collision between the Rat's policy and the evangelical movement's leaders. It was signed by the parishioners of at least five of Strasbourg's parish churches, and advertised itself as a formula for ending division and discord. Most of the townsfolk, it claimed, were "inclined toward the Scriptures", but certain others, who had never heard the Gospel preached and who were incited by "perverted pastors and monks'- preachers", bitterly opposed the movement. There was a simple solution, which would dry the stream of petitions troubling the Rat: to negotiate the turnover of all pastorates to the Rat and to the parishioners. It was their right, according to divine law; neither incorporations nor ancient custom was sufficient grounds for refusal. Second, the Rat should require the return of rich parish revenues to their proper recipients, the parish's pastors and ministers. Third, the absurd chanting of canons on holy days should be abolished; working people deserved peace and quiet after the sermon and divine offices.[168]

The petition asked the Rat to reverse its previous policy of providing evangelical pastors only for those who wanted them, of giving legal sanctuary to ideas which pleased a large group of citizens, and to undertake the repression of the old religion. It asked for a Rat-enforced evangelical monopoly on Strasbourg pulpits, and for steps to be taken against the cultus which had defined the canonical life of the chapters. While it did not demand forcible seizure of the parishes, it did demand that the negotiations for them succeed.

Faced by this petition, which claimed the support of such a large group of citizens, the Rat took the matter to the Schöffen. As the representatives of the leadership of each guild, the Schöffen could keep the gap between Rat and citizenry from growing too wide through influence on both sides. The Schöffen agreed to the response the Rat had planned, which was then summarized and made public.[169] First, the Rat asserted, the forceful seizure of long-held property (harbrochte besitzung) would be profoundly dangerous. Not only could the canons appeal to powerful outside authorities -- Emperor, Pope, the Reichsregiment, and the Landvogt -- but such seizure violated Strasbourg's own laws. Such acts would rapidly destroy the town's "brotherly peace." And yet the parishioners had no ultimately compelling reason for their request, since the matter of paying pastors' salaries (as distinct from choosing pastors) had nothing to do with the salvation of souls. Therefore: in order to "advance and support the Gospel", the Rat would retain control of the parishes it already possessed until the end of the Speyer Reichstag,[170] and would pursue negotiations for the release of the other parishes. In the meantime, it demanded peace, and an absolute moratorium on actions for which citizens had no legally recognized right.[171]

The Rat had simply refused to change its policy. It was willing to cede a certain measure of ground to the evangelicals, namely by publicly affirming the connection between the appointment of evangelical preachers and the salvation of souls, but it had a prior commitment to the security of the city. The evangelicals proffered a new divine law which absolutely superceded "human" law and customs in religious matters; the Rat regarded Strasbourg society as a tissue of human conventions -- old duties and freedoms, long-held properties -- a fabric already under strain by its own campaign to change the clergy's legal status. Unilateral, illegal attacks by unauthorized groups on the clear rights of the canons flouted the Rat's pretention to offer justice to all, and, more deeply, violated its basic conception of community. Such attacks would destroy the foundation of social cooperation in Strasbourg.

Close examination of the decision shows the Rat continuing to protect itself from accumulations of power in the hands of its subjects. The Rat's outline of points to be presented to the Schöffen states that even if the latter think that the parishioners should be given the right to appoint pastors, the Rat thinks it better that the pastorates be left in its own hands.[172] The Rat was beginning to accumulate units of power knocked loose from the medieval religious edifice; the alternative was to permit the establishment of powerful institutions, governed by Strasbourg laymen, but not subject to the Rat. The Rat had consistently resisted the formation of any organization, especially composed of lower class workers, which might form a basis for challenge of the master artisans' hegemony.[173] Yet many parishes were dominated by lower-class, highly volatile wage earners,[174] and no form of government of the parishes had been developed which would guarantee the power of "responsible", settled, wealthier burghers, as had long before been accomplished in the guilds. The evangelical movement disrupted religious government, leaving yawning (and, to the upper classes, dangerous) power vacuums, and yet provided no acceptable institutions to replace them. By filling the void with its own authority, the Rat both confirmed the Reformation institutionally and denied other social movements an institutional lever.

On August 31, the evangelical preachers themselves submitted a petition to the Rat, attempting to resolve some of the ambiguities in the Rat's response to the parishioners' petition. The Rat had not directly taken up the issue of the suppression of Catholic preaching. Rather, by insisting that the canons be protected by the same structure of law as everyone else, the Rat had seemed to maintain its neutrality. The preachers' tactic was to place the most optimistic interpretation possible upon the Rat's words. They wrote that they had carefully considered what could be the source of the current discord among citizens. Since it was certain that the Gospel produced only patience and peace, they thought it clear that Catholic clerics were responsible for inciting certain citizens against the Gospel and for trying to factionalize the city. They congratulated the Rat, therefore, for its decision to be faithful to the Gospel and for the consequent decision to take over the parishes. They then suggested a way to eliminate the false preachers who were at the root of the trouble. The Rat should renew the mandate of December 1, 1523, ordering the exclusive preaching of the Gospel, adding a clause requiring proof from Scripture for any doubtful doctrine. A committee of ten or twelve _Ratsherren_ should then review all controverted teachings which concerned matters of faith accessable to all Christians, and silence those preachers judged to distort Scripture. The preachers conceded that some citizens would still not change their minds, but explained that since the true Christian would be patient and tolerant, unconvinced but decent citizens could live in the community in peace. The preachers then turned to religious reforms in the Rat itself. The _Ratsherren_ should translate their profession of faith into action. The chapel attended by the Rat (the St. Erhardtskapelle) should be de-catholicized -- the Mass abolished, pictures removed, candle-burning stopped, the chant of the Wilhelmites silenced. Finally, the preachers asked for consideration to be given to the establishment of schools.[175]

The preachers' petition neatly sketches the ambiguities of the Rat's earlier decision. The Rat had not formally embraced the preachers' program. It had not given divine law an absolute priority over human convention, except in "eternal" matters, conceived narrowly. It had not shifted its policy from granting new ideas legal sanctuary to repressing old ideas. It had not asserted a unilateral right to "administer the temporal", giving it power to sequester ecclesiastical property. By crowding the Rat on these issues, by over-interpreting the Rat's concessions, the preachers attempted to push the Rat towards clear commitment to the new religion and repression of the old, under the banner of peace and unity.

The Rat did not respond to the preachers' petition, and on September 5 it made another pronouncement fully continuous with its decision on the parishes. Some parishioners had taken the canons' removal of silver icons as an excuse for them to remove the wooden ones themselves. The Rat bluntly prohibited this unauthorized innovation.[176] Yet the popular agitation, to which all contemporary documents witness, was growing too rapidly to contain. Convinced by the preachers' polemics, twisted by the rejection of old values and patterns, frustrated by the slowness with which legal institutions gave ground, Strasbourg town dwellers focused on the irritating way in which the remaining Catholic preachers called their new understandings heresy and their reforms disobedience.

As Conrad Treger's little book gradually spread from the Augustinians' monastery where it was sold, the anger found an object. The man who, evangelical burghers thought, had flown behind the Bishop's skirts to reneg on a challenge to dispute with the evangelical preachers, had dared "to describe the honorable Rat and honorable citizenry as damned Bohemian heretics led astray by our preachers, and [to say] that we are rebellious and no longer obey Your Graces." On September 5, a select committee of citizens appeared before the Rat and charged Treger with violation of the December 1, 1523 mandate forbidding provocative language, and of having slandered the Rat. They demanded he be compelled to defend himself publicly. Before the Rat's delegates could reach Treger, however, a mob had invaded the cloister, seized the Provincial, and pulled him before the Rat, which took him into custody.[177]

The Treger affair has been clearly narrated elsewhere, and there is no need to do so here.[178] During the succeeding weeks, the stage was shared by four parties. The citizens' select committee [Ausschuß] put distance between itself and the violent "rabble," but it firmly demanded that Treger be forced publicly to answer for his calumnies and to back up his charges against the preachers. Many within the walls, however, expressed their feelings more directly than the Ausschuß permitted. Several large mobs gathered, one of which pillaged the food stores and wine cellars of St. Arbogast and the Carthusian cloister. Treger's powerful friends, from the Bishop of Strasbourg to the Rats of Freiburg and Baden, demanded his immediate and unconditional release. The Rat was left desperately juggling its interests. The population's demand for a disputation directly violated the explicit order of the Emperor not to hold disputations until a General Council was convoked, and the external threat hung very heavy. Treger refused to accept any compromise. After long negotiations in the first days of October, the Rat released Treger after he swore a solemn oath, and it then permitted the evangelical preachers to publish treatises attacking Treger's earlier-published "Hundred Theses", which had attacked Lutheran ecclesiology and the sola scriptura principle. The Rat had successfully avoided having to take actions which would have left it exposed to its enemies from without, or which would have discredited it in the eyes of its citizens. But the Treger affair had made the general acceptance of evangelical ideas among the "common folk" unmistakable. The Rat could continue to make certain compromises to avoid gross offense to authorities outside the walls, but it had little room to negotiate and no means at all of disguising the fact that Strasbourg had become an evangelical town.

This was immediately apparent in its negotiations with the chapters. We have seen that the Rat's proposal in July, still moderate in some respects, was replaced in November by a return to what had been an extreme bargaining position in 1523: demanding the clergy's subjection to citizens' burdens and to full secular jurisdiction. At the end of October, the Rat ordered the removal of icons from city churches[179] and in early November it suspended the five yearly masses said for the city and diverted the money which had gone for candles to the city leprosarium and orphanage.[180] These steps unmistakably declared the Rat's allegiance to the evangelical party; they were unequivocal rejections of elements of the sacral system of piety. The canons' self-exile on December 6 reflected their own assessment of the city's status. On New Year's Day, 1525, the Rat issued a mandate clearly reflecting its new position. It reminded city dwellers of the December 1, 1523 mandate, which had prohibited talk which would provoke other people or be injurious to the Christian faith. Yet lately, words had been exchanged between clergy and laity which "not only disrupted our peaceful and brotherly way of life, but gravely insulted the honor of God and his holy Word." The order to abstain from slander was repeated, with the emphatic insistance that "God's Word and commands" be held in respect.[181]

On January 10, the newly elected Rat and Ammeister

received a sharp letter from the Reichsregiment, the official administration of the Empire in the Emperor's absence. It had received notice through official protests from the Bishop and the chapters of the innovations in the clergy carried out by the Rat. It demanded an explanation.[182] The Rat answered briefly on January 23: it had the right and the power from "divine law" to undertake such steps.[183] A second letter from the Reichsregiment on February 3 formally labeled the changes "outrageous, criminal, against law and ancient ecclesiastical custom", and demanded complete restoration of the status quo ante.[184] In response, the Rat sent a delegation to Esslingen, the seat of the Reichsregiment. It carried with it the Rat's defense of its own actions regarding the Schirm, the provision of pastors, the removal of icons, and the seizure of chapter property after the canons' self-exile. In addition, the delegation brought a defense of the preachers' illegal actions written by Bucer, covering the full range of the issues presented by the canons; two of Capito's tracts, including Dass die pfaffheit schuldig sei, burgerlichen Eid zu thun, a restatement of Capito's position on clerical citizenship; and Bucer's long Grund und Ursach, a full explanation and defense of the liturgical changes of the last year. The Rat's approval of the changes could scarcely have been clearer.[185] In March, 1525, the Rat prohibited concubinage for lay and cleric alike, enforcing equivalent sexual standards for all estates. By Easter, it took the major repressive step that signalled the full allegiance of Strasbourg to the cause of the Reformation: with the exception of the churches of the four chapters, all churches in Strasbourg were forbidden to celebrate Mass, the heart of medieval Christianity.[1

The Rat and Evangelical Ideas

In 1523, the Rat launched a major drive to end what it regarded as the clerical disruption of the city's secular life. By suspending the Schirm and permitting the repurchase of annuities, the Rat decisively moved to neutralize the effects of clerical immunities on the community. It thereby put into action a program developed during generations of struggle. Two years later, in 1525, the attack had succeeded. Uniformly, Strasbourg clergymen were citizens, fully subject to local laws, taxes, duties. Their interests were bound to the community's. But now, most clerics were married, too. Except in the shrunken chapter choirs, the Mass was no longer said in Strasbourg. There were few candles, few icons left in the bare churches, and no processions in the streets. The new Rat had bluntly rejected an order by the Imperial administration to reverse its "criminal" religious innovations.

This profound religious change had been no part of the Rat's original project. That had matured in the world of the fifteenth century, designed to work around the laws of papacy and Empire, shaped to conform with medieval piety. It had never occurred to the fathers of the new Ratsherren that controlling the public behavior of mass-priests might lead to the abolition of the Mass itself. Yet it was a Rat filled with the sons of pious men which protected and then institutionalized the new religion. How did it come to pass?

It is clear that, at least in part, the Rat's protection of the "Gospel" tended to further its own political objectives. A good deal has been said of the manner in which the Rat's decisions to protect evangelical preachers tended to cut Strasbourg off from the jurisdiction of the Bishop. Limiting the Bishop's direct power in town life had been one of the town's major goals since the Battle of

Hausbergen in the thirteenth century. Even his religious activities had been restricted by the Rachtung of Speier, negotiated with Bishop Wilhelm von Diest in the fifteenth century; a layer of locally resident officials were inserted between the Bishop and towndwellers, and the rights of Bishop, Chapter, and Rat were defined so that unilateral action by the Bishop was difficult.

During the evangelical movement, the Rat made increasing use of the Scripture principle and the threat of riot in order to cut the Bishop off further. It protected Zell because he taught "in accord with Scripture," in effect robbing the Bishop of jurisdiction over sermons preached in Strasbourg. Later, when the Rat was slow to protect the benefices of married priests, it did protect their bodies; neither Bucer nor Firn was exiled. It eventually decided that in the case of clerical marriage as well, the Bishop's religious government was acting against the town's interests. It asserted that the population was near the bursting point, and further, that the Scriptures left the issue of clerical marriage in doubt. The question should be put to a new council, not decided by a local bishop. When Wilhelm von Hohnstein proceeded to excommunicate the priests, the Rat defended their positions, their privileges, and their incomes. The Rat justified its subsequent decision to take all parish pulpits into its own hands by the "eternal" importance of preaching the Word. The Rat admitted that it was an appropriate issue on which to defy human law. By this time, the Bishop's administration had been pushed far into the background of Strasbourg life. His only ecclesiastical influence was as an ally of the Empire, the only potent antagonist to the preachers which remained.

It is obvious that these actions were in some measure consistent with the Rat's ancient purpose to hobble the Bishop. The Scripture principle offered the Rat a pious, quasi-legal weapon to attack church administration, effectively insulating the town from any form of episcopal interference. Yet the fifteenth century Rat had never intended to destroy religious government as such. It had tried to buffer the power of its religious lord by constructing checks and balances, not to end medieval religion.[187] The medieval Rat had attempted to find its way around the law, to preserve the core of religious government; the new Rat presided over the dissolution of these institutions. By 1525, the town's religion had changed, for which the Rat was held responsible by the Reichsregiment in the most explicit terms. That change was hardly the fruit of fifteenth century policy.

The issue of clerical immunity displays similar disparities. The form of the Bürgerrecht which the Rat offered to the clergy had been drawn so that the sacral functions defining the clerical estate need not be impeded, nor its consecration profaned. Further, the Rat meant to force the clergy to compromise by using political pressure, which, if dangerous, was still legal. By 1525, clerical immunity was abolished, but the sacral system defining medieval religion had largely vanished as well. The church's institutional structure had been torn down by town-dwellers' vigorous use of "divine law" and by violence. The Rat had been pushed in directions in which, with good reason, it feared to go. Its safety in the Empire was compromised; the integrity of law and custom, on which it essentially depended, was threatened. It is clear that evangelical ideology assisted the Rat to achieve long-desired objectives; it is also clear that it did so by destroying old values and endangering political interests which the Rat had always protected.

In part, then, we may interpret the Rat's support of the evangelical movement as a search for weapons to further its own institutional objectives. Elements of evangelical ideology threatening those objectives were resisted. The Rat was very slow to accept clerical marriage, even after its majority was convinced that Scripture did not forbid it. If it early enshrined Scripture as the only valid standard for judging doctrine, not until 1525 did it publicly recognize divine law as providing valid grounds for clear violation of canon and Imperial law. It resisted residents' demands for separation of their parishes from the chapters, arguing that ancient possessions must not be seized unilaterally. It consistently attempted to slow "innovations" which could threaten its security in the Empire.

The preachers and their followers, however, resisted any effort to keep change within fifteenth century boundaries. In the end, the Rat approved the attack on the sacral system itself, including gross violations of law which endangered its position. The impulse to carry out its own reform program cannot account for those actions. They also represent real penetration of the Rat by the preachers' ideology from within, and unbearable pressure for change from below.

From the beginning, the preachers' program was understood and (with reservations) actively supported by a circle of influential families, including those of Ratsherren. The wives of Friedrich Ingolt and Reimbolt Spender accompanied Firn's concubine to the altar. Other important council members, including Nikolaus Kniebis, Daniel Mieg, Bernhart Wurmser, Martin Herlin, Matthew Pfarrer, and Jakob Sturm, came to share the preachers' conviction that the sacral system itself was at fault for the current religious malpractice and the clergy's obnoxious social position. These views of this minority slowly gained ground in the Rat as a whole. The spontaneous defense of Zell, the breakdown of the lay-cleric ethical distinction in the defense of Firn, the removal of icons and abolition of the Mass are evidence that, at the very least, an influential minority of _Ratsherren_ was able to persuade other members to undertake evangelical changes in the city's religious life.

Where the minds of council members were not changed, the threat of violent uprising forced compromise with the general population. The push from the citizenry played a role in all of the Rat's actions in support of the movement. Even in cases such as the defense of Zell, in which the Rat appears to have reacted spontaneously, the danger of unrest figured in its arguments to others. The pressure from below -- the placards, petitions, demonstrations, riots all giving testimony to the boiling unrest -- proved irresistable.

The evangelical movement was a means for the Rat to fulfill some of its oldest objectives; it also posed the Rat with basic threats. The Rat's hesitations, its ambivalence, the slowness with which it was won to the preachers' program all indicate that its final support of the movement was less the result of its own institutional motives than it was the fruit of the preachers' victory in the population as a whole. The Rat's position in Strasbourg society did not permit it oligarchic independence. On one hand, it could not easily develop values far removed from those of the social groups from which its members came; if it had, it would have found any resulting policy difficult to sustain. Both the noble and the artisan members were appointed annually by procedures ensuring responsiveness to those holding economic and social power in the city. If certain highly active members of the Rat were regularly reappointed, they did not constitute a closed oligarchy. They were rooted by marriage, family, and _freundschaft_ in the prosperous and stable strata of Strasbourg society, and their opinions could not diverge too far from their associates'. Strasbourg Ratsherren never possessed the social isolation permitting the development of ideas radically different from their fellows'. Further, had this dependence not been enough, it would have remained true that the Rat relied on moral authority alone for enforcing its decisions. It was in no position to impose resented programs on large or influential groups of its citizens. Again and again, we find the Rat consulting with the Schöffen, the leadership of the guilds, before the announcement of its policy, in order to assure popular support. Both the formal political structures and the social position governing the Rat assured that its members' unconscious values and conscious opinions would not grossly differ from its subjects'.

On the other hand, the class origins and the experiences of office of Ratsherren reinforced certain values and objectives. Two cases were particularly important. Many Ratsherren were drawn from strata relatively dependent on Strasbourg's secure status in the Empire; at the same time, constant diplomatic activity intensified their consciousness of their duty to the Empire and of the concrete dangers of disobedience. Second, they naturally reflected the dispositions of those classes having the greatest stake in the economic and social status quo; that conservativism was reinforced by the formal responsibility for and active practice of the maintenance of legal rights.

With these conditions in mind, one can see that the penetration of the Rat by evangelical ideas and the political pressures that forced it to support actions it feared proceeded from the same source. Ratsherren were gradually convinced by evangelical ideas, only one part of the diffusion of evangelical ideas throughout the classes from which the Rat was drawn. The Rat was not likely to oppose what most upper class citizens wanted; it tended to reflect the same values. When the reinforced conservative inclinations of its majority isolated it from too large a spectrum of Strasbourg society, unrest and riot forced it to accept a faster rate of change. The Rat's growing acceptance of evangelical ideas, no matter whether free or coerced, reflected the rapid growth of adherence to the preachers' program in all sectors of Strasbourg society.

Chapter 4

The People's Gospel

By the end of 1524, the Rat had consented to move with the current of change sweeping throughout all of Strasbourg. There was no question of holding out alone. If the Rat's social position tended to give its values a more conservative cast than other residents', no radical difference could be sustained for long. By stymying episcopal repression and establishing "evangelical" reforms, the Rat acted in concert with the wishes of (or, at times, in response to the threats of) the effective majority of Strasbourg's population. The Rat was organically linked to the rest of the town. Where it supported the "Gospel" of its own will, as in its defense of Zell in December, 1522, its action illustrated the dispersion of sympathy for Zell and for some form of the Scripture principle in the classes from which it was drawn. In other cases, in which the Rat was coerced to travel further or faster than it wanted by the danger of alienating large sections of the population, the potency of "evangelical" sentiment throughout the population was illustrated. The Rat was not the prime mover in the Strasbourg reformation. Its actions mirrored the society of which it was a part, though with the peculiar cast given to its values by its own social position.

The irresistable acceleration of change which invaded Strasbourg between 1522 and 1525 was the work of the whole lay population's energy. The behavior of other institutions reveals the powerful shift in popular feelings as clearly as the Rat's does. The Catholic establishment stammered and fell silent, not because it had been refuted or because the Rat forbade it to speak, but because it feared the violence of a population in which it no longer had a strong enough foothold. The evangelical preachers, in turn, felt that they could safely turn their polemics toward the remnants of the medieval cultus; the basic changes in the population's attitude toward the clergy had largely been accomplished. The direct evidence of popular opinion is unequivocal. In spite of the resistance of pockets of determined Catholics[1] and the undoubted indifference of many townsmen, on the occasions when the population could express its views -- the upper strata of artisans, through the guild masters in the votes of the Schöffen; a broader social spectrum, through the Ausschüßen of the Treger affair and in parish votes; or through the lower strata's ancient substitute for the plebescite, the unruly demonstration -- it was clear that by fall in 1524, the great majority of those who cared gave their voices to some form of the "Gospel."[2]

But how did the people understand this "Gospel", and what relation did that understanding have to the ways in which the evangelical preachers intended their ideas to be used? Even if one were interested only in the changes accomplished by the fiat of the Rat, it would be of interest to examine the values which drove residents to exert pressure for change. And the Rat's actions only account for a part of the total change in the clerical estate in Strasbourg. Within the legal parameters which the Rat constructed, there was room for many different resolutions of the clergy's status.[3] It was the initiative of the evangelical preachers and, above all, the attitudes which prevailed in the general population which left the clergy as a class of socially integrated religious "experts." Further, the attitudes finally enshrined in the protestant society of the late sixteenth century only represented a few of the forms given to the "Gospel" during the evangelical movement. The hearers of the Word heard it in many different social contexts. Some of the new structures of understanding and value which they built around these 'Words' fell by the road or were violently repressed by the new religio-political establishment. In this chapter, we shall examine the ways in which Strasbourg people understood and used the "Gospel", creating mental structures to fit their own social context, and thereby remaking their relations with the class of religious leaders.

Within these different appropriations, however, there is an identifiable continuum in the manner in which laymen grasped the preachers' ideas. Two major currents emerge clearly from the struggle we have narrated: the burgeoning hatred of the clergy and the great moral confidence of lay residents. Most Strasbourgeois were led to discredit the medieval sacral system, coming to interpret it as an invention by a clerical estate intent on dominating laymen and keeping an easy and splendid life for itself. The Scriptures gave laymen a set of quasi-legal standards to use against the legal walls of the clergy. On the other hand, most laymen did not feel threatened by "divine law." It universalized and legitimated their own norms. God approved of good citizens. That is to say that Strasbourg residents involved in the evangelical movement used "divine law" radically and destructively against the ideology of the medieval clerical estate, and conservatively and constructively in respect to their own values. Yet "divine law" also provided the members of the mainstream with grounds for selective religious conservatism; some institutions could still be regarded as religiously useful, rooted in Scripture. "Divine law" was sufficiently capacious to protect many components of the medieval religious order, though in revised form. However, more radically alienated residents were not obliged to use these principles so conservatively. The rejection of religious mediation could cut much more deeply into the sacral structure; the principles could also be turned against secular institutions, or function as the ideology for political revolution.

*   *   *   *   *

To reconstruct the ways in which town residents appropriated the preachers' ideas is obviously best done from direct evidence, from analysis of residents' written explanations of what they thought and did, from the words they traded in pamphlets and the suits they launched in court. That evidence is very fragmentary, and not enough is known about the religious sociology of late medieval towns to permit full reconstruction. The problem is further complicated by the fact that common citizens were only likely to write down what they thought about religious or political matters when extraordinary circumstances required it. Yet townspeople in the mainstream of religious change could enter the first stages of commitment to the preachers' Gospel -- attending evangelical sermons, withdrawing from the medieval system of piety -- anonymously, without crime or scandal, that is, without creating the sorts of situations which would be likely to provoke written self-expression. Normally, only when residents' new values were well-developed would conflicts be provoked which required written self-explanation: calling a pastor, demanding the right to interview a relative "imprisoned" in a cloister, demanding relief from the tithe, or quarreling with other residents with sufficient violence to leave legal records. The preachers considered it the proper function of their estate to publish all the necessary written rationalizations for innovations; they tended to crowd out more naive versions which might have illustrated the population's understandings.[4] Laymen outside the mainstream of change were no more likely to write about religion than their conservative fellows. Seditious residents were unlikely to run the risks of publication, if word of mouth could serve; and on the Catholic side, even priests were quite reticent after the Treger affair. Thus it is clear that not only do we depend on the random preservation of documents from four centuries of violence in Alsace, but that some of the most interesting stages of attitudinal change are intrinsically unlikely to be represented at all. What does remain can hardly pretend to completeness. Yet as a set of illustrations it may still be useful, freeing us from total dependence on inferences made from indirect evidence.

The indirect evidence, however, can help fill in the blank areas. It establishes the limits and directions of the mainstream's changes in attitude. For example, the preachers' attacks on the clerical estate were acted upon. The fact that most monasteries closed their doors, many of their members breaking their vows under pressure from relatives, friends and from the city as a whole, and that the chapters were changed beyond recognition demonstrates the general disaffection from traditional evaluations of clerical prayer and contemplation.[5] The catastrophic decline in the purchase of masses shows that, for whatever reasons, the population was alienated from the central constitutive symbol of the priestly mediation of religious meaning.[6]

The Starting Point: Pre-Reformation Anticlericalism

The stream of anticlerical propaganda with which the evangelical preachers attempted to woo towndwellers itself provides a prima facie case for the existence of strong anticlerical feeling on the eve of the Reformation. The Rat's attempt to subject the clergy to secular taxation and legal jurisdiction while leaving its religious office intact, mirrors the peculiar nature of this pre-Reformation anticlericalism. Largely unfocused resentment of the clergy coexisted with a profoundly traditional "churchly" piety.[7] Popular engagement in the medieval devotional system did not wane significantly until Zell's attacks had been underway for some time. There is evidence that by 1520 the market for indulgences had reached a point of near-satiety; financial returns dropped sharply, and cases of public contempt for indulgences were brought to the Rat's attention. Yet Strasbourg cloisters were hard pressed to say all the masses ordered by the people.[8] The early evangelical preacher, Tylman von Lyn, by his account, was protected from excommunication because the prior of his order had no mass-priests to spare.[9] Throughout Strasbourg, religious brotherhoods flourished. These fellowships provided a group of men with insurance of adequate involvement in the sacral system. They provided for burial and masses at death; they founded masses, gave candles or other sacred objects to their chosen church, and attended holy rituals together. In 1514 Nikolaus Kniebis, the most influential artisan in Strasbourg during the evangelical movement, joined the Brotherhood of St. Sebastian, founded to promote piety in city government by the city secretary, Sebastian Brant. In 1519, Martin Herlin and Mathis Pfarrer (who later became strong supporters of the evangelical movement while in the Rat) headed the "Brotherhood of the Passion of Jesus Christ and of His Mother, Mary Perpetual Virgin", responsible for the yearly passion plays. There is no evidence that other brotherhoods, such as those for journeymen, declined in fervor.[10] In fact, the monasteries most overburdened by the demand for masses and prayers were the ones which served the lower classes in Strasbourg. Pre-reformation anticlericalism in Strasbourg cannot be shown to have placed the essential religious activity of the clergy in question.

If the ideal role of the clergy in the sacral system was not popularly rejected, however, that does not imply that the clergy's execution of that ideal escaped criticism. The most visible attacks on clerical iniquity were made by the circles of learned reformism which centered around Wimpheling, Sebastian Brant, Hieronymus Gebwiller, and Geiler von Keyserberg.[11] A similar distinction to the one we noted in the Rat's anticlericalism exists here, too. These circles' stock in trade was violent criticism of the clergy's derogations from medieval clerical ideals. If the bitter tone of the criticism and the burning demand for reform lent themselves to radicalization, the standards upon which the criticism was based were wholly conservative.

The reformist circles were not isolated from the community at large. Several of the town's secular leaders, certainly including the two _Ratsherren_ most prominently associated with the evangelical movement, Jakob Sturm and Nikolaus Kniebis, had close connections with them. Since such _Ratsherren_ were not in the clergy, we may assume that they did not share the others' natural bias in favor of clerical privilege. But they clearly were capable of understanding the reformists' ideas. Further, the reformists' influence was not confined to the social elite. One of their lay patrons established a _Predikatur_ at the Cathedral for Geiler von Keysersberg, expressly for the purpose of preaching, in order to bring about a general reformation of morals. For an entire generation, Geiler preached to huge audiences from his pulpit, criticizing all estates and demanding reform. For Geiler, the betrayal of medieval religious ideals was universal; no class, lay or cleric, escaped his tongue. Yet he chiefly held the leaders responsible, above all the custodians of holy things, the preachers, the priests, the spiritual lords, whose utter failure to live and function as they ought, he alleged, corrupted their example and obstructed the means of grace. Geiler's ethical standards were conservative, his view of the priesthood's function wholly traditional, even his dedication to clerical immunity fierce. Yet his attacks on those who derogated from those standards were equally fierce, and those attacks were pounded into the Strasbourg population during decades of preaching. If Geiler can be said to have aroused anticlerical feeling, however, it was anticlericalism profoundly shaped by medieval religion. Indeed, such popular resentment as there was to clerical concubinage might well be traced back to Geiler and his circles of learned, pious friends; but the later resistance to clerical marriage might well be traced back to the same source. If Geiler popularized sulphurous criticism of clerical greed, laziness, and sexual vice, he did so by painting the consecrated, exalted, "separate" character of the clergy as brilliantly and attractively as possible.[12]

Pious anticlericalism similar to Geiler's was endemic in Strasbourg in the decades preceding the evangelical movement. Yet among laymen, resentment focused not only on the clergy's failures, but on its social position. The Rat's broad assault on clerical immunity clearly witnesses to social grievances held against the clergy throughout the upper strata of lay society, grievances which, by the Rat's own judgment, no reformation of morals could resolve, but only social relocation of the clerical estate. There is other evidence of upper class anticlerical feeling. The sharp decline in major benefactions to the church reflects not only general retrenchment in response to inflation, but also in some measure a judgment on the "rich" upper clergy. Families still sent children to the cloister, but much less of their property went with them.[13]

We have no such means of estimating the sentiments of lower classes. The plume of anticlerical fury thrown above the peasant uprisings in Alsace brilliantly illustrates the feelings of their fellows in the countryside.[14] In Strasbourg itself, however, the evidence is less clear; the records of criminal trials do not present patterns of anticlerical violence. Yet there is no reason to think that poor laymen would have resented the clergy less than wealthy laymen did. Popular anger was cold and unfocused, and it refrained from attacking the proper religious functions of the clerical estate. Yet it was felt widely.

We have observed that both Bucer and Zell sought to radicalize popular anticlerical feeling in order to discredit the sacral system. To medieval religion they opposed the "Gospel", promising freedom from human religious law and free access to a merciful God. Did endemic late medieval anticlerical grievances actually function as tinder for the "Gospel's" spark?

The First Impact

Early in 1523, Eckhart zum Treübel published a short treatise in Strasbourg, _Ain dümietige ermanung_ (A Humble Admonition).[15] It is an example of the first inroads of evangelical ideas on the consciousness of pious but mildly anticlerical laymen. Eckhart was a knight and a citizen of the town, born into a prominent and politically active patrician family. Although in the latter part of his life he retired to his castle at Hindescheim, he retained his citizenship and remained in intimate contact with affairs in the town.[16] If his rather chaotic German tends to indicate that his education had not been prolonged, he was still able to boast of voyages to Russia, Poland, Wallachia, and

Turkey.[17] Eckhart appears faithful to his class. As a landed knight, he need have had no affection for merchant commerce; his pamphlet, reflecting this on a religious level, is an assault on the currently reigning commerce in holy things.

Ain dümietige ermanung is appropriately subtitled, "one should not have anything to do with money in church." Eckhart introduces himself as an ordinary layman, but one deeply troubled by the "manifold disorders" in the faith, especially by the way in which "God, Heaven, the saints, even the Mother of God, and all our sacraments and Christian things" are openly put up for sale. "The entire order of the Christian church" is bought and sold. The penny has greater honor than God.[18] Eckhart focuses on the destructive effects of such commerce on the Eucharist, the cornerstone of the medieval sacral structure. When people attending Mass toss coins on the altar, Eckhart writes, two grave evils occur. The person who pays the money sins, because he is trying to buy grace.

> He does not so much trust in God, that [God] is full of mercy and that through that mercy he can or will forgive him, prevent one thing [from happening], or grant another. Rather, he means to purchase it with money, to move [God] with money,... and thus [he] places his faith more in the penny than in the mercy of God.[19]

The priest who sees the money is not hurt any less. Standing in God's place, he ought to remain undisturbed in his devotion. If the sight of money distracts him, his devotion will collapse. He will forget God and follow his greed. Eckhart than expands this theme into a general polemic against mixing money and holy things. Money is the seed of the devil. Christ avoided it, and Judas, who carried the purse for the Apostles, was perverted by it. Thus, he pleads, as Christ cleared the temple, so should usury, simony, and retail commerce (Gremplerei) be kept away from God and his saints.[20]

Eckhart closes by excoriating Christendom's sinful resistance to God. "That, however, is caused by our religious leaders, who give us such an utterly poisoned example. But the Lord lives!"[21]

Ain dümietige ermanung was composed before Eckhart had assimilated the evangelical preachers' program. In all formal respects, he shows himself to be traditionally pious. The purpose of his pamphlet is to preserve the consecration of holy things: the Eucharist, the clergy, the "whole Christian order." His understanding of the priesthood is medieval. He chooses the priest's celebration of Mass as the central clerical function endangered by greed, unlike Zell, who chose preaching. For Eckhart, the priest still stands in God's place.

Not all of Eckhart's attitudes are quite so conventional. Of course, his extreme description of the greed-prompted corruption of the church was little stronger than some of Geiler's own attacks on abuses. The contrast he depicts between trust in God's mercy and attempts to purchase God's favor was not new. By emphasizing trust in God's mercy as the decisive element of the Eucharist, rather than magnifying its objective and sacrificial aspects, he did nothing that his fathers would have found wholly alien. The sum, however, was to exaggerate certain elements common to late medieval piety in ways suggesting liasons with the sermons of the evangelical preachers. The pamphlet reflects the preachers' caricature of late medieval religious activity as petty commerce which was designed to obscure the truth that interior dispositions, faith and trust, which were all that were really necessary for acceptance by God.

The major theme of Eckhart's pamphlet, however, is an attack on what he considers to be a commercial market in the sacred. He clearly regards the 'fiscalization' of religion as antithetical to and destructive of true piety, thinks that it corrupts the means of grace radically.[22] He associates the current state of affairs with Judas, or with the Temple before Christ drove out the moneychangers who had rendered it a den of thieves. Eckhart expliticly links the clergy's sale of holy things with precapitalist commercial practices -- usury and retail trade -- in which the factor profits from others' labor without any contribution of his own. These practices traditionally excited great resentment among artisans and those associated with the rural economy. Linking greedy priests with such "middlemen", popularly regarded as essentially egotistical and exploitative, Eckhart cites a Scriptural maxim to the clergy: "Freely have you received, freely give."[23]

This association was current among other laymen.[24] The analogy between priests' exploitation of sacred mysteries and usurious and monopolistic practices was harped on in the tracts of Mathias Wurm von Geudersheim, another Strasbourg knight.[25] Already in August, 1522, the Rat itself had told the Bishop that he should appoint learned, pious priests who "would expound the teaching of God and the Apostles, and not say anything to serve their greed and their own profit."[26] This identification of sacred commerce with self-seeking business practices, together with the conviction that such activity traduced and destroyed the religious value of the "goods" so sold, left a fertile field for the evangelical preachers. They argued that the sacral system was the tool of a clerical conspiracy to defraud and tyrannize the laity for self-profit. We have seen that Zell began the Christeliche Verantwortung by alleging that his accusers cared for nothing more than their bellies; like the image-makers who rioted against Paul in Ephesus, they would do anything to keep their "sacred" businesses intact.[27] From there, it was a short step for Zell to persuade his audience that the sacred goods themselves -- the masses, indulgences, candles, clothing, special times and places, the whole sacral system -- were nothing more than fictions designed to serve this conspiracy. At this point, the evangelical preachers employed their keenest weapon, the Scripture principle. God's own law knew nothing of these human inventions. Thus, the preachers argued, the traffic in such useless goods should be abolished, and the money turned to the service of the community.

It is certain that it was at least in part by these means that Eckhart himself was radicalized. Between the latter part of 1523 and 1524, he wrote a series of pamphlets praising evangelical progress in the community, urging the Rat to remain faithful to the Gospel, and praising the Rat for its new welfare system. The latter was, he wrote, a Gospel-inspired redirection of money from nonsense like bells and organs to the poor.[28] In 1528, Eckhart wrote a treatise describing true Christian faith and practice for his children. In one section, he reviews the old inventions used by the priests to cheat the laity: purgatory, indulgences, penances, Masses, and the like.[29] For Eckhart, initial distaste for commerce in holy things, including authentic concern that such commerce would destroy their religious value, had become a rejection of much of the medieval sacral system on the grounds that it was invented to serve the interests of the clerical estate.

There can be no question that the storm of anticlerical hatred grew in intensity as the preacher's ideas were disseminated. Almost every document from the first years of the evangelical movement witnesses to extraordinary tension in Strasbourg, to a near-universal fear of an anti-clerical uprising. Even the tracts of the preachers in 1523 attest to it; Zell, Brunfels, and Bucer all go to lengths to warn against pseudo-evangelicals who, unlike true Christians willing to suffer outrage, are prepared to act on their grievances by force.[30] Capito's main concern in the summer of 1523 was to bring cooler heads of both sides together, before it was too late and war broke out.[31] In almost every pronouncement by the Rat on religious issues, it cited the threats to the city's internal peace. It cannot have been empty rhetoric; such arguments moved the chapters to compromise. In 1524, the lightning struck; only rapid action to resolve lay grievances against the church quieted the city after the Treger riots, as Alsace moved towards the explosion of the Peasants' War.[32]

During the decades preceding the Reformation, the propaganda of the learned reformists mirrored one element of the laity's attitude toward the clergy: loyalty toward old religious ideas, coupled with the conviction that the modern clergy traduced those ideals. But the reformists offered nothing to deal with another element of lay anticlericalism: resentment of the clergy's social position. By explaining the clergy's malpractice and its social status as the fruit of a massive clerical fraud, the evangelical preachers were able to persuade much of the population that large parts of medieval religion were fraudulent inventions of a self-seeking clergy. Eckhart's pamphlet exemplifies a development of consciousness particularly inviting to laymen who resented pre-capitalist business practices and who were ready to see such economic 'egotism' as a radical disease of the entire social fabric. Priests could be lumped with other middlemen, their mediation of grace 'exposed' as a technique for unfairly profiting from goods necessary for the soul's salvation. The evangelical preachers' claim that Christ saves those who trust him, irrespective of any "holiness" no matter how derived, was calculated to reveal the medieval religious system as a confidence game and the clergy as swindlers. In this context, Bucer's promise of a new cooperative society oriented to the common good could take on anticlerical overtones quite audible to laymen.

The Gospel as Social Elevator

The evangelical movement derived a good deal of its energy from radicalized lay anticlericalism extended to the medieval sacral system. There is evidence that some laymen also had in mind the quite concrete benefits which elimination of the medieval clergy could provide. By reinforcing the Rat's objective of economic control over the clergy, the "Gospel" helped merchants harness their most active and powerful competitors. The total demoralization of the Strasbourg clergy left Strasbourg commercial figures with a dominant position in local markets, the possibility of purchasing ecclesiastical lands at favorable prices, and sharply reduced "sacral" expenditures.[33]

For many others in the town, hopes focused on relief from heavy clerical taxation. The fact that the preachers devoted a large volume of their propaganda to Christian non-resistance of evil, heavily underlining that the illegitimacy of the religious government did not imply laymen's right unilaterally to withhold the tithe, strongly suggests that the question of non-payment was posed with some force. In 1524, a substantial group of gardeners, suffering from a bad harvest, refused to pay the canons of St. Thomas the tithe they owed as members of the incorporated parish of St. Aurelien. Only after protracted negotiations, mediated by the Rat, did the two parties agree on a reduced sum. The gardeners' action was closely related to a wave of tithe withholding which rose during the two years preceding the Peasants' War.[34]

Some groups experienced economic dislocation, especially those who supplied goods for the sacral system. In 1525, the painters and sculptors, pleading that their crafts had been set aside by the Word of God, were granted priority for positions with the city adminstration.[35] Other groups, however, found new opportunities opened to them. For example, the gravediggers asked the Rat to outlaw the fees they paid sacristans and priests for permission to bury bodies in city churchyards. They pictured the fees as kickbacks, extorted from their already meager incomes, undermining their efforts to raise their children decently and have them carry on in the craft. They asserted that they provided an honest service; they deserved full pay. Once again, the clergy appears as a profittaker, sucking from others and contributing nothing itself. The clergy's discredit appeared to be to the gravediggers' advantage.[36]

The apparent economic benefits of discrediting and harnessing the clergy did not exhaust laymen's understandings of how the Gospel could enhance their social position. For some, confirming the merit of lay values at the clergy's expense 'boosted' them psychologically and socially. For others, the new arrangements offered religious means to achieve self-respect and community standing, means not offered by the normal social hierarchy. An example of the latter was provided in January of 1524, when a group of parishioners from St. Aurelien submitted a petition to the Rat, requesting the appointment of Bucer as a supplementary preacher.[37] It is not possible to determine the composition of the group with precision. According to lists of occupations of parish members compiled between 1540 and 1560, the outlying part of town which the parish occupied was relatively poor. One fourth of the parishioners of St. Aurelien were gardeners, another fourth were day laborers and servants, and the remainder were involved chiefly in clothing trades, woolworking, and ropemaking.[38] However, it was the church trustees (Kirchenpfleger), laymen who oversaw parish affairs and who therefore were probably drawn from among the better established members of the parish, who signed the second petition in April in the name of the "entire parish community", having presided at the general parish meeting which chose Bucer as the permanent pastor.[39] It is likely, then, that the petitions reflected a fairly broad social spectrum, numerically dominated by the poor, but with significant influence from somewhat more prosperous members.

The language of the parishioners' petitions is highly suggestive. During the first set of negotiations with the Rat and the Chapter of St. Thomas during January and February of 1524, the petitioners had insisted that they be provided with a preacher "who preaches like the others in the city", not one who "saws on the same old fiddle."[40] In April, they formally expressed their motives for choosing Bucer as their permanent pastor:

> In recent days, some of us humbly presented Your Graces with a supplication on behalf of the parishioners of St. Aurelien, [describing] the lack we have had due to our pastor's unfitness for daily preaching of the divine Word. We requested a preacher who preached the holy Gospel rightly, according to your Graces' mandate, to be supported at our own cost, so that among us we be directed to one Christ and

> unanimously live to God's praise, Your Graces' pleasure, and the good of the common city [gemeyner stat].[41]

After making that request, they had gone ahead and had Bucer preach to them, "so that we not be robbed of the most needful thing in this time, the divine Word." "By God's grace, we heard and grasped [the Word] in such a way that we are all of one heart and spirit, [determined] to hear the holy Gospel from him from now on and daily to direct our lives according to it."[42]

The original negotiations in February leave the reader with the sense that the petitioners refuse to be left out of the main current of city life any longer. Others, living in the center of the town, had preachers in the new style; even if they from the outskirts had to pay the salary themselves, they wanted one too. The April petition amplifies these feelings, already showing the influence of Bucer's sermons. Faced with the illegality of their actions, the parishioners insist that they do not mean to be subversive of the social order. In fact, they claim, their intentions are the opposite. They understand Scripture as a rule by which they can direct their lives in order to live in full social confidence. The fruit of Bucer's preaching, in the petitioners' eyes, is the ability to achieve fully respected status before God (living to his honor and praise), before the Rat (to its pleasure), and in the social life of the city (to its good and welfare).[43] Full social integration and confident status in the community awaited those who directed their lives according to Scripture.

The petitioners appear to have understood Bucer's sermons to have promised that in the new cooperative society, social respectability would be measured by the brotherly service resulting from Scripture-directed lives. One did not need to change classes in order to lay claim to the community's esteem; the new religious understandings promised to carry with them new standards for measuring one's value in the community.[44] Not only were the poor to be freed from competition for religious status with the clergy and the rich,[45] but Bucer's argument that the social order depended upon the reversal of egotism through faith was understood to offer lower class laymen enhanced social standing and self-consciousness as well. The parishioners of St. Aurelien hastened to grasp this religious upward mobility with both hands.

The writers of the petition also betray a changed attitude toward religious authority. For them, it is the Scriptures alone that provide the new standards for life. The petition asserts that Bucer was chosen on grounds of his expert skill in expounding the right sense of the Scriptures to the community. It was on grounds of this professional capacity that the city's Doctors and preachers had recommended Bucer to the parishioners; he was the most able and skillful (<u>täuglichsten</u> <u>und</u> <u>geschicksten</u>) man available.[46] Bucer's function in the community, then, is as a skilled guide to the real source of authority, the Scriptures. Neither charisma nor ecclesiastical consecration appears to be considered relevant, only skill and the people's choice. If Bucer is regarded as qualified for any reason other than his training and the fruit already appearing from his sermons, it is as an exemplar of the conduct appropriate for all estates, ordering one's life according to Scripture:

> [The fact] that he has a wedded wife [by itself] caused our community, which viewed the scandal and vice of our previous unmarried pastors with great offense, to

> choose precisely him as pastor. For the Holy Spirit, whose mandates matter more than all [other] mandates and human statutes, wants a pastor who has a wedded wife. Thus there is no way that even the Imperial Mandate...can forbid that a married priest serve a Christian community....[47]

Bucer has followed the Holy Spirit in Scripture, has married, and is devoting his life to the service of the community. He thus is a model of what the petitioners regard as ideal citizenly virtue. Preachers are especially good citizens.

The St. Aurelien petitioners understood the Gospel as an ideal of lay life which imposed new, socially integrative standards on the clergy which sprang from typical lay values. Bucer did skilled work for pay for the common good, he was married, and he was subject to the Scriptures in precisely the same mode as laymen. But these standards were attractive to the petitioners as well. Faithful attention to divine law allowed anyone, poor or rich, to achieve a life of pious service rooted in the divine order of the universe, worthy of full human approval. The fact that most Strasbourg workers took no part in the peasant uprisings in 1525, and that for a generation Strasbourg economic life was marked by unusual calm even in the face of significant worsening of the material conditions of life for workers, tends to indicate that this religious social elevator was taken earnestly by many.[48]

Confidence in Divine Law

A good deal of moral self-confidence floated on the surface of the Strasbourg evangelical movement. The evangelical preachers promised laymen that a society grounded in faith and ordered according to divine law would be characterized by the respectability, cooperation, and concern for the common good which were valued by all good citizens. Strasbourg laymen naturally brought aggressive confidence to the defense of an ideal which so faithfully represented many of their own values. It was natural, too, that this should be sharpened and hardened to compensate for the painful internal dissonance caused by the rejection of their fathers' religious values. Evangelical residents could not bear to be told that they were heretics or rebels. Already in the _Christeliche Verantwortung_ Zell mentioned his partisans' temptations to violence when they were called such names.[49] Treger's pamphlet, openly calling residents "Bohemian heretics", was greeted by riot and looting, and its author was imprisoned and ejected from the city.[50] Yet the charge that evangelicals were harming their society would seem undeniable; the new doctrine obviously posed grave dangers of social disruption. The Rat, for one, repeatedly recognized that "divine law" posed threats to the human agreements defining orderly city life. Further, no socially significant group, whether the Rat, a monastery or chapter, a family, a parish, a guild, a brotherhood, or the town itself was immune from schism over the new ideas.

In response, the preachers had been concerned to demonstrate the absolute priority of divine law over human law. Yet Bucer also insisted on the positive social effects of the Gospel. The Word would usher in a renewed social order founded on brotherly unity. Among others, the parishioners of St. Aurelien were intent on publicly displaying their unity and spirit of cooperation. They called themselves a community (_gemeyn_); they underlined the unanimity of their mutual commitment to direct their lives according to Scripture. That standard, they assured the Rat, would cause them to live to the Rat's pleasure and the good of the entire city.[51] Yet they did not mention the Catholic minority in the parish, which had requested a traditional priest of its own.[52] In good measure, the evangelical movement's obeisance to ideals of brotherly unity and its touchy, bantering confidence were reactions to the bitter disunity and doubt sweeping the city.

In the late spring of 1524, a case came to the Rat's attention which illustrated many of these matters. In mid-May, the Rat received a supplication from a citizen named Augustinus Trenß, lodging charges against Caspar Hedio, Michael Rott, and Nikolaus Kniebis.[53] Trenß sketched a lurid conspiracy in which Rott, a doctor of medicine, had allegedly invited Trenß' widowed mother and sister to his house, as a pretext for illicitly inducing the mother to give her daughter in marriage to Hedio, the new evangelical preacher in the Cathedral. When the mother resisted, Trenß alleged, Rott called in Kniebis, a relative, to use "smooth words" to persuade her to comply. Hedio, who had been lying in wait in the house, assured Agnes Trenß that Rott and Kniebis could prevent any offense to the family's _freundschafft_ and talk her son out of his opposition.

Trenß based his appeal squarely on the Rat's responsibility to preserve law and custom. It was against the city's own articles as well as universal custom to take a child away from its father without permission, or, if the child was an orphan, without the permission of its guardian. Yet the object of the defendants, he wrote, was precisely to bring his mother to act against the will of the girl's brother, her guardian, and the family's _freundschafft_. For his part, he had ordered his sister to let priests alone and find a decent burgher to marry, since clerical marriage was a legal nullity, an impossible disgrace:

> The Doctor [Hedio] is a clergyman. Such marriages are not only not normal, not customary, but

> contrary to all the law, both religious and secular, that has been in use in Christendom for more than a thousand years. And more than a little shame and scandal to me and mine will grow out of this business. A properly acting, responsible magistrate in Christendom would not permit this sort of thing. It would forbid it; in no way would it allow it. And one would think that it would so act, since it is incredible that a few people could criminally overturn and spurn papal and imperial law.[54]

Trenß then listed the concrete injuries he expected. His sister would rightly be regarded as a public sinner and whore. Since before the law she would be an unmarried cohabitor, she would be ineligible for inheritances from her mother or grandmother. Great dishonor would fall not only on him and the family, but upon its freundschafft as well. The Rat thus should order Hedio to cease and desist; if it refused, it should at least not oppose him when he looked for justice outside the city walls. "For if it should come to pass that any priest or monk can properly cheat and defraud a citizen of his child or his relative without his knowledge or consent, my Gracious Lords...can judge for themselves what will come of it."[55]

In spite of Augustin Trenß' clear expectation that the Rat would be reluctant to act in his favor, if only because of Nikolaus Kniebis' eminent position, he depicts himself in a light meant to appeal to men of high standing who had remained faithful to the attitudes of the preceding decade. The anticlericalism traditionally directed at promiscuous monks and priests and the old suspicion of clerical trickery are now directed at Hedio. Above all, however, Trenß brings to the fore Hedio's subversion of the fabric of medieval society. Trenß charges Hedio with an assault on the integrity of a father's authority over his children, on the unity of the extended family, on the family's freundschafft, on the Articles of the city, and on the laws of Papacy and Empire. For Trenß, Hedio's suit for his sister was just another priest's strategem for battening himself on the lives of decent citizens.

Responses were not long in coming. Kniebis, the most active member of the Rat during the evangelical movement, immediately sent an angry, cold letter to the Rat, refuting Trenß' account.[56] He launched no philosophical defenses of clerical marriage; he cleared his own name, and then turned the onus on Trenß to defend his own 'slanders' and threats. According to Kniebis, there had been no conspiracy. The betrothal had been carried out in proper form long before, with the mother's consent. The Trenßes, mother and daughter, had visited Rott unexpectedly, as he was conversing with Hedio at home. All agreeing to an immediate marriage before local gossip waxed hotter, Rott went to Kniebis' home and pulled him away from dinner. The company of friends which assembled at Rott's house then asked Kniebis to give the pair together in marriage. Initially, Kniebis wrote, he had refused, saying that he was not a priest. In the end he gave in, and then took part in the wedding feast. The next day he had approached Augustin Trenß, in order to make up the differences. Trenß, furious and raving, would only shout that he would pursue Hedio until he caught him, and then would strangle him. Kniebis had ended up officially warning him to let Hedio, his sister, and his mother alone. Trenß was the troublemaker; he should be silenced and charged with all court expenses.

Kniebis' petition kept rigidly to the facts of the case; it included no ruminations on the nature of the Gospel.

The cold, proud fury with which he dissected Trenß' account was to be expected from an eminent burgher of any religious persuasion, when personally attacked by a common citizen; it was no Gospel-fostered confidence. But his account itself is revealing. Upon persuasion, Kniebis was willing to perform a ceremony of marriage, presumably in virtue of his office as Ratsherr and former Ammeister. Yet Kniebis, in utroque iuris licentiatus,[57] cannot have misunderstood what it meant to displace a priest. Marriage was henceforth a holy estate belonging to civil jurisdiction, not a sacrament belonging to priests. Further, as a member of the Rat, he had officiated in an action which as unequivocally as possible violated the laws of Papacy and Empire, on an issue in which the Rat had tried to maintain legal regularity. Ratsherren could use their prestige of office to protect and advance the movement even when the Rat as a whole could or would not. Under their aegis, whole families could act on the "Gospel", cushioned from the effects of conspicuous disobedience.

Caspar Hedio also submitted a petition to the Rat.[58] Although he further clarified the details of the case, he chiefly was concerned by Trenß' charge that he, as a representative of the new Gospel, had subverted established authority. The ambiguity of the evangelical preachers' position--divine law which drove them to submit to the Rat's taxation but not to the Emperor's prohibition of marriage--was painfully in evidence. Hedio asserted that it had never been his intent to violate God's command to obey one's parents and the Rat, so long as they did not resist God. He underlined his wife's mother's free assent to the marriage, formal permission which, he thought, should satisfy the Rat's articles. But as to Augustin Trenß' claim that the marriage was illegitimate on grounds of religious and secular law: God is the Lord, above all law and all kings of the earth, and he had never forbidden marriage to anyone. It was Gregory VII's forceful, arbitrary, and tyrannical enforcement of clerical celibacy that had given the church's law currency, "to the great injury of all decency."

> No Christian authority which acknowledges Christ as the head above all legislators can support and confirm such a law.... Rather, the Word of God, which is valid and endures forever, and through which heaven and earth were created, quashes [such laws], powerfully trampling to the earth not only canon law but the whole earth, hell, and the devil--whoever presumes to build against the counsel of God.[59]

As an upright (frumm) man, he had the right to take an upright woman to wife. It was also God's law that, once married, a man must not part from his wife; Hedio absolutely refused to leave his. No doubt, he writes, the members of the Rat will support him, as lovers of God's commandments and of Christian freedom.

Hedio's statement illustrates the way in which militant evangelicals used Scripture to revise social standards. Even though the laws of Papacy and Empire protected the consecration of the priesthood from profane institutions such as marriage, God's laws (which happened to conform to what most laymen considered respectable and upright for themselves) took priority. But Hedio also argues that this divine law will not subvert other lay institutions, those which provide for social control. Obedience to the secular magistracy and parental government of the family are commended, not suspended by divine law.[60] Hedio portrays himself as an upright citizen, subject to the same social controls as others.

At the same time, he cannot promise absolute obedience. Rat and family may be obeyed only as long as they do not violate God's commands; he implied that he would refuse an order to leave his wife. If the clergy was subject to social controls, society did not have the right to set all its own standards. Divine law could be used to appeal from any human statute. This principle, one may note, left the new religious "experts" with a good deal of power. When determination of divine law was normally left in their hands, the new clerical estate could easily come to resemble the old.[61]

The most revealing of the petitions submitted to the Rat was that of Agnes Trenß, the mother of Hedio's bride. Profoundly humiliated by her son's public exposure of the family quarrel, she begins by apologizing for the slander on the characters of honorable people which he had circulated. Hedio, she said, had acted in a manner proper for any upright, modest man. In some detail she described the history of the negotiations with him, how she had cautiously assessed the merits of the marriage, all with her son's permission. Then, egged on by anti-evangelical companions "who live in such a way that it is not without cause that they hate the light of the Gospel," he suddenly asserted his opposition. Hoping that through the daily preaching of the Gospel her son would change his mind, she let the matter ride for a time.

> I hoped that he, like I, ...would recognize that holy matrimony is permitted by God to all, and that (since until now marriage was forbidden to the clergy and thus great scandal and vice was current) every pious Christian ought to help drive off the improper, shameless lives of some clergymen through divinely blessed marriage however they can. But this knowledge did not come to my son, perhaps because of the conspiracies of the godless.
> Now, since I had given way to him enough, far

> more than I was obliged to as a mother, and in view of the fact that he does not oppose this marriage for any good Christian reason, I [was] moved by the daily clear preaching of the Gospel in this City of Strasbourg (which Your Graces certainly would not allow, nor such a respectable citizenry listen to, if it were not Christian and godly) [to] promise my daughter to Doctor Caspar as his wife, with not a few of my relations, friends, and well-wishers, decent, honest, respectable people...[agreeing] with me. I have no doubt that, since such a marriage is God-pleasing, it should also be proper and wholly advantageous for my daughter.[62]

Agnes Trenß concluded that her son should be ordered to let everyone alone. For her part, she wrote, if he did not repent of his scandalous conduct and of his disobedience both to God's commands and to her will as his mother, she would henceforth refuse to recognize him as her son!

Agnes Trenß thought that Hedio was a good marriage prospect for her daughter. He held high office, had a good income, and enjoyed powerful connections. One may wonder whom else Agnes Trenß, the widow of a gardener, could have found for her daughter who could have attracted Nikolaus Kniebis to the marriage supper. The new clergy was an untapped resource in the marriage politics of Strasbourg families.[63] It was now a part of lay society, available. Further, although clerical marriage was obviously still a matter of some controversy, the fact that Agnes Trenß consented to Hedio's suit indicates a change in popular feeling. Her petition indicates how carefully she had considered the problem, and how sensitive she was to the climate of opinion. The new clergymen were beginning to be regarded as common citizens, part of the web of Strasbourg bourgeois life.

For Agnes Trenß too, divine law came to supply the standards for proper conduct, although the certificate of social acceptability given to divine law by the Rat and the population clearly mattered as much as her independent judgment. But she displays a tough confidence soon to appear elsewhere in the citizenry. The discord is not the fault of any "innovation" of hers, but of her son's failure to listen to and receive the Gospel. It was he who violated due obedience, by slandering upright people, disobeying her and resisting the Gospel. Her further suggestion, that he had been perverted by unnamed evil Catholic companions, shortly found echoes. The dissonance experienced by newly converted evangelicals could be redirected as hostility to representatives of the old order.

On June 4, Augustin Trenß responded, abashed but unconverted.[64] He asserted that he had told the truth as far as he had known it, without meaning to injure anyone. He acquiesced to the others' accounts of the affair. But his mother's polemic left him an argument not to be missed:

> This new Evangelical teaching is now supposed to be working so much, that father and mother and their children, and marriage alliances, and friendships are brought to hostility and division, as, God pity it, [is the case] between [me and] my dear only sister and my mother who...does not want me for her son any more. None the less, I certainly shall acknowledge her as my mother my whole life long, without regard to this new teaching.[65]

He did not yield on the issue of clerical marriage, however.

It was against all custom and law: "Your Graces might consider...my family and my honorable <u>freundschafft</u>, which has endured both good and bad with this city for many years, and show consideration so that the innovation does not begin with me and my <u>freundschafft</u>."[66] Trenß made the best of his opportunity to show that the "Gospel" split and ruined the basic social units of medieval life.

Agnes Trenß' petition illustrates a crucial step in the institutionalization of the preachers' ideas: the evangelicals' brassy inversion of responsibility for the discord filling the city. Residents converted to "divine law" could accuse traditionalists of resisting the absolute claims of God's ordained order. Internally torn by their own conflict of values, and witnesses to a popular conflict which Strasbourg's social compact could not sustain for long, it was natural to find scapegoats where the preachers told them to look: in the persons who kept reminding them that their new values violated the religion in which they had been brought up. Agnes Trenß' attack on her son was less typical of other citizens' reactions to disunity than her references to the machinations of certain wicked resisters of the Gospel who had corrupted him. During the summer of 1524, rumors of Catholic subversion filled the city. Word came from nearby cities and the countryside that canons had been seen organizing bands of criminals to start fires; others were reported to be laying the groundwork for an attack by neighboring princes.[67] The rumors led to violence, and the canons of Young St. Peter, who had figured prominently in the rumors, fled the city.[68]

A few days thereafter, a petition was presented to the Rat which demanded that steps be taken to end Catholic resistance to the "Gospel." It claimed to represent the opinion of the residents of five parishes.[69] The petitioners alleged that the discord in the city was the work of certain of their fellow citizens, who without ground or reason felt "anger, discord, displeasure, and annoyance at us." Yet the petition attached no great blame to such people; they opposed the Gospel because they had never heard it, and perhaps also because certain "perverted" pastors and monastic preachers had incited them. For that reason, the Rat should provide evangelical preachers for all parishes. And further, the petitioners wrote, they were honest, quiet, hard-working people who wanted peace and quiet on feast days. They should be dispensed from the noisy, irritating splendor of chapter ceremonies; they wanted neither the canons' goods nor their labor.[70] For the petitioners, reminders of the old order should be stamped out.

To the petition was appended a theological rationalization of the requests. The Gospel could not be held accountable for the discord. It brought peace. If only all residents would listen to it, it would irresistably bring peace in its wake. There was no alternative; "without friendship towards God, there will never be true friendship among us." Bucer's ideas take the stage: faith is the foundation of society.

This petition brings together the themes of many earlier documents. The confidence of its tone is striking. It claims to represent the desires of common working people who want no more spectacles of glorious holiness from the Kapitelherren, or self-seeking (eigensüchtig) sermons from old pastors, but rather the respectable, hard-working, obedient tranquillity promoted by the "Gospel." It seems obvious to them that the new religious arrangements will not interfere with the unified society which the Rat seeks to defend. The new religion is basically supportive of respectable citizenly life; the old religion and its clergy are destructive. Evangelical preachers are the agents by which decent, peaceful society can be established and guarded; peace with God will produce peace in the town.[71]

The majority of Ratsherren still refused fully to

accept these principles in September of 1524. They agreed to appoint evangelical pastors, but their treatment of the request for separation of parishes from the chapters was blunt. The city's peace rested on keeping its laws intact. People had no business robbing other residents of long-held possessions on their own authority. This sensitivity to law, however, was shortly forced to give way before an outburst of redirected anger from the population. After the Treger riots, the evangelicals on the Rat had the upper hand, and the public dismemberment of the sacral system could proceed in earnest.[72]

There is no stronger indication of the transformation of the general conception of the proper place and role of the clerical estate than the collapse of monasticism in Strasbourg. By 1530, only a tiny minority of the former population remained in the cloisters. If members of orders were free to go to houses elsewhere, the influence of the new atmosphere caused a substantial number simply to give up their vows altogether.[73] The Rat encouraged the change by opening the cloisters to social and ideological pressure. In response to a series of petitions from citizens, it ordered that relatives be granted access to the enclosed, and that they be given opportunities to persuade them to come out.[74] It further ordered that evangelical preachers be given regular hearings in several convents, expounding the "Gospel" and then offering free exit and a pension to any who wished. For those who did leave, the Rat helped to ease the transition. It granted many requests for pensions from those who could not make their own way, and those who married were given stocks of grain and wine in order to set up housekeeping.[75]

One petition to the Rat for a pension, somewhat more revealing than most, was presented by Andreas Waldner, who had held minor posts in the Johannites' house at Strasbourg. The devaluation of the monastic life is nearly complete:

> [It is] necessary that Your Graces consider the poor religious, who have wasted their capable years in cloistered life, and who now leave the monastic life for conscience' and God's sake, even though they are unfit for any secular occupation. For from the opened Word of God they know that all their establishments are against faith and love. For that reason, those who acknowledge God and who consider the future life withdraw from them, which people Your Graces have provided be given adequate pensions, as justice indicates, since it was from a universally held error that they lived in places where, under the appearance of service to God, they were put away, grew old, and became incapable.[76]

He narrates his rather checkered career, attempting to establish his rather shaky claim on a share of the Johannites' "excess" revenues. Finally, he states, he left the cloister permanently, driven by the Gospel, to give himself into the "common vocation" and earn his living with his hands. A combination of persecution of the Gospel and illness had prevented him from doing so, and thus he appeals for relief from his distress.

The themes of this petition are mirrored in many others. Very frequently mentioned is the new, Gospel-established freedom to marry. Now that the Word has shown that God is not well served in the cloister, monks' "work" has been exposed as idleness and their sexual consecration as presumption. Thus they mean to become respectable.[77] A way of life originally chosen because general opinion gave it the highest standing is to be deserted, now that the old standards have been reversed.

In Strasbourg, what it meant to be pious had changed.

The old system was understood as the enemy of citizenly virtue, the new one as its friend. The new clergymen were understood as examplars of good citizenship and respectability. Like the town's legal experts, they were professionals, valued for their skill and learning. The eternal importance of the matters they dealt with, their place in the limelight as the conduits of God's Word to the community, and their conspicuous piety all contributed to their moderately high social status and inevitable aura of religiosity. Yet they were part and parcel of bourgeois protestant society, citizens, married, working for the community, excelling in virtues which had once been left for laymen.

Cutting Deeper

The deconsecration of the clergy is only one aspect of the general sweeping away of much of the old sacral system. If the preachers retained a sacred cosmos, inhabited by angels and devils and subject to special providences of God, yet the old divisions of the material and social world into sacred and profane were altered. As their sermons gradually changed public opinion, the preachers began the concrete abolition of sacral customs. Gradually, they cast off vestments, candles, relics, pictures, processions, choirs, liturgies, ancient services, and sacraments.[78] Yet as the identification of these sacral objects with priestly "tyranny" became current, radicals became increasingly impatient with the trappings of the old system. Disagreements over the pace of change were the first symptoms of the later cleavage between the established evangelical preachers and religious radicals.

In the legal aftermath of the Peasants' War in 1525, a stream of people relocated in Strasbourg, many purchasing the *Bürgerrecht* both as a legal shield and as a sign of their identification with the Strasbourg Gospel. One such peasant, Wendelung Murer, a former resident of Zabern suspected but later cleared of participation in the rebellion, submitted an interesting petition to the Rat.[79] In it he attempted to clear himself of responsibility for a disturbance which had occurred during a return trip to Zabern. Sitting in an inn in Zabern, he wrote, another peasant had told a story of one time when he had been suddenly overcome with illness. Sensing death coming, the peasant had said, he ran to the graveyard in a local church to mark a shady spot for his last lying place, and then to his master to beg him to bury him there. Wendelung had felt impatient. He had told the man he was a fool to wish to be buried in one place rather than another. Once dead, it didn't matter. For his part, Wendelung had said, they could throw his body in the Rhine. If the fish got it, the worms wouldn't. The sacristan of the church, who was sitting nearby, replied that he wanted to be buried in consecrated ground, especially at his church. In the heated discussion which followed, Wendelung denied that the graveyard could be any more consecrated than any other place; God had created and blessed the whole world. Even if the church owned a papal letter consecrating its churchyard, the Pope was only a man, and no man could outdo God. The sacristan said that Wendelung was a false prophet, and told him to go back to Strasbourg and the Lutheran heretics, where he belonged. After further exchanges between them, a fight broke out.

Wendelung's account may well varnish the facts for the Rat's benefit. Yet that is merely to say that he expected the Rat to approve the opinions he expressed. In fact, the Rat defended him in the ensuing litigation.[80] No doubt other citizens would have expressed themselves more prudently; Wendelung's strident impiety would not have recommended itself to all. Yet only his rhetoric, not his principles, went beyond what Bucer had published in 1523.[81] The universe had been blessed by God and so could not be thought profane, but the old sacral differentiation of places, times, and human beings was stripped down to a few "external" agreements by which the community could be provided with the Word. The preachers could even use the remnants of the sacral cosmos against medieval religion; they made much of God's threats through natural catastrophies and human discord as a lever to force the Rat to abolish the masses permitted to the chapters.[82] Medieval sacral differentiation, however, was discredited. In 1528, citizens were taking up gravestones to use in buildings.[83]

The preachers, however, considered it important to keep some elements of the old church structure, in revised form. Although neither Scripture nor the preaching office nor the sacraments could guarantee God's favor in and of themselves, the preachers thought, they were the reliable means by which God extended his Word to men's hearts and instructed his people in his law.[84] Yet an extension of the same principles by which they had attacked the medieval church could be used against the preaching office and the sacraments. In 1523, Zell and Bucer had exulted in the triumph of the small over the great through the Word. The Spirit could call laymen as his prophets; the Scriptures were filled with the shepherds and workmen, people without external qualification, through whom he had spoken. Further, the preachers had attacked the medieval sacramental system on the grounds that faith alone, not any external action, could justify men before God.[85] If this opposition of internal to external were extended, any institutional mediation of the means of salvation, whether through official preachers of communal rites of any sort, could be challenged. The evangelical preachers had made the old sacral system and official clergy the villains of a conspiracy against laymen's goods and freedoms. The more radical the alienation of people from the old church, the more chary they were likely to be of a new one.

These tendencies emerged early in Strasbourg. Beginning as pressure for accelerated reform of liturgy and sacraments, the push for radical change gradually revealed its ideological roots in a more or less extreme dissociation of religion from "external" institutions. Especially before the violent suppression of the peasants' economic Gospel in 1525, this radical alienation from the medieval system was often linked with a parallel economic radicalism.

Strasbourg's most conspicuous early representative of this radical interpretation of the Gospel was Clemens Ziegler, a gardener who worked leased plots of land around the city. Between 1524 and 1525, Ziegler wrote and published five pamphlets, expositions of the Gospel, rambling attacks on sacramental practices, and christological analyses of doubtful orthodoxy. He championed tithe withholding, and on the eve of the Peasants' War he toured through Alsace preaching to peasant congregations, asserting the Gospel's condemnation of usury, the tithe, and economic exploitation of the poor, but preaching pacifism. Faced with an ultimatum from the Rat after the outbreak of violence, he returned to Strasbourg before the catastrophic battles that brutally put down the revolt.[86]

In Ein fast schon büchlin...von dem leib und blut Christi, written in 1524, Ziegler confronts those who criticized him for an earlier pamphlet on the Eucharist, and those who told him that his calling was to work, not to preach.[87] At length, Ziegler cites passages from the Scriptures to prove that God uses the lowly as his prophets. God will not withhold knowledge of the Scriptures from any believer; his Spirit has been poured out on all flesh. Like anyone who sees a neighbor in danger of harm, Ziegler claims the right to save his neighbors from the eternal loss which threatens them. People should not regard the personal estate of the preacher, but pay heed to the Word he proclaims. Ziegler does not threaten the bond between the prophet and the Scriptures; in his early works there is no question of special revelation. He does no more than to use the preachers' own principle of the absolute authority of Scripture to justify his own exegesis-based attack on their slowness to demand the reform of sacramental practice. Yet for him, the Spirit's gifts are given to many, not to a few "expert" members of the clerical estate. He does not mention the community's choice of preachers, and he lists no qualifications for the prophet except asceticism and hunger for Christ's promises. Bypassing the new establishment, Ziegler disrupts the preaching office as the stable, normal, "expert" estate providing the Word to the community.[88]

Ziegler's treatment of the sacraments reveals the same anti-institutional bias. He radically spiritualizes the Eucharist. Arguing that both Christ's 'carnal' and 'glorious' bodies are unavailable for literal presence in the bread and wine, Ziegler separates the partaking of the body and the blood from any sacramental rite at all; true faith in Christ's suffering is all that is necessary.

> Where that happens in the heart of a person, wherever he may be, cutting wood...or going to the field...or watching over the cattle in the pasture, when such thoughts are present in him...he certainly partakes of the body and blood of Christ. And if no priest and no altar and no external sign are there, still Christ's body and blood are surely there.[89]

It is possible to partake under the wine and bread of the altar, too; if it can be done anywhere, why not there as well?[90] But it is not necessary, and it is an abomination to think Christ is there in a different mode than anywhere else.[91]

Ziegler's position is still far from full spiritualism. He insists on the bond between Scripture and Spirit; if he approaches Carlstadt's view of the Eucharist, he is still far from rejecting all external means to which the Spirit might bind himself. Yet it is clear that he has no brief for the reconstruction of a religious establishment around a core of Word-supporting offices, as the evangelical preachers did. The preachers still considered themselves members of the clerical estate; Ziegler considered that estate dissolved. It was another issue which most clearly distinguished Ziegler from the established evangelical preachers in Strasbourg. Although Bucer had condemned merchants in 1523,[92] his description of the cooperative society did not dwell on the economic adjustments which love-filled believers should be expected to make. It offered enhanced status through religiously-motivated service, not through the reform of economic institutions. In contrast, Ziegler strongly pushed the standards of Old Testament law and New Testament love, both requiring that economic exploitation of the poor be stopped. In 1524, he refused to tell peasants to pay their tithes; if God had once made such a law, it was suspended now.[93] The text of a sermon on the Our Father, preached in 1525 near St. Odile shortly before the first uprisings began, has been preserved.[94] In it, Ziegler begins by attacking the clergymen who call themselves fathers and who make laws for others; God alone is Father, and his will alone is to be done. The sovereignty of God cuts away the human hierarchy of authority.

"Give us today our daily bread." Every man has

> a right to daily bread. Consider the Law: "In regard to the poor man, you shall not be a creditor, you shall not require interest of him. And if you take the garment of your neighbor as a surety, you shall return it to him before sunset, since it is his only covering." "If you buy a property from your neighbor, you shall preserve for him the right of repurchase." By this collapse all rights of lease, all the land rents. You tell me the law is no longer a norm for us. Well, then, listen to Christ: "Lend," he says, "without hoping to receive."[95]

Later clauses of the prayer forbid avarice and usury. On the other hand, the words "deliver us from evil" rule out taking one's liberation in one's own hands. Vengeance belongs to God.

For Ziegler, as for the land-tilling poor with whom he identified, the new cooperative society based on faith in God and free from human religious law had to bear fruit in economic reform. Precisely the commercial practices which for him discredited the sacral system were breaking the backs of the poor. The same merchants who were in the temple, plagued the countryside too. Religious techniques to rob the poor jostled with straightforward usury and market speculation.[96] For many of the poor within city walls, Ziegler's economic Gospel was very plausible.[97]

Ziegler's economic orientation raises the question of that of the evangelical preachers. The preachers' integration in Strasbourg society, their identification with its values did not make them slow to criticize abuses, it merely limited the keenness of their vision into Strasbourg's exploitation of the countryside.[98] They were married, resident in the town, citizens, salaried. They depended on the governmental support of *Ratsherren*, of bankers and merchants, of the hundreds of citizens receiving income from leased lands or loans to peasants. It would have been difficult for them to look beyond the walls. And their ideas gave them no very great stimulus to do so. Their Gospel did not promise economic equality, but internal peace and confidence even under the gravest oppression. The enhanced status their restored society promised was religious, not financial. If usury and economic exploitation were obviously wrong, yet other evils were far more profoundly dangerous, since they threatened the faith which was the source of just behavior: blasphemies against God such as the Mass, the grave need for schools to educate children in piety, the threat of religious radicals, public indifference to their preaching, the lack of church discipline, and many more.

Yet it would be facile to describe Ziegler and the established preachers simply as the ideologues of different classes. Both retained significant independence. To Ziegler, the Word which enjoined non-resistance to evil was more important than his identification with peasants' economic grievances. The preachers, in turn, continued to regard themselves as the clerical estate, responsible to the Word at any cost, obedient to human authority only when it heeded divine law. Tension between the preachers and the Rat persisted, preachers arguing the absolute claims of the Kingdom of Christ, the Rat guarding the fabric of the social order. After the Augsburg Interim and the city's agreement to let the Mass be said in the Cathedral, Bucer wrote to Jakob Sturm from exile in England: the city should rather have fought to the last man and been burnt to the ground, before letting that blasphemy come back in the walls.

* * * * *

The evangelical preachers demanded change in the clerical estate because a new concept of justification caused them to regard the clergy's pretension to mediate grace as an unjustified invasion of God's prerogatives. The consecration which had protected the clergy's sacral role was thus unjustified as well; all Christians were subject to the same laws and open to the same freedoms. The medieval clergy had no right to live in splendid immunity set above the rest of society. It was no better than any other means of living off the sweat of others.

Strasbourg townsmen had sought change in the clerical estate for a long time. Anger at clerical unworthiness joined with resentment of the clergy's social, political and economic position. Yet this anger had not extended to the clergy's religious functions; they were still valued highly. Both medieval law and medieval piety kept reform programs within more or less strict limits.

The evangelical preachers' presentation of a divine law exposing the clergy's consecration as a class ideology and its 'holy' functions as a conspiracy against the freedoms and goods of laymen, offered Strasbourg residents an effective solution to their dilemma. Those who obeyed God's law could by definition regard themselves pious, submitting to a rule of law that preceded any human law, no matter how well accepted. Divine law obliged all Christians, lay and cleric alike, to follow standards remarkably similar to the norms for lay life prior to the coming of the "Gospel." The story of the success of the preachers' concept of the clerical estate is one of the progressively growing confidence among townsmen that God approved of respectable, hardworking, pious laymen of all stations, and that he refused to condone their exploitation and misrule by a class of counterfeit holy men. The Gospel liberated and enhanced lay life.

The preachers, however, had not 'liberated' lay life

from the sacral system out of love for liberty or the urban life style for their own sakes. They had done so in order to free men for true faith and diligent service, founding a new society growing up into the kingdom of Christ. No one was free from divine law; no one lived for his own sake. The Word was prior to the whole world, the city included. The tensions between those who resented the "new Papacy" founded on divine law, the preachers themselves, and those who chiefly valued the integrity of the social fabric helped write the history of Strasbourg during the following decades.

Epilogue

Analysis of the struggle in Strasbourg over the nature and social position of the clerical estate leaves us with an enlarged view of the Reformation. It was more than a reformation of abuses or a revolution in doctrine. It was in some respects an ideology intended to resolve specific problems of late medieval society. The change in the clergy in Strasbourg was fueled by popular grievances, long angers at old "abuses." The preachers' ideology radicalized the grievances, 'revealing' the source of "abuses" as the religious function of the clergy itself. It then offered a radical solution: social redefinition of the clergy, based on a new concept of justification. As support it offered the Scripture principle, a legal standard which could be used to overturn law, a pious means to revise religion. The Reformation was not simply a paroxysm of disgust or a mass revival of religious sentiment. The preachers' ideas had a clear social direction; they offered a highly plausible and attractive solution to problems which had seemed utterly intractable. Zell, Bucer and Capito did not create social tension in Strasbourg, but they inflamed it and opened a new direction for it. Reformed theology offered a surprising outlet for old pressures, one that was far from necessary. It is in this sense that we proffer the evangelical movement in Strasbourg as an example of the possibility of a positive relation between religious ideology and social change.

Our excursion into the struggle in Strasbourg ended well before institutional changes in the clerical estate had come to a close. In the first months of 1525, the bloody suppression of the economic Gospel in the Peasants' War, the struggle with spiritualist radicals, the absolute prohibition of the Mass, the establishment of an official church order, the transformation of the Chapter of St. Thomas into a scholarly foundation, the long fight over discipline, and the cataclysm of the Augsburg Interim still all lay in the future. Yet the seeds had already been planted; the central changes in the clerical estate had been made.

For better or for worse, the preachers were wed to lay society. From one perspective, the clergy had come down from heaven to dwell with men. Like laymen, Bucer and Zell and Capito had homes and wives; they lived in the warmth of household life, part of the old circle of human affection. They suffered too, like laymen, when the plague carried off their families, when the city they loved was shadowed by the smoke of war. Part and parcel of town life, they could minister to their fellows not as lords or angels but as common men. Freed from the strain of reaching for superhuman perfection, they were capable of exemplifying common virtues consistently. There was no longer any question of using a special status as a platform for exploitation or abusive religious government. Pastors were good citizens.

Yet the destruction of the clerical autonomy which made integration possible also opened the way for the preachers' Word to be consumed by urban culture. The original preachers kept a strong sense of their membership in the first estate, ministers of the Word of God, which was subject to no man; yet the institutions which could maintain that independence after the first generation had been demolished. Without sociological guarantees for keeping values distinct from those of laymen, clergymen could not develop an exploitative ideology. They could, however, become ideologues for others. Scripture remained sovereign, in principle. But the movement in Strasbourg had left the enforcement of the preachers' interpretation of Scripture solely in the hands of the Rat. The preachers had to go to the Rat for permission to print controversial books, for the administration of congregations, for church discipline, for their houses and salaries, for the official definition of teaching, and even at times for the content of their sermons. As became clear in the battles over the Mass and discipline, the Rat had reference to values other than the preachers' Gospel.

The medieval clergy was open to the accusation of having used its consecration not for the sake of the people but for itself. In response, the evangelical preachers demanded that the clergy be domesticated, that it make its home with men, that it serve the citizens of Christ's kingdom. Yet once tamed, it was vulnerable to a less noble servitude.

Appendix

The date of Zell's Christeliche Verantwortung is obscure. Most historians place its publication shortly after the first appearance of Zell before the Vicar, thus in the first weeks of 1523, (Röhrich, Mittheilungen, 3, pp. 112-113). Chrisman, p. 101, treats the CV as the text of what Zell said before the Vicar at the December 22, 1522 hearing, published the following year. Adam, however, dates it on Christmas of 1523, perhaps misled by the final leaf, which reads, "Als man zählt nach dem Geburt Christi xxiii," no more than a fanciful way of saying "Anno domini." (Adam, p. 34.)

A March 10, 1523 letter of the Bishop of Strasbourg to the Rat provides an externally documented terminus a quo. (AST 47) The Bishop protests against the unruly behavior of Zell's supporters: "So bewegen wir doch, das gemelter Meyster Mathis ime selbs/ ein solchen grossen anhang macht/ der im trotzlicher weiß one [?] widerrede/ in der Rechtfertigung/ darzun er yetzt gegen unserm Fiscal steet/ mit vielerley bösen freveln hochmutigen unerbern wortten und geperden bystand thut." The use of the present tense rules out any possibility that the Bishop is refering to the CV itself. Further, had Zell already published a vernacular appeal for support as obviously radical as the CV, it would seem extremely odd that the Bishop did not complain of that, rather than of the unruliness of Zell's supporters. Clearly, Zell was in the process of delivering a legal defense against the Fiscal's charges at the time the Bishop wrote. (See above, p. 8, n. 8 for further evidence of the occurrence of a second hearing.) The publication of the CV therefore followed the hearing.

The text of the CV confirms this later date. Zell's remark that it has been decided that there are to be no more disputations probably refers to the Nürnberg Mandate, published in Strasbourg on March 6 (CV Z4r; Chrisman, pp. 107-108). A clearer reference, however, is the citation of an opponent's sermon, a "bruder" who "zu Ostern dissz jars/ der dreyen Marien salben ußgelegt hat." (CV L1v.) Easter, 1523 fell on April 5. Thus the earliest possible date is late spring, 1523.

A terminus ad quem is provided by Otto Brunfels' Von dem evangelischen Anstoß (Simonis et Iude, 1923, = October 28, 1523), which mentions the prior publication of Zell's "Artikel buch." (C1r). This is confirmed by Wolfgang Köppfel's prefatory letter to Capito's Verwarnung/ der diener des Worts, published in early 1524. Köppfel writes that the CV appeared before the Entschuldigung of Capito. The latter was completed November 11, 1523 (Entschuldigung, AA2v).

Greater precision may be purchased at the price of less certain evidence. There are references to "other preachers" being persecuted together with Zell, which may possibly refer to Bucer's presence in Strasbourg (CV b3r-v). Zell also mentions the persecution of runaway monks: "Und wundert mich warumb man einen guten bruder oder tochter ubel redt/ die...[ihren klöster]/ härauß kummen/ es sey yo durch erläubnüß des Babsts oder nit." (CV T3v). Both Bucer and his wife were attacked in Strasbourg during the summer of 1523 for having abandoned their monastic vows. The reference is rendered still more suggestive by the fact that Bucer had obtained a papal dispensation (DS I, pp. 156-159).

Analysis of Zell's ideas suggests a still later date. Prof. Marc Lienhard has pointed out to us a possible dependence of the CV on Luther's treatise, Das eyn Christliche versamlung odder gemeyne recht und macht habe, alle lere tzu urteylen. (May, 1523; WA 11, pp. 401-419). In this treatise, Luther interprets the verse, "My sheep know my voice" (John 10:4), as asserting the power of the individual believer and thus of the Christian community to recognize God's Word, to evade or depose false shepherds, and to install true ones (WA 11, pp. 401-410). One passage in the CV employs the same biblical passage in a very similar manner: "Ich mich auch bekenne gesagt haben/ das ein pfarrkindt nit eben bey einer todsünd schuldig sey in seiner pfarr predig zu hören/ vorab wo er vernäm das jm sein zugeteilt hyrt nitt das recht gottswort predigte/ oder es fruchtbarlicher von eim anderen hören möchte/ welches auch ein yeglicher mensch wol urteylen kan und sol/ dieweil das urteyl bey den schäflin ist/ obs die recht weyd sey oder nit. wie der herr lernt/ das die schäflin jrs hyrten stymm erkennen. welchs wo geschähe/ warumb solten sy jm nit nachfolgen/ und die falschen propheten vor denen er sye auch treülich gewarnet hett/ meiden." (CV D2v-D3r).

The strength of this argument for a later date of the CV is partially sapped by the fact that Luther's treatise Vom Mißbrauch der Messe (WA 8, p. 496 ff.), written in 1521, also insists on the power of Christians to judge doctrine. Further, like the CV, Luther there mentions the power of the community to elect a pastor only as an historical footnote, still regarding appointment by the hierarchy as the normal method (WA 8, p. 502). We do not think that the far more radical ideas of Das eyn christliche versamlung were fully exploited by a Strasbourg preacher until Bucer published his Summary (August, 1923; DS I, pp. 82-86). Yet Luther does not use the John 10 passage in the CV's manner in his 1521 treatise. The parallels between the language and order of argument of Luther's 1523 treatise and the CV are so strong that we continue to think it probable that Zell had read, if not fully accepted, the later work. The text of Das eyn christliche versamlung could not have reached Zell before June.

Another passage of the CV probably relies on Bucer's lectures in Zell's home, which began in June (DS I, p. 17). In a brief outline of the Gospel, Zell describes the source of the Christian's ethical drive: "Wann so wir ye gott nichts thun künden/ wann er ye unserer güter nit bedarff/ es ist vorhyn alles seyn. er gibt uns/ wir künden jm nichts geben oder thun/ so geben wir dz selb unseren nechsten/ dem wir thun/ helffen und rathen/ ein yeglicher mit dem er kan und vermag." (CV Q4v.) This is the idea that Bucer develops in his first publication, Das Ym Selbs (August, 1523; DS I, pp. 29-67). In the foreward, Bucer writes that he composed the treatise at the request of people who had attended his lectures, and who wished to hear this concept more fully discussed. (DS I, p. 44.) We think it highly probable that on this point, Bucer taught Zell and not vice versa. The passage in the CV is not amplified anywhere else, standing as an isolated remark. In contrast, the idea dominates Bucer's ethics and social philosophy in Das Ym Selbs, standing at the heart of his reform program.

Given the presence of material from Luther and Bucer that could have reached Zell no earlier than June, we think it likely that the CV was not completed before June.

Several considerations lead us to fix the end of the summer of 1523 as a terminus ad quem. First, Zell apparently has not had time to develop the new ideas of June. Second, in spite of the vague references to other preachers, Zell clearly still regards himself as the sole established preacher of the Gospel in Strasbourg. In early summer, that would still have been possible. Capito was at odds with Zell, and Bucer still regarded himself as a temporary refugee, seeking positions in other cities (DS I, p. 151). But after Bucer and Capito's sermons and publications in late summer, Zell could not have retained so strong a sense of isolation.

A final indication that Zell completed the CV in the summer of 1523 is the apparent interaction between him and Bucer in the CV and Das Ym Selbs on the issue of prayer for the dead. In a passage early in the CV, Zell defends the practice at length, basing his argument on the communion of the saints and a citation from Augustine asserting a "middle state" for the dead, neither saved nor damned, but suffering (_CV_ G4r ff.). Yet in a later passage, Zell argues that the concept of purgatory is _ungewiß_, that in such weighty matters we should rely on Scripture alone, and that Augustine's treatise is self-contradictory and thus no authority (_CV_ M1v ff.). Early in the _Summary_, Bucer attacks purgatory and intercession for the dead with violence (_DS_ I, p. 101). Later, he retreats. He says he has no advice to give on the subject, except that after praying for the dead a few times, one should assume God has heard and stop (_DS_ I, pp. 124-125). It would seem possible that each gave way to the other, thus placing the _CV_ in the summer of 1523.

Footnotes

Introduction

1. See Bernd Moeller, "Piety in Germany around 1500," in The Reformation in Medieval Perspective, ed. Steven Ozment (Chicago, 1971).
2. See Peter Berger and Thomas Luckmann, The Social Construction of Reality (New York, 1966), and Peter Berger, The Sacred Canopy (New York, 1967).
3. The word "evangelical" refers to the "gospel" preached by Mathis Zell and his colleagues, fostering radical religious change; "Catholic" refers to rejection of the evangelical program.

Chapter 1

1. The first years of the Strasbourg reformation and the career of Zell, who dominated the infant movement, are relatively obscure; historical interest has focused on the long-range constitutional and social consequences of the formation of Protestant established religion. Prof. Marc Lienhard is currently preparing a biographical and theological study of Zell. Other sources for Zell's career include Timotheus Wilhelm Röhrich, Mittheilungen aus der Geschichte der Evangelischen Kirche des Elsasses (Strasbourg, 1855), vol. 3, p. 91 ff.; Johann Wilhelm Baum, Capito und Butzer (Eberfeld, 1860), p. 195 ff.; and Miriam Usher Chrisman, Strasbourg and the Reform (New Haven, 1967), pp. 91-92, 100-111.
2. Adolf Baum, Magistrat und Reformation in Strassburg bis 1529 (Strasbourg, 1887), pp. 15-16. It is possible that Graf Sigismund von Hohenlohe, dean of the Cathedral Chapter, already sided with the evangelicals. His efforts on Zell's behalf may have reinforced the Chapter's traditional reluctance to give the Bishop any voice over its internal affairs.
3. Johann Adam, Evangelische Kirchengeschichte der Stadt Strassburg (Strasbourg, 1922), pp. 30-31; Chrisman, pp. 100-101.
4. Mathis Zell, Christeliche Verantwortung (Strasbourg, 1523), aa1-bb2 (hereafter cited as CV); Adam, pp. 35-37, summarizes the articles.
5. These protests were retained in the printed version of the CV. They refer to allegedly unfair legal procedures: Zell being required to be personally present and to respond under oath, though his accusers were not; being confined to a response of "credit" or "non credit" when the charges were read; etc. Zell, CV b4v-c1v.
6. The CV has never been carefully examined and dated. Most treatments of the evangelical movement identify the CV as the text of a self-defense presented by Zell at the Vicar's hearing at the turn of the year 1522-1523. This is incorrect on two grounds. First, in the opening speech printed in the CV, Zell refers to it as his second appearance, following protests against the legal form of the first hearing (CV a3r). A letter from the Bishop to the Rat in mid-March, 1523, refers to a self-defense by Zell which is still in progress. Thus those portions of the CV which appear to be the text of an oral self-defense are probably from the latter hearing. Second, the CV is textually complex. Zell refers to it as "the reply...which I made first in Latin and afterwards in German." (CV a2v). While it may be assumed that certain portions of the CV are relatively straightforward translations of the March hearing before the Vicar, the CV is obviously a major expansion and reorientation of that defense, containing extensive materials composed well after March.

Its final form dates from the summer of 1523. See Appendix.

7. See Appendix.

8. Zell, CV a2v.

9. See Appendix.

10. The audiences to which the CV is addressed depend on Zell's tactics for reform, still wholly dependent on the self-reformation of the clergy. He hopes to find support in the ecclesiastical hierarchy of Strasbourg against the coterie of 'hypocrites' which has deceived the Bishop. Accordingly he appeals not only to the Bishop personally but also to the Dean and Chapter of the Cathedral, traditional rivals of the Bishop (CV a3r). Later he expands his appeal to all "sincere and worthy" priests, who will help him cast out the exploitative hypocrites in the upper clergy (CV A3r-v). Zell appears to have begun to look for resources outside the clergy, however. He argues that the whole church is concerned in the 'case' of the Gospel (CV b2r), including all estates both temporal and spiritual (CV a3r), even the Rat.

11. Köppfel writes a prefatory letter to Capito's Verwarnung der diener des worts (Strasbourg, 1524), an edifying mixture of evangelical sentiment and mercantile avarice, to advertise the evangelical books he published: "It is my plea that you, Christian reader, will desire to confirm your spirit in God through exercise in the Scripture; and so that your reflection may be aided, that you will wish to read M. Mathis' reply [(Verantworten)] diligently, which is to be used as a summary of the teaching of the Apostles and David's weapon chest."

12. Zell, CV a2v.

13. Zell offers extracts from old sermons in CV F3 ff., G4 ff., P2v ff.

14. Steven Ozment, Homo Spiritualis (Leiden, 1969), pp. 105-109.

15. Jaroslav Pelikan, Spirit versus Structure; Luther and the Institutions of the Church (New York, 1968).

16. Martin Luther, De Captivitate Babilonica Ecclesiae, in Werke Gesamtausgabe (Weimar, 1883 ff.), vol. 6, p. 484 ff. (hereafter WA); Martin Luther, An den christlichen Adel deutscher Nation, WA 6, p. 381 ff.

17. We do not argue that Zell was original in treating reformation ideology as a solution for political, social, and religious problems allegedly caused by medieval ecclesiology. This inversion is characteristic of many of Luther's reform treatises as well. Zell closely follows portions of Luther's 1520 propagandistic treatises, such as those cited above.

18. Here we deal only with Zell's intentions. For an analysis of late medieval popular anticlericalism, see chs. 3 and 4.

19. Zell, CV a3v-a4v.

20. Zell, CV d1v-d3r. Using an image readily understood by his urban audience, he compares the right use of the Fathers to a Rat, where each one speaks his opinion and all the listeners then decide. Since all believers possess the same Spirit as the Fathers, all may judge and even improve on their opinions (Zell, CV f3v).

21. Whenever possible, Zell links his arguments with anticlericalism, e.g. his attack on canon law: "If some canons of religious law are no longer being observed, as, for example, those dealing with benefices and clerical morals and the like, one wonders why they retain them and have not torn them out a long time ago. [The reason is] that they don't want to betray or shame the canon law, [to make it appear] as if it had erred somewhere and were not all directly from the Holy Spirit, who does not err, and, his word once spoken, will have it kept uncontradicted. As he spoke by his prophets, 'I will watch over my word,' and many of the Scriptures say that God's word will endure eternally, that not a letter will be lost. But man's word is not so, but today announced, tomorrow contradicted, as we see every day. The same may have occurred in this case, since an error is a sure indication of the absence of the Holy Spirit, since he is the Spirit of Truth." Zell, CV c4v. The abuse of benefices and sexual irregularity were stock targets of late medieval preachers. Zell introduces them here, but as a springboard for his attack on all human religious law.

22. Zell reshapes the definition of "heresy" so that it, too, will expose his clerical opponents as antichristian. The traditional definition, contumacy in error, he redefines as stubbornly self-serving abuse of Scripture. He lists motives: the emotions of debate, or pursuit of glory, riches, high status, power, or land and people (Zell, CV d4v-e1r). The real heretics, then, are not those who try to render the sense of Scripture humbly and faithfully, even if they err; they are those who pervert Scripture so as to serve their own interests--the belly-serving hypocrites in the clergy.

23. Zell certainly did not intend his anticlerical invective to appear irreligious. He claims to attack false religion and evil practice for the sake of the true and the good. Regardless of his radical theories, he cultivates his links to the model of the medieval preacher against abuses, e.g. Geiler von Keysersberg. Thus he rarely attacks an object of popular piety frontally (e.g. clerical celibacy). Rather, he glorifies other objects of traditional piety (e.g. Scripture as divine law, respectable lay sexual behavior), and shows that the clergy has used the object under attack to foster its tyranny, while subverting the latter objects. His argument against clerical legislation proceeds by praising Scripture (always an object of great reverence in the Middle Ages) as God's law--a fully sufficient law, from which the church has no right to differ. When his opponents attempt to counter by minimizing the role of Scripture as the church's lawbook, he can accuse them of impiety and of usurpation.

24. Zell's most coherent discussion of the church as creature of the Word occurs in his reply to the twenty-second article (Zell, CV Y3r ff.), a faithful restatement of Luther's thought.

25. Zell, CV d2v, e3v.

26. Zell draws his descriptions of Luther's exegesis of these passages from Luther's treatise, Vom Miszbrauch der Messe, printed in 1521. Luther, WA 8, p. 496 ff.

27. Zell, CV f4r-v. Following Luther, Zell makes vigorous use of

Conciliarist exegesis rebutting theories of papal autocracy. For the origin and broad diffusion of non-papalist exegesis of these passages in medieval canon law, see Brian Tierney, Foundations of Conciliar Theory (London, 1955).

28. Ibid. Zell argues that his opponents have collapsed the power of the keys into a license for an ordinary government, founded on the power of men to invent laws. He points out Christ's rejection of temporal power, including--a lively popular grievance--Christ's refusal to divide an inheritance. Medieval church courts traditionally claimed the exclusive right to adjudicate wills, and the Strasbourg Rat had been making forays into this jurisdiction for half a century in order to stem the flow of land to the church. See below, p. 108 ff. Restriction of the church to governing consciences spiritually, by the Word, implied obvious advantages for city government. Zell's exegesis offers townmen an opportunity to attack the Church's previously invulnerable legal position while remaining pious. It is the clergy's pretensions, no longer the town's, which are religiously illegitimate.

29. Zell, CV g1r.

30. Zell, CV g1v. One should note that Zell only redefines the clergy's divine powers; he does not abolish them. True preachers receive the Word from Christ just as he receives it from the Father.

31. "The disciples of Christ are commanded to feed [weyden] [his sheep]. If their successors do so, too, they also are disciples of Christ and rightful successors of the Apostles. If not, they are...brooks without water, and day laborers...." Zell, CV q1r-v.

32. Zell, CV g2v. See also s1v, where Zell compares the preacher's power to that of a city's delegation to the Emperor. It may alter the wording of the Rat's message, but not its content; anyone changing the message is a traitor.

33. Zell, CV g2v-g3r.

34. Zell uses antipelagianism politically, as an argument against medieval ecclesiastical government. That humans can take no initiative in the process of salvation is understood to imply that only God, not humans, may create laws and institutions governing that process. Zell's argument in this passage, that human religious government may not exceed its divine mandate, is later expanded into a general polemic against any human legislative authority at all in religious matters. In CV N4r-v, Zell constructs an absolute opposition between human opinions [gutduncken] and divine commands. Humanly invented religious ordinances are incapable of pleasing God, for it is satanic pride to seek to displace God as sole religious legislator. Zell's target, of course, is the political expression of that 'pride', the church hierarchy. One may speculate that evangelical preachers' antipelagianism became intelligible to their audiences in part because they expressed it politically, against a resented governing elite.

35. Zell, CV g1v. Here Zell parallels Bucer. See below, p. 48 ff.

36. "You ought to be servants of the New Testament, not of the letter, but of the spirit. That is: not of the law, but of grace. You should set forth the grace of God, not law. Moses gave the law, but

truth and grace is through Jesus Christ." Zell, CV g3r-v. Zell obviously is aware of the theological significance Luther gave to the opposition between law and grace, but again his discussion of it occurs in a political context. Here, to preach grace simply means not to make laws. See also Zell, CV h1v-2v, z2v, O3r.

37. John 21: 15-17.

38. Zell, CV p4v. The principle of salvation by faith in the Word is, of course, presupposed by Zell's reduction of the clergy's activity to preaching. But because his argument is not scholastic but popular and anti-hierarchical, only here does he explicitly introduce the theological principle itself. It is taught in part through the political program it produces.

39. Zell, CV i1r-p3v; r3r-y2r.

40. Zell's forceful distinction between works of love--caring for the poor--and the "selbs ertichten wercken" serving the bloated clergy had immediate political resonances in Strasbourg. Between October, 1522 and August, 1523, the Rat was preparing to establish a system of public welfare, to be paid for by the negotiated release of all ecclesiastical incomes stipulated for the poor. See below, p. 122 ff. Zell appears slow fully to assimilate Luther's understanding of justification. He retains the conviction that love of God must be the source of any activity which can please God, although he makes a Lutheran concept of faith the source of that love (Zell, CV i2r-i3r). While he insists that good works come from the believer as spontaneously as fruit from a tree, he later makes works of love to be works required by the law, lacking the 'joy' offered by merit-earning invented works (Zell, CV i3r-v). The point of his rather clumsy discussion is that the simple, ordinary, lay life of faith is all the Scriptures demand, and that medieval "extras" were commanded by the clergy for self-serving motives. In the Christeliche Verantwortung, the principle of faith is important chiefly in so far as it makes "simple" lay Christian life the norm for all.

41. Zell, CV i3v-i4v; k2r-v. The clergy's additions to Scripture, Zell argues, are no help at all to the pious life; they simply serve the clergy's interests. Christians should struggle against base desires, but one can keep a true fast even when eating meat, and be a glutton while 'abstaining'. Regulating fasts by law has had the effect, not of enforcing asceticism, but of creating an artificial hierarchy of religious status.

42. Zell, CV k2v-k3r; see also n4v. For the history of the reformation polemic against mandatory celibacy, see Steven Ozment, "Marriage and the Ministry in the Protestant Churches," Concilium 8, 1972, pp. 39-56. Zell here exhibits a common feature of the early polemics. He is relatively little concerned to praise marriage for its own sake, or to attack sincere celibacy. He is content to argue that salvation may be found in either estate, and to underline the disreputable consequences of the absolute prohibition of marriage to the clergy. It is clear that in Strasbourg, clerical 'chastity' was one of the best defended of the social distinctions of the clergy from the laity, and a point at which lay self-confidence was least well developed.

There was widespread resistance to clerical marriage in 1523 (see below, p. 149 ff). Instead of making a direct appeal to lay sexual norms by praising marriage, Zell argues by indirection: in practice, the law against marriage has destroyed common decency, and tortures the consciencious, even although a pious life is still possible within marriage.

43. Zell, CV k3v-k4r.

44. Zell, CV n2r-n3r.

45. Zell, CV y1v.

46. Zell's object is the distinction between lay and cleric. "Now, I could well say that St. Paul knew very little of this distinction between spiritual and secular [persons] in the form it takes now, though he was worried that such things would happen in the last days.... Is it not to prohibit marriage, having so many healthy, strong people, men and women, live outside of marriage in promiscuity or in unbearable temptation: who could be helped by the medicine of marriage, permitted for all by God?" Zell, CV 13r. "Great anguish arises from this prohibition of the estate of marriage, or establishment of the estate in which one undertakes to withstand the force of nature with prohibitions and eternal vows." Zell, CV 12r. See also n2r. Zell represents the Scriptures as attuned to natural human sexual desire, and thus permitting marriage to all; the lay state is thus both natural and in accord with Scripture. Mandatory clerical celibacy is neither, merely a prop for illegitimate religious status. In this connection, Zell attacks the traditional interpretation of the word "wife" in the verse, "A bishop shall have one wife," (I Timothy 3), as meaning that a bishop shall have only one diocese. A wife means a wife, not a benefice. Zell, CV 13v-14r. Chrisman's attribution of a poem, allegedly against Zell, to Hieronymus Gebwiller is incorrect (pp. 103-104). The line, "He twists the Epistle around so deftly/ that "woman" comes to mean a benefice," could hardly be directed against Zell. Röhrich identifies it correctly as a part of Stefan von Bullheim's poem in defense of Zell, here attacking the conservative schoolmaster, Gebwiller (Röhrich, Mittheilungen, 3, p. 101).

47. Clerical marriage will support the stable patriarchy of respectable urban life: "So you ask, would all promiscuity end if the clergy had wives? And I say, there would not be the twentieth part of what there is now. It could just about be rooted out from the world, since precisely clerical chastity is a cause for just about all of Christendom being full of whores.... Don't you think that if the clergy had to be married, they could rebuke other people for their promiscuity, and that they couldn't support so many loose women, who thus would not run away from their fathers and friends? Wherever they went, they would find marriage in the way.... Before going into a common brothel, they's stay home and work." Zell, CV 12v.

48. Zell, CV k3r, n1v-n2r.

49. Zell associates the clergy's 'indecency' with the nobility's. Both classes' sexual morés conflict with a citizen's respectability. Not incidentally, both classes were old antagonists of the artisan-controlled commune. The cleric-noble link is underlined on other issues. The

epithet "idler" [müsziggänger], with which Zell and Bucer derided clerics while contrasting them to hard-working common folk, was in use against noble families. Zell often refers to clergy as "Junckherr".

50. Zell, CV 14r-v.

51. Zell, CV 11r-13r, m1v, n1v, n2v, n4r. This portion of the argument chiefly addresses the clergy, but it also has the effect of persuading the laity that its own estate, marriage, is fully legitimate religiously.

52. It is at this point that Zell reintroduces the polemic against clerical conspiracy. "So then why don't we come to the aid of this poor lot with fitting, godly means from Scripture? Is it in order to get money and goods? Has the spotless bride of Christ become a decoy-bird so that one may accumulate money and goods, get land and people?...Why don't we [the clergy] travel overseas like other merchants, work like they do, risk our bodies and goods like they do? To obtain our goods, do we have to risk the souls [of our charges], hazard so many suffering consciences?" Zell, CV n2r. "And as far as clergymen's marriage is concerned, it is obvious that it is prohibited out of sheer hypocrisy, so as to deceive the people....Although these days we practice little enough hypocrisy; even if we once leapt up and won our kingdom through it, no one can take it away from us any more, so there's no further need for much pretense or hiding. Even if we're public whoremongers, who's to prevent us?" Zell, CV x4r. See also m4r, n4r-v.

53. Zell raises a live political issue. Since the mid-fifteenth century, the Strasbourg Rat had sought to restrict clerics' inheritances as a means of protecting the town's tax rolls against erosion. See below, p. 108 ff.

54. Zell, CV x3v-x4v; v3v; y1r-y2v.

55. Zell, CV n3v. See also n4r, v3r.

56. Zell, CV x4r.

57. See below, pp. 109-110.

58. Zell, CV s3r-s4r.

59. See, for example, the portion of Wimpheling's "Responses and Objections to Enea Silvio," written in 1515 to restate the Gravamina nationis germanicae, a bill of complaints drawn up at the behest of Maximilian I in 1510 (Manifestations of Discontent in Germany on the Eve of the Reformation, ed. Gerald Strauss (Bloomington, Indiana, 1971), pp. 40-46). Martin Luther, De Captivatate Babilonica Ecclesiae, WA 6, p. 484 ff.

60. Zell, CV s4r, t1v.

61. "Well, these are carnal things, about which I don't complain as much when we speak of the church's imprisonment. It would be a small thing, as far as temporal goods and even the body go...to bear such an imprisonment to the end.... But that our poor souls should be imprisoned as well, in an imprisonment that serves to damn us eternally--that is to be pitied!" Zell, CV s4r-v. See also t3v-t4r, B 1v-B3r. On this principle, Zell suggested that many papal laws, those inflicting fiscal or political hardship, should be obeyed, but

that where the soul was placed in jeopardy they must be broken. This became a popular way to seek "higher ground" during the first years of the evangelical movement, e.g. when the parishioners of St. Aurelien appointed Bucer preacher in 1524, conspicuously at their own expense. See below, p. 168. The pacifist propaganda of the evangelical movement, which denied its intention to rob priests and asserted that lawbreaking must be strictly confined to cases in which souls were at stake, was an important ingredient in the wealthy and law-respecting Rat's tolerance and final embrace of the Reformation.

62. Zell, CV t1v-t2r. See also CV x1.

63. Zell, CV t2r-v.

64. Zell, CV q2 ff, r4r, s2r, s4v, t1v, S1 ff.

65. Zell, CV q2v. Zell is to be understood as a radical disciple of Geiler and Wimpheling, in so far as they struggled to build up the secular clergy - common priests and preachers - rather than monks, friars, and the hierarchy, out of pastoral concern for the common folk.

66. "One has to pay a great deal of money to establish a preacher's benefice, or to turn a vacant, idle benefice into a useful preacher's benefice,...though preaching, as Paul said, is ten thousand times more useful." Zell, CV t1r-v. Zell may be referring to the extremely expensive negotiations that finally won the establishment of a Predikatur for Geiler von Keysersberg. Zell did not argue that the chant of monks or canons was simply worthless or unlawful; rather, that it was much less useful than preaching. See Zell, CV q3r, F2v.

67. Zell, CV t1r.

68. Zell, CV v1v. See also CV o4r-v. These discussions reflect Luther's Vom Miszbrauch der Messe, WA 8, p. 496 ff.

69. Zell, CV v1v-v4r. In one passage, Zell appears to make salvation conditional on faith alone, even without baptism: CV s3v.

70. Zell, CV v2r-v.

71. Zell, CV v2v-v3r.

72. Zell, CV v3v.

73. Zell here indicates that some sort of legislative authority in church affairs should continue; useful and proper regulation of the Mass and communion are praiseworthy. "But that it has been made into a legal requirement, so that both the server and the communicant must suffer injury and imprisonment of body, goods, and conscience, is to be pitied." Zell, CV x2r. He does not clarify who should make these rules.

74. Zell, CV x2r-v.

75. Neither in the case of the ban (excommunication) nor of marriage did Zell advocate wholesale abandonment of church-related legal administration. He insists on the ban's validity as a public declaration of an individual's preexistent rupture with Christ; as we would expect, he criticises its self-serving abuse by the clergy, including its enforcement by the secular magistrate. Zell, CV p1r-v. Zell deals with impedimenta matrimonii in two long discussions, in which he proposes a

simplified set of rules. The dissertation of François Wendel, Le mariage à Strasbourg à l'époque de la Réforme 1520-1692 (Strasbourg, 1928), was unfortunately written without knowledge of Zell's proposals.

76. See above, p. 18.

77. See above, pp. 27-28.

78. Zell, CV y2v. Denying the charge that he called bishops and the pope "scarecrows and masks [hypocrites]", Zell writes (not without irony), "Why would I be so irrational?... They are our spiritual lords [oberen], and I know well that one ought not to speak ill of lords.... A pope is a glorious thing, since he is the one who should care for all Christendom; a bishop likewise over a whole country; and thus they rightly should be honored wherever they are found." Zell, CV T4v.

79. Zell, CV y2v; F1r-v.

80. Zell, CV p2r ff.

81. Zell, CV A1r.

82. Zell, CV r3r. This is a reappropriation of the Conciliarists' anti-papal use of the classical legal concept of "equity", under which the letter of the law can be distinguished from the intention of the law-giver. The papacy was divinely instituted for certain ends; if a pope defects from them, he need not be obeyed. Zell's new step is to find in the Scriptures a fully adequate description of the ends of ecclesiastical institutions, sufficiently clear to justify disobedience. That, however, is not to say that Scripture provides Zell with an ersatz canon law, a fully adequate compilation of positive law. Rather, it offers him legal standards for overturning law.

83. See Zell, CV p 2r; y3v-y4v; B1; T4v-V1v.

84. Zell, CV y2v.

85. Zell argues that God normally employs the orderly, institutional means of projecting his word, but that he will not permit corrupt institutions to frustrate his purpose. "I see quite clearly that the cause of divine, evangelical truth must be renewed once more only through the small, the inconsiderable, the unlearned, as at the beginning of the church. If the great learned ones don't want any part of it, still God wills to have his word unsilenced, if even the stones must speak." Zell, CV a2v. "I must [attack abuses], since I am a preacher and called to the office of preaching...And even if I were not called with a regular [ordenlich] vocation, and rose up and cried out anyway..., and took [God's] word in my mouth, ...don't you think that would be a vocation? What is a right and true calling but that the spirit of God--that is, a just zeal concerning the dishonor of God and the leading astray of his people--drives one so that he takes [God's] word in his mouth and to [God's] honor fights against his enemies? Do you not think that God could call [men] outside of the human order, where he saw that vocation [dz beruffen] was imprisoned by the human order? Who sent the prophets, Elijah, Isaiah? etc. Should Elijah have waited until Ahaz had sent him in order to speak against him? ...And just so the others, whom God himself authorized to arise, without any orderly vocation from the men against whom they were to preach." Zell, CV y3r-v. "It could be understood from that that everyone should be allowed to preach...

although, strangely, we don't like it when a layman arises to preach, which is never prohibited [in Scripture], much rather permitted, as we have said, above all where the harvest is great and ripe, and our 'noblemen' want no part of it. Perhaps they fear that they'll turn black in the sun." Zell, CV Elr-v. This may be referring to Karsthans, a radical peasant preacher whom the Bishop had moved against in the summer of 1522. The Bishop's twenty-four articles alleged a link between Karsthans and Zell. When the CV reaches those articles, though Zell is reticent about his relation with Karsthans, he writes: "Who knows from what judgment of God laymen are now beginning to preach, while the most learned and elevated prelates have had [preaching] in contempt for a long time." Zell, CV Llr.

86. Zell, CV A4r-v.

87. "And, in a friendly manner, I also request that the people absolutely not adopt any improper means, neither indecent words nor, still less, deeds, since the Antichrist must be vanquished, not with iron weapons, but with the breath of the mouth--the word of God. Thus I think anyone who takes iron sword in hand acts greatly against God.... [The only proper means] is to pull the masks from their faces through the word of God." Zell, CV Blv. The last sentence shows Zell's dependence on the late medieval model of the preacher as critic of abuses. That his exposure of 'hypocrisy' was based on more radical principles than Geiler's, need not be labored. For Zell at the time of the composition of the CV, the evangelical movement is still a preachers' reform.

88. "I have faithfully admonished the people often and forcefully to be still, [to use] good, friendly words toward the clergy, and, still more, friendly deeds--not to quarrel with them; ...to give to everyone what they owe.... I said, too, that the Gospel does not take or withhold another's possessions, nor reviles people with words or works; rather it gives everyone its own possessions and takes nothing from anyone; is friendly with everyone; hits no one; quarrels with no one; humbles itself before all; is obedient to all, especially authority; gives tribute, tax, honor to whom it is owed. Oh, how faithfully again and again I have admonished [them] to obey authority, temporal and spiritual, in those things not against God. Have you never heard from me how I came before some foolish people with evil designs, who considered that since the Gospel demands brotherly love and community of goods and that no one constrain the other [?] with seizures, with taxation, or other unjust things, that therefore they need not pay interest [Zins] or fees [Gülten] or similar debts to anyone, especially those who had more than they; saying, the Gospel makes all things common, etc., no one should constrain others, and such. Such designs, not only once but as often as they were presented, I boldly stood against, and spoke as above, that the Gospel yields to everyone what belongs to him. I said also that the Gospel does indeed require friendliness, but does not coerce anyone to be friendly. Thus, whoever wanted to be evangelical should do so: pay, forgive, lend, give, suffer, help, divide one's goods, etc. No one else should or might be forced to do likewise.... [After seeing an example of true evangelical behavior], if anyone wants to be like that too, fine; if he will not, he commits it against God. The Gospel is free. It should certainly be preached to everyone, and whoever has grace will accept it. No one should be compelled, however, since God

wills to have free service." Zell, CV B1v-B2r. Here Zell uses precisely the same argument against religious revolutionaries that he brings against the clerical government: the Gospel does not admit of coercive government, especially as regards property, etc. To Zell, the radicals seem only to be the mirror image of their enemies in the hierarchy and in the city. The Gospel requires generosity and love in the social order, but does not offer the right to resist, but only to suffer. For the importance of Zell's position to the success of his movement in Strasbourg, which depended on the support or compliance of the wealthy and respectable, see Ch. 3. It is important to note that the preachers' Gospel was not the only one being hawked in Strasbourg. A radical religious ideology, exploding in the Peasants' War in 1525 but resurfacing repeatedly long thereafter, was present from the movement's beginnings. The evangelical preachers' antirevolutionary ideology was not developed only in defense of their new establishment in the 1530s, but in the very process of winning city-wide support for their Gospel. The tension between Zell's refusal to use coercive force, and the need to build a politically effective program to take over Strasbourg ecclesiastical life and actually to supplant the old clergy, is obvious. The preachers and evangelical citizens did so chiefly by appealing to the 'secular magistrate', the Rat, to take coercive action on their behalf. Thus the appeal for magisterial intervention is part and parcel of the evangelical movement, and not only the product of a second, conservative, "establishment-building" phase of the Reformation.

89. Zell, CV D2v-D3r; K2v-n4v. Zell recommends that even food regulations be obeyed, since the soul is not endangered by keeping them: Zell, CV K2v; l4v-m1r. See also Zell, CV z2v ff, L1 ff., N1r-v.

90. Zell, CV N1v.

91. See Appendix.

92. Zell, CV a3r.

93. Zell, CV l3v. The Rat can punish its own subjects, the loose women, but not necessarily the clergy. Again, Zell insists on a rigid distinction between the spiritual sword of the Word of God and the secular sword, and he does not place the normal holders of the spiritual sword, the preachers, under the secular sword's jurisdiction. See Zell, CV z2r, J4v-K1r.

94. Zell, CV a2v; y4r-z1r.

95. Zell, CV q2v-q3r; S2r ff; E1v. As corruption has been imitative, so reform can be imitative: Zell, CV q3r-v.

96. Zell, CV A3r-v.

97. Zell, CV q3r; e1r-e2r.

98. In places, the concept of the 'small' rebuking and converting the 'great' through God's Word appears to be transposed into the language of overthrow: "It shall be that just as the small book [Scripture] has done to the great books, the small and simple people who have abandoned themselves to the small book alone shall also vanquish and dishonor the great men." Zell, CV y4v. See also Zell, CV a2v.

99. Geiler could not have considered it theoretically impossible that God raise up prophets from without the ecclesiastical government. In practice, however, he constantly reaffirms the validity and stability of hierarchical church government. For Geiler as a conservative, "churchly" nominalist, see Jane Dempsey-Douglas, Justification in Late Medieval Preaching: A Study of John Geiler of Keisersberg (Leiden, 1966). Zell follows Geiler's model as a preacher against 'abuses', and especially as a partisan of the secular, preaching clergy, not (of course) as a defender of the hierarchy. Zell, like Geiler, still relies on repentance brought about by preaching.

100. Zell, CV C3v-D1r. Zell admits the need of administration so that people will speak in order and so that business will be handled by those who are earnest and competent. But it does not follow that the latter are essentially different than their fellows, "just as in a council [Rath] all are alike, yet one is commissioned to a greater and graver care than others.... But that same ampmeister of a council is not more than the others, if one disregards his commission, nor of a different estate: so also in this case." Zell, CV D1r-v. Zell goes realistically to observe that while ammeisters may yield to pride, and consider themselves above others, there should be no similar failing in the spiritual government.

101. Zell's self-defense is based on the premise that he, as a local pastor, had the right to read Luther's books and to adopt and preach ideas that he personally determined to be in accord with Scripture. To that end, he discounts the hierarchy's power to define doctrine. See above, p. 13 ff.

102. Zell, CV y1v-y2v.

103. The CV handles the priesthood of all believers with extreme reticence and caution. The doctrine is left unmentioned until the latter half of the book, where Zell must explicitly answer a charge that he taught it. Even before he affirms it, he immediately introduces the distinction between sacerdos and presbyter, to deny laymen a voice in church government (CV D1-E2v). He denies that the concept of the priesthood of all believers played any significant role in his sermons (CV E4r). Zell turns the charge that he thinks women ought to be permitted to consecrate the Host into a joke (CV M4 ff.).

104. Zell, CV E2v. Indeed, Zell defends the local preacher's independence from the hierarchy on the grounds that only so can he effectively pacify and govern an otherwise unruly populace (CV c3v-c4r).

105. This is most obviously true of charismatic prophets, who, however, do not oversee the Church but only preach to it. Zell envisions the choice of preachers either by the hierarchy or by the community (CV E2v-E3r, D3ff), though he does not develop the latter option. Yet in neither case does the human choosing of the preacher-overseer produce valid human control of him, except by admonition through the Word.

106. Zell's practical conclusions from believers' power to recognize God's Word are extremely conservative. Indeed, believers can judge what is true pastureage and what not. But in the CV, that leads to the practical conclusion, not that parishioners may depose and appoint preachers, but only that they may attend sermons elsewhere than their parish church. Zell denies them the right, however, to choose where they will

hear mass or make their confession! Zell, CV D2v. Zell's delicate handling of the rights of parish clergy further attests to his political situation and his search for clerical support in 1522.

107. Zell, CV E3v-E4r.

108. Zell, CV E4r.

109. Zell, CV G4r-H2v.

110. Zell is confident that dissolving legal obligations will not bring about a mass defection from religious practice, but rather better observance. "If we were to follow the Word of God, there would not only be no contempt, but also a friendly, willing obedience in the whole wide world, which would soon return to one fold under one shepherd, Jesus Christ." Zell, CV K3r. See also, CV o3v.

111. Zell lacks Luther's emphasis on secular vocation as the nearly essential condition of faith. See Gustav Wingren, Luther on Vocation, trans. Carl C. Rasmussen (Philadelphia, 1957).

112. This does not open the way to religious pluralism. The only options Zell holds forward are piety and impiety.

113. Zell, CV O2v.

114. Some elements of Zell's polemic were quite familiar in Strasbourg. Both Wimpheling and Geiler had preached and struggled in favor of the secular clergy and the rationalization of church government. See Charles Schmidt, Histoire littéraire de l'Alsace (Paris, 1879), vol. I, pp. 31-67; 75-86. Zell, however, gave these already controversial issues a radical ecclesiological foundation.

115. Wolfgang Capito, provost of the Chapter of St. Thomas, and Sigmund von Hohenlohe, dean of the Cathedral Chapter.

116. See above, pp. 24-25. Zell consistently links the obnoxious monasteries and chapters with nobles and rich citizens, e.g. his derisive use of noble titles such as Junckherr.

Chapter 2

1. The circumstances of Bucer's arrival in Strasbourg are summarized in Bucer, DS I, pp. 31-32, 71-75, 151. See also Bucer's Verantwortung an den Rat, DS I, pp. 293-301, and the discussion in J. Adam, pp. 47 ff.

2. Bucer, DS I, pp. 291-292.

3. The Strasbourg Rat's own account of this is printed in DS I, pp. 346-347.

4. Edited in DS I, pp. 31-184.

5. A French translation of Das Ym Selbs, including notes and introduction, was made by Henri Strohl, "Traité de l'amour du prochain," Cahiers de la revue d'histoire et de philosophie réligieuses, No. 32, 1949. An English translation was published by P. T. Fuhrmann, Instruction in Christian Love (Richmond, 1952). My translations are my own. Das Ym Selbs is described by R. Boon, "De Eerste Drie Geschriften de Straatburgse Reformator Martin Bucer: Het Begin van de Ontwikkeling zijner Theologie," Nederlands Archief voor Kerkgeschiedenis, vol 39, 1952-1953, pp. 193-218.

6. Bucer, DS I, pp. 45-46, ll. 13-17, 26-36. Bucer had pursued the study of Thomistic theology as a Dominican, especially at Heidelberg. The Thomistic basis of his ethics is evident. See the introduction to Das Ym Selbs, DS I, pp. 34-35.

7. Bucer, DS I, p. 45, ll. 20-26.

8. Bucer, DS I, p. 45, ll. 19-20.

9. This is one example of Bucer's adjustment of Thomistic ethics to fit Reformation theology.

10. Bucer, DS I, p. 47, ll. 23-33.

11. Bucer, DS I, p. 46, ll. 9-17.

12. Bucer, DS I, p. 46, ll. 32- p. 47, ll. 2, 8-14.

13. Bucer, DS I, p. 48, ll. 1-16. Man's dual nature thus implies that two kinds of social service are possible: spiritual and corporeal. This justifies the existence of the first two estates, the religious office and the secular magisterial office; corporeal service includes, of course, the third estate as well. However, just as in man spirit and body are not independent, so in the social order the first two estates work together.

14. Bucer, DS I, p. 48, ll. 17-24. This service extends beyond one's family to all men: DS I, p. 50, ll. 38 - p. 51, l. 7.

15. Bucer, DS I, p. 48, ll. 24-35.

16. Bucer, DS I, p. 48, l. 36 - p. 49, l. 15.

17. Bucer, DS I, p. 50, ll. 17-38. The fact that even sinful men can still use some creatures properly means that the effects of sin are limited. The effects on human society, however, are graver than on the capacity of humans to use physical creation.

18. Bucer, DS I, p. 51, ll. 32-34.

19. Bucer, DS I, p. 58, ll. 21-38.

20. See below, p. 95 ff.

21. Bucer, DS I, p. 51, ll. 34-39.

22. Bucer, DS I, p. 51, l.39 - p. 52, l. 7. See also DS I, p. 52, l. 14 - p. 53, l. 16. The political importance of Bucer's argument is obvious. Evangelical preachers were accused of betrayal of their estate by siding with lay attacks on clerical revenues and immunities. Bucer offers an alternate definition: the faithful clergyman is he who sacrifices all he has for the good of the community. However, too facile an identification of Bucer's "community" with the political unit of Strasbourg should be avoided. Note also that even in this treatise, where Bucer is using language as conservative as possible, that he reserves the office of salvation to Christ alone. The clergy only preaches.

23. Bucer, DS I, p. 53, l. 24 - p. 54, l. 6.

24. Bucer, DS I, p. 54, ll. 13-15.

25. Bucer, DS I, p. 54, ll. 7-37.

26. Bucer, DS I, p. 55, ll. 1-7.

27. Bucer, DS I, p. 55, ll. 11-21.

28. Bucer, DS I, p. 55, l. 22 - p. 56, l. 7.

29. Here again Bucer draws on the conventional wisdom of the later Middle Ages. Secular government normally functioned as the defender of the faith, punishing if not defining heresy, assisting the church's administration of the means of grace and helping to enforce its discipline.

30. Bucer, DS I, p. 57, ll. 10-14.

31. Bucer, DS I, p. 56, ll. 25-31.

32. Bucer, DS I, p. 56, ll. 14-20. This contrasts with Luther's exhortation that a ruler use his reason vigorously, not placing excessive confidence in written law of any sort, even 'divine': WA 11, p. 272. For Luther, a Turk might govern without being a tyrant.

33. Bucer, DS I, p. 56, l. 31 - p. 57, l. 24.

34. Bucer, DS I, p. 57, ll. 25-30.

35. Bucer, DS I, p. 58, ll. 1-4. The editor of the DS notes the parallel passages in Luther's *Von Weltlicher Obrigkeit* in notes 79 and 80.

36. Bucer, DS I, p. 58, ll. 21-25. In 1523, Bucer was well aware that the magistracy was not uniformly acting as the "motor" of the Reformation. Hutten's defeat, the prohibition of Lutheran ideas at the Diet of Worms, his own flight from Wissembourg, and his chilly reception by the Strasbourg Rat could have left few doubts. Thus, again parallel with Luther's treatise of 1523, *Von Weltlicher Obrigkeit*, Bucer's concept of the religious responsibilities of the magistrate is a defense against magisterial hostility.

37. Bucer, DS I, p. 58, l. 26 - p. 59, l. 10. Bucer's hostility to merchants is wholly traditional. The merchant merely profited from an exploitative exchange, not producing any good thing. Bucer's Dominican background left him grudgingly open to certain forms of lending (DS I, p. 144, ll. 7-12). *Contra* Bernd Moeller, however, in 1523 Bucer's economic opinions were scarcely better adapted to an urban audience than Luther's. Moeller's opinion that Bucer's and Zwingli's "urban" theology accounted for their success in winning cities to the Reformation is open to grave doubt, if only because he abstracts from the actual struggle in the cities. He cites from treatises composed by Bucer well after the evangelical movement had won in Strasbourg. Further, it was Zell, and not Bucer, who first assembled the nucleus of popular support which led to that victory. In chapters 3 and 4 of this study, we provide an account of the decisive steps and combinations of ideas and issues which dominated the actual course of the movement in Strasbourg. For the issue of Bucer's supposedly "urban" theology of "community", see below, p. 92 ff. Bernd Moeller, *Reichsstadt und Reformation*, Schriften des Vereins für Reformationsgeschichte, 180, Jarhrgang 69, (Gütersloh, 1962).

38. Bucer, DS I, p. 59, ll. 11-26.

39. Bucer, DS I, p. 59, l. 28 - p. 60, l. 1.

40. Bucer, DS I, p. 60, ll. 1-6.

41. Bucer, DS I, p. 60, ll. 6-13. For Bucer, faith is not only a principle which, remaining hidden, sustains the elect until the future coming of Christ, as it is for Luther. It is a firm and public basis on which the whole of society can begin its restoration immediately.

42. Bucer, DS I, p. 61, ll. 11-14, 16-21. See also DS I, p. 60, l. 21 - p. 61, l. 6.

43. Bucer, DS I, p. 61, l. 32 - p. 63, l. 6. Faith thus satisfies the full range of human need, including the needs of the conscience. This satisfaction 'spills over': those who are aware that God gives them all things are grateful, and thus they serve others. Further, their natural desire to seek good things for themselves sated through faith, they are left free to regard the need of their neighbor.

44. Bucer, DS I, p. 63, l. 22 - p. 64, l. 14.

45. Bucer, DS I, p. 64, ll. 15-28.

46. "From all this...it may well be concluded that if we are to be restored to our original just and godly state, in which we were created to praise God, to be of use and service to all creatures, and in no way to seek our own profit [nutz] ..., it is faith that must accomplish all this: the true righteousness, in which the just lives toward God, men, and all creatures." Bucer, DS I, p. 64, l. 29 - p. 65, l. 3.

47. Bucer, DS I, p. 65, ll. 4-10; p. 66, l. 18 - p. 67, l. 1. Good works do not become for Bucer a secondary cause for justification. The believing man's nature is to perform good works, just as it is a fish's to swim, but he is restored to that nature exclusively through faith. See DS I, p. 65, ll. 26-39; p. 66, ll. 6-16.

48. Bucer, DS I, p. 64, l. 39 - p. 66, l. 6.

49. Bucer, DS I, p. 67, ll. 2-17.

50. A useful summary of Bucer's career in Wissembourg is available in DS I, pp. 71-75.

51. This is Bucer's own estimate of the proportion of the population that would have opposed his exile. Bucer, DS I, p. 134, ll. 15-17.

52. This grief is evident in the long defense of his departure appended to the Summary, Bucer, DS I, pp. 130-138.

53. See below.

54. Zell was not excommunicated until 1524, after his marriage, at the same time as the other recently married evangelical clergy in Strasbourg.

55. See Bucer's letter to Beatus Rhenanus after the Heidelberg Disputation of 1518: WA 9, p. 160 ff.

56. Bucer, DS I, pp. 379-384.

57. Bucer, DS I, pp. 285-290.

58. Although Bucer denied the charge brought by the Bishop of Strasbourg to the Rat, that he had been excommunicated in Speyer, citing a legal

technicality ("Verantwortung an den Rat," DS I, pp. 299-300, Verantwortung, DS I, pp. 176-177), he was certainly so regarded by the Catholic party, and no subsequent ban was pronounced.

59. See the June, 1523 "Verantwortung an den Rat", DS I, pp. 293-301, where Bucer seeks to obscure the legal case against him by technical appeals at the same time that he boldly asserts his right to marry, etc.

60. Bucer, DS I, p. 80, ll. 18-22.

61. Bucer, DS I, p. 81, ll. 22-23.

62. Bucer, DS I, p. 80, ll. 22-34; p. 81, l. 27 - p. 82, l. 9.

63. Bucer, DS I, p. 81, ll. 15-26.

64. Bucer, DS I, p. 82, l. 28 - p. 83, l. 6, 11-17. Compare Bucer's strong assertion of the powers of the believer with Zell's relatively timid suggestions.

65. Bucer, DS I, p. 85, ll. 14-22, 24-26. Although Zell argues that the possession of the Word is the only necessary qualification for God's special prophets, he emphasizes the utility of normal human qualifications, an emphasis which Bucer had come to share by the time of his conflicts with religious radicals. See Steven Ozment, Mysticism and Dissent (New Haven, 1973), p. 17 ff.

66. Bucer, DS I, p. 96, l. 26 - p. 97, l. 8. See also above, p. 94, n. 49.

67. Bucer, DS I, p. 130, ll. 16-28; p. 135, ll. 30-39; p. 136, ll. 14-31.

68. Bucer, DS I, p. 83, l. 25 - p. 84, l. 3. Bucer's chapter headings express this clearly; e.g. "Grace to understand Scripture is given to the simple and humble and taken away from the clever and proud." Bucer, DS I, p. 85. In parallel with Zell, Bucer launches a major polemic against those who deny that the Holy Spirit is the author of Scripture. See Bucer, DS I, pp. 86-89.

69. Bucer, DS I, p. 84, ll. 21-31. See also Bucer, DS I, p. 136, ll. 14-23.

70. Chrisman's suggestion (pp. 85-86) that Bucer offered a middle ground between Luther's "God-centered determinism" and medieval "free will" is confusing. She correctly observes that Bucer retains Luther's concepts of faith and of election (see DS I, p. 90, esp. l. 30), which, however, exclude any concept of human free will in matters concerning salvation. On the other hand, for Luther no less than Bucer faith was obtained (though never "obtainable") through Word and sacrament. The controversy over the Eucharist was produced precisely by Luther's suspicion that Zwingli and Bucer were threatening the status of preaching and sacrament as institutions in which the Word of grace was obtained. See Ernst Bizer, Studien zur Geschichte des Abendmahlstreits im sechszehnten Jahrhundert (Gütersloh, 1940).

71. "[They are] false Christians who represent themselves as Christ, who alone saves us, as if they saved us. Part of them through their power, as the Pope, and Bishop, among others, who have promised and sold heaven to us by their indulgences. The other part through their own good works, as monks, nuns, and all the tonsured...." Bucer, DS I, p. 102, l. 37 - p. 103, l. 4. See also DS I, p. 120, ll. 25-37, and passim.

72. Bucer, DS I, pp. 100-103, 108-109, 110-116, 122-124.

73. Bucer, DS I, p. 144, ll. 22-26.

74. Bucer, DS I, p. 144, ll. 26-29.

75. See, for example, the discussion in D. Luthers leer, DS I, p. 327, ll. 7-22, where the clergy is not only made subject to the Word, but is also made servant of the faithful and not lord. Bucer clearly regards the clergy's claim to high social status to rest on its claim of salvific power.

76. See above, p. 54 ff.

77. See below, p. 76 ff.

78. Bucer, DS I, p. 86, l. 27 - p. 87, l. 5. To show that the clergy is idle, he must discredit the "work" for which they are valued: the Mass and prayer.

79. Bucer, DS I, p. 87, l. 9 - p. 88, l. 3.

80. Bucer, DS I, p. 88, ll. 14-23.

81. Bucer, DS I, p. 88, l. 23 ff. Bucer's polemic against the greed and fiscal exploitation practiced by clerics is as bitter and sustained as Zell's.

82. Bucer, DS I, p. 89, ll. 11-18. See the continuation, DS I, pp. 89-91.

83. Bucer, DS I, p. 91, ll. 15-29; p. 92, ll. 1-10.

84. Bucer, DS I, p. 92, ll. 5-8. In 1523, Bucer had not yet made of discipline an essential mark of the true visible church. Here it is only one of a variety of services a spirit-filled believer can render.

85. Bucer, DS I, p. 92, l. 30 - p. 93, l. 18; p. 98, ll. 8-16.

86. Bucer, DS I, p. 93, ll. 19-35. See also DS I, p. 97, l. 19 - p. 100, l. 6.

87. Bucer, DS I, p. 93, l. 38 - p. 94, l. 10.

88. Bucer, DS I, pp. 94-97. The editor of the Summary calls attention to Bucer's use of the vocabulary of traditional mysticism. Bucer, DS I, p. 94, n. 94. Bucer's intention, however, is to describe how tribulation ("frembd werk gottes" is Luther's "law") destroys trust in self and in creatures, leaving the soul capable of trust in God alone. The influence of German mysticism on Bucer proceeds through Luther's transformation of mystical thought. See Ozment, Mysticism and Dissent, pp. 17-25.

89. Bucer, DS I, p. 97, l. 25 - p. 98, l. 5. Bucer combines an old-fashioned humanist critique of monastic hypocrisy with the more radical claim that God does not want monastic "work" at all.

90. Bucer, DS I, p. 99, ll. 4-14.

91. Bucer, DS I, p. 98, ll. 8-16.

92. Bucer, DS I, p. 98, ll. 21-23.

93. Bucer, DS I, p. 99, ll. 29-34.

94. Bucer, DS I, p. 100-102; 108-109; 110-116. After several passages con-

demning the doctrine of purgatory, however, Bucer makes a concession to Zell, who had defended prayer for the dead in the CV: "I have no counsel to give you about the dead, since Scripture teaches us nothing about them....I do not want faithful prayers to the Almighty for the dead prohibited, so long as one trusts that he hears such prayers, so that after it has happened once or thrice, one believes that God has heard us on their account, and thereafter they are to be left alone." Bucer, DS I, p. 124, l. 33 - 125, l. 7.

95. Bucer, DS I, pp. 103-113.

96. Bucer, DS I, p. 102, ll. 3-23; p. 115, l. 27 - p. 116, l. 33.

97. Again, only after the Mass has been shown to be valueless can the class of "Mass-priests" be considered useless and parasitical.

98. Bucer, DS I, pp. 116-123.

99. Bucer, DS I, p. 123, ll. 22-34.

100. The sources for Bucer's positive concept of the ministry include not only the three works printed in 1523, Das Ym Selbs, the Summary, and the Verantwortung, but also an unpublished treatise probably composed in October or November, 1523, "Das D. Luthers und seiner nachfolger leer...christlich und gerecht ist....", edited in Bucer, DS I, pp. 304-344.

101. Bucer, DS I, p. 170, ll. 26-31. (Verantwortung).

102. Bucer, DS I, p. 321, ll. 8-11, 15-22 (D. Luthers leer).

103. Bucer, DS I, pp. 326-327 (D. Luthers leer).

104. Bucer, DS I, p. 327, ll. 3-6 (D. Luthers leer).

105. Bucer, DS I, p. 327, ll. 1-3 (D. Luthers leer).

106. In D. Luthers leer, Bucer denies the clergy superior social status, but strongly affirms the importance of its function as proclaimer of God's Word. As with Zell, Bucer limits the clergy's power by tying it to the Word. "Since all true apostles are servants [knecht] of Jesus Christ, and set over his flock as servants [diener] and not as lords (I. Pe. 5:3), to which they should present not their own but only God's Word..., so all preachers and teachers should be careful to preach nothing but the single certain Word of God expressed in divine Scripture." Bucer, DS I, p. 316, ll. 26-33 (D. Luthers leer).

107. See below, p. 86 and Bucer, DS I, p. 127, l. 33 - p. 128, l. 4; p. 143, l. 33 - p. 144, ll. 6, 26-29. (Summary)

108. Bucer, DS I, p. 162, l. 32 - p. 163, l. 3 (Verantwortung).

109. Bucer, DS I, pp. 164-165 (Verantwortung).

110. Bucer, DS I, p. 340, ll. 15-17, 19 (D. Luthers leer).

111. Bucer, DS I, p. 164, ll. 27-30 (Verantwortung).

112. Bucer, DS I, p. 165, l. 24 - p. 166, l. 38 (Verantwortung). The vow inverts the proper responses of believing people. Faced with need, the believer spontaneously wishes to give; monks are sworn to do nothing but take.

113. Bucer, DS I, pp. 166-169, esp. p. 168, ll. 12-16 (Verantwortung).

114. Bucer, DS I, p. 328, ll. 1-6 (D. Luthers leer).

115. Bucer, DS I, p. 333, ll. 3-5 (D. Luthers leer).

116. Bucer, DS I, p. 167, ll. 28-36 (Verantwortung).

117. One example, among very many, from the Summary: Bucer, DS I, p. 97, l. 22 - p. 98, l. 5.

118. Bucer, DS I, p. 121, ll. 27-35; p. 143, ll. 12-16; l. 34 - p. 144, l. 6 (Summary).

119. Bucer, DS I, p. 59, ll. 1-10 (Das Ym Selbs).

120. See above, pp. 58-59.

121. Bucer, DS I, p. 128, l. 14 - p. 129, l. 6 (Summary). This theme was taken up and amplified by Otton Brunfels, Bucer's old friend and correspondent, in an October 1523 treatise, Von dem Evangelischen Anstosz (Strasbourg, 1523).

122. Bucer, DS I, p. 176, ll. 5-10, 15-19 (Verantwortung).

123. Bucer, DS I, p. 316, l. 33 - p. 317, l. 1 (D. Luthers leer).

124. See Heiko Oberman, Forerunners of the Reformation (New York, 1966), p. 121 ff.

125. Contra Moeller, Reichsstadt und Reformation, p. 38, who argues that because Bucer and Zwingli emphasize the ethical results of faith strongly, they lose Luther's keen awareness that active love is always a "gift".

126. See Bucer's attack on 'externals' in D. Luthers leer, DS I, pp. 320-326. Compare with Luther, WA 7, pp. 20-38.

127. Bucer, DS I, p. 321, l. 33 - p. 322, l. 4 (D. Luthers leer).

128. Cf. Moeller, Reichsstadt und Reformation, who argues that the communal, corporate categories of Bucer and Zwingli appealed to city dwellers threatened by expanding 'lordship' better than Luther's; the latter distinguished too sharply between political community and the church, which was only an invisible minority of true believers.

129. See Gustav Wingren, Luther on Vocation (Philadelphia, 1957).

130. This is not to say that Bucer lacked the conceptual resources to admit that legal and vocational coercion might have social utility. His comment that Adam's family before the fall lived "in accord with the entire divine law without law" (DS I, p. 48, l. 34. Das Ym Selbs) might be construed to suggest that if pressed, he might have admitted that a minimum level of cooperation can be compelled by law. He certainly thinks that the magistrate can restrain evildoers. Yet in 1523, such resources for the stability of the social order are very far from Bucer's mind. The theme of Das Ym Selbs is that egotism has ruined the ministry and the magistracy, and that faith alone produces the love that brings true human society into existence. In contrast to Luther, who seeks non-religious sources of social stability, Bucer emphasizes society's utter dependence on faith.

131. Bucer's concept of justification dissolved the soteriological pretensions of all such corporations, eliminates the cult around which they turned (e.g., the Mass, the monastic cycle of prayer, prayer for the dead, the cult of the saints, etc.), and redirects religious activity into "authentically" religious channels, i.e. the service of one's neighbor. For one example among many, see his attack on religious confraternities (Bucer, DS I, p. 84, l. 29, Summary).

132. See below, p. 141.

133. See below, p. 210 ff.

134. See below, p. 168 ff.

135. Annales de Brant, Fragments recueillis par l'Abbé Dacheux, Fragment de anciennes chroniques d'Alsace (Strasbourg, 1892-1901), vol. III (hereafter cited Annales I,) p. 245, no. 3476.

136. In spring or early summer of 1523, Wolfgang Capito, an associate of Erasmus, took up the position as Provost of the collegiate chapter of St. Thomas in Strasbourg. Attempting to pacify the religious conflict in the city, he asked Zell to leave Strasbourg. See below, p. 128.

137. See Bucer, DS I, p. 128, l. 24 - p. 129, l. 6.

138. Moeller argues that while Luther was content to regard tiny evangelical minorities in cities as fully sufficient churches, for Bucer and Zwingli only the creation of a visibly evangelical religio-political community was adequate (Reichsstadt und Reformation, p. 35). Although it seems obvious that Bucer had much greater hope than Luther in the renewal of human society through the Word, even before 1525, we insist that Bucer's ideal community did not essentially depend on the capture of an entire political community, including its magistrate.

139. See above, p. 72.

140. Ibid.

141. See Bucer, DS I, pp. 366-372. This organizational activity rendered him subject to charges of subversion. His first attempt to preach was stopped by the Rat in June, 1523 (see below, pp. 149 ff.); even in November, his application for the Bürgerrecht was rejected. See the Summary, Bucer, DS I, p. 128, ll. 6 ff.

Chapter 3

1. For example, Zell and Bucer give teeth to the old charge that the clergy is idle, by arguing that what had been considered useful service to God and man, such as the chant, prayer, etc.--goods for which there had been a brisk demand throughout the fifteenth century--was in fact useless. Yet their argument is based on a new understanding of what is useful to salvation and to the spiritual welfare of the community. Only if justification occurs solely through faith does preaching become the primary useful commodity the clerical estate offers. Consider, for example, the petition from an aged monk to the Rat in 1525, requesting a pension, discussed below on p. 220 ff. To him it was the universally accepted belief that the monastic life was service to God which had led him into the cloister; the Word exploded that belief, and so he has left the

cloister. The changed norm of what constitutes service to God and man is what permits the social "insight" that the contemplative clergy is idle and useless.

2. The best treatment of the constitution of Strasbourg in this period is Otto Winckelmann, "Strassburgs Verfassung und Verwaltung in 16ten Jahrhundert," Zeitschrift für die Geschichte des Oberrheins, N. F. 18, 1903. See also Chrisman, pp. 14-31.

3. Chrisman, pp. 93-96.

4. For the struggle between Rat and Bishop, see Chrisman, pp. 16, 35-41; Karl Stenzel, Die Politik der Stadt Strassburg am Ausgange des Mittelalters, Beiträge zur Landes und Volkeskunde von Elsass-Lothringen und den Angrenzenden Gebieten XLIX (Strassburg, 1915), pp. 84-168; and especially the forthcoming thesis of Francis Rapp, Institutions écclésiastiques et gens d'église: Abus et réformes dans le diocèse de Strasbourg 1450-1525, thesis presented for the Doctorat d'Etat in history, Université des Sciences Humaines de Strasbourg, (Strasbourg, 1972), which I consulted in manuscript.

5. For an introduction to the development of clerical immunity, see Konrad Hofmann, Die Engere Immunität in Deutschen Bischofsstädten im Mittelalter, Inaugural-Dissertation for the University of Tübingen (Paderborn, 1914).

6. Gerald Strauss, ed., Manifestations of Discontent in Germany on the Eve of the Reformation (Bloomington, Ind., 1971).

7. Rapp, Institutions, livre 5, p. 34 ff. See also Hofmann, Immunität, p. 32 ff. and Bernd Moeller, "Kleriker als Bürger" in Festschrift für Hermann Heimpel zum 70. Geburtstag II (Göttingen, 1972).

8. Moeller, "Kleriker als Bürger", regards the struggle over immunity as the struggle of "citizenly" life to assert its control over an alien "clerical" life, and emphasizes the continuity between the fifteenth century struggle and the assault on clerical immunity during the evangelical movement. We would supplement him by insisting on the self-protective rather than aggressive character of the lay government's campaign, and on the discontinuity between the fifteenth century Rat's unwillingness to attack the clergy's religious office and the fundamentally unmedieval character the evangelicals' demand for clerical citizenship took on.

9. See below, p. 116 ff.

10. AST 176 Varia Ecclesiastica XI, 29 v ff. Dr. Sebastien Brant Im Rechten gegründetes Bedencken ob und auff waß weyß wider die Geistl. der güeter halb ordnungen gemacht werden können oder sollen.

11. "I have looked into the business of the Beswärung of the clergy, so far as time and other business of your Wisdoms permitted. Indeed, it may be regarded as the weightiest matter ever to come into my hands, on which counsel is to be taken carefully and [the matter] handled with consideration. For when I seek means [Vermög] and the content of both canon and imperial law, every side I find that no [?] or secular power or authority should nor may establish, enact, order, or either command or forbid anything to the dispossession or decrease of the possessions and goods, or to the hindrance of any present or future good of churches,

houses of God, or clergy in the community, or to [dissolve] any of their traditional or acquired liberties..." AST 176, 29v.

12. "As imperial law states: 'Null and void are all laws and customs introduced, established, or employed against ecclesiastical freedoms or religious persons by city or secular power, the lords of a Rat, or any other persons, other than those allowed by canon and imperial law. Such arrangements and laws, improperly done, shall be regarded powerless before the law, and those who make or establish such arrangements themselves shall suffer the heavy penalties they usurped, to wit, expulsion from their power and government, together with the infliction of the imperial ban on the city of [?] [?] and the fine of a thousand silver marks for all those who establish, counsel, help, dictate, and write; and all those who give judgment according to [those laws] are impeached, and whatever they do or judge is powerless.'" AST 176, 29v.

13. "In addition, canon law inflicts the papal ban on all who through secular power forbid their subjects to sell something to the clergy, or to buy from them, or to mill or bake for them, or who forbid anything else of service." AST 176, 29v.

14. "Many famous doctors [teach] that a statute or order could well be made by lay people against clerical bequests, since it would concern their own goods and land, which a community certainly controls itself." AST 176, 29v.

15. AST 176, 29v.

16. See below, p. 194.

17. See Chrisman, pp. 55-58; also Charles Schmidt, Histoire littéraire de l'Alsace, (Paris, 1879).

18. Martin Herlin and Mathis Pfarrer, two of the city's most eminent supporters of the Evangelical Movement on the Rat, in 1517 were the heads of the brotherhood which directed the annual passion play. Nikolaus Kniebis, perhaps the most renowned Evangelical Ratsherr, joined the Brotherhood of St. Stephen, founded by Brant to promote piety in government. Jacob Sturm, Kniebis' counterpart, famous in Protestant diplomacy originally planned to be a priest, and grew up under Wimpheling's tutelage. Throughout the fifteenth century, the Rat's conspicuous piety, displayed in founding masses, in elaborating the city's pious rituals, etc., was great. For a useful account both of the Rat's anticlericalism and of its piety, see Rapp, Institutions écclésiastiques, Livre 5.

19. Note that one of Zell's major complaints concerning the use of the church's ban is that the secular magistrate must enforce it. CV H3v, J4v ff.

20. Annales II, 4407, 17 January 1522: "Several vicars and clergymen committed outrages at night with women, for which the city arrested, imprisoned, and punished them. The Chapter complained of this, and argued that it was improper for this magistracy to imprison and punish clerics. The Rat replied that it was in accord with the Rachtung of Speier, since the Rat understood it to provide that in citizenly or ceremonial matters it could command nothing, but when outrage or crime was committed, my gracious lords stood here as the magistracy to punish

it, since the Rat here has a merum et mixtum Imperium." The distinctions made here between "ceremony" [für, feier], citizenly matters, and outrage [frevel] distinguish three areas of conduct in which any resident might engage. The Rat here claims no jurisdiction over religious conduct for anyone, over daily secular conduct only for laymen, but over criminal actions for all.

21. Annales II, 4399. This celebrated affair is most accurately narrated by Rapp, Institutions écclésiastiques, livre 5, p. 201 ff.

22. Hofmann, Immunität, pp. 89-115; Rapp, Institutions écclésiastiques, livre 5, p. 34 ff.

23. See Moeller, "Kleriker als Bürger", p. 205 ff.

24. To surrender the freedoms of one's estate was generally considered treason against one's estate. In Strasbourg, the question of actually violating the oath of ordination was clarified by the Weihbischoff's practice to require an oath to preserve clerical immunities of all holders of benefices. Capito goes to some length to prove the invalidity of this particular oath in Das die Pfafheit schuldig sey Burgerlichen Eyd zuthun...(Straßburg, 1524), p. a4r ff.

25. Moeller, "Kleriker als Bürger", p. 214.

26. Contra Moeller, "Kleriker als Bürger", who overemphasizes the fundamental cultural opposition between burghers and the clergy: "Beide Sozialkörper, der Klerus und die Stadtgemeinde des Spätmittelalters, standen einander mit ihrer Tendenz zur Ausschießlichkeit im Weg." (Moeller's emphasis). (page 203). Thus the push to bind the clergy to the city is viewed as an expression of bourgeois cultural imperialism, held back by an ideological failure to dissolve the clergy as a distinct class, a failure made good by Reformation ideology (pp. 209-210). In our view, the attack on immunity did reflect a limited alienation of citizens from the clerical estate's values, but a far more central motive was citizens' desire to protect themselves. The Rat's language does not suggest a desire to make laymen out of clergymen, but to adjust governmental jurisdictions so that it could govern the "bürgerlich" life of all residents in a coherent manner, leaving "geistlich" life to the religious government. We do not think that late medieval Rats lacked the ideological resources to carry through such a reform; it was their lack of political resources, and their unwillingness to run the risk of exclusion from the Empire and Christendom, that held them back. Reformation ideology radicalized a coherent late medieval reform, turning it into something other than it had been.

27. Moeller, "Kleriker als Bürger", pp. 207-209. There is no reason to think that these purchases of the Bürgerrecht were ideologically motivated; personal circumstances of each individual dominated.

28. Rapp, Institutions écclésiastiques, livre 5, p. 38.

29. Annales I, 3465, 3466, p. 224; A. Baum, Magistrat und Reformation, p. 53, n. 1.

30. Rapp, Institutions écclésiastiques, livre 5, pp. 39-50.

31. Rapp, Institutions écclésiastiques, livre 5, pp. 50-53.

32. AST 176, Varia Ecclesiastica XI, 29 v. ff.

33. Karl Stentzel, Die Politik der Stadt Strassburg am Ausgang der Mittelalter (Strassburg, 1914).

34. Rapp, Institutions écclésiastiques, livre 5, p. 52 ff.

35. The clearest narration of the events is still A. Baum, pp. 51-73.

36. See Otto Winckelmann, Das Fürsorgewesen der Stadt Strassburg vor und nach der Reformation bis zum Ausgang der sechszehnten Jahrhunderts, (Leipzig, 1922); A. Baum, pp. 56-62; Chrisman, pp. 275-283.

37. Contra Winckelmann, p. 69, and A. Baum, pp. 60-61. In this respect we agree with Chrisman, p. 277-278, that the reform of the welfare system was not directly linked to the Reformation. To go further as she does, however, and to assert that it was merely a coincidence that at the time of welfare reforms, the monastic foundations were collapsing and thus vulnerable to seizure of revenues is, we think, excessive. It ignores the relation between the bourgeois drive for coherent self-government and the success of the evangelical movement.

38. Winckelmann, Fürsorgewesen, p. 98.

39. See above, p. 10.

40. Otto Brunfels, a Carthusian monk who took part in the movement in Strasbourg, displays a good deal of concern to maintain the spontaneity and visibility of public charity by individuals: Von dem Pfaffen Zehenden/ Hundert unnd zwen und fyertzig Schlussreden (1524); b4v.

41. See below, p. 145 ff.

42. See Röhrich's description of pamphlets written by Eckhardt zum Treubel in 1523 and 1524, Mitteilungen III p. 20-28. Eckhart praises the new system as an evangelical redirection of money from bells and wax to the poor.

43. Brunfels and Hedio both describe the secular magistrate's proper use of the tithe as the protection and support of the poor (Brunfels, Von dem Pfaffen Zehenden, a3v-a4v, clr ff.; Caspar Hedio, Von dem zehenden zwo trefflicher predig/ Bescheen im Münster zu Strassburg/ uff den tag Novembris (1524) blv, b2r, clearly in support of the new system. Brunfels extends the system's attack on the rich beggars who divert gifts from the poor to the clergy. Why should these rich beggars, oppressors of the poor, who have horses, who swill and devour, and who are foreigners, be supported by our gifts (i.e. tithes)? Brunfels, Von dem Zehenden, dlr-dlv.

44. A. Baum, pp. 51, 54.

45. AST 87/5. Artcel der Priester so das Burgrecht kauffen oder empfahen. Another text is found at AST 170 f. 39, perhaps earlier since it requires the normal fee of 1 pfund 7 schilling, while this text requires 3 pfund 7 schilling. See Moeller, "Kleriker als Bürger", p. 212, note 105; A. Baum, p. 55, n. 2. Chrisman, p. 112, misinterprets the document. Clerics must join guilds, and they do not receive full political rights. See Moeller, pp. 213-214.

46. Contra Moeller, "Kleriker als Bürger", p. 212: "Die geschichtliche Bedeutung dieser Bestimmungen liegt, wie mir scheint, nicht in den Modifikationen, die außer der Zunftpflicht der Tradition folgten, sondern in dem Erlaß als solchem: Es wurde eine einheitliche Rechtsgrundlage für das Bürgerrecht der Geistlichen geschaffen, die Aufnahme von Geistlichen wurde zu einem mit einigen Ausnahmeregelungen versehenen Normalvorgang des städtischen Rechtslebens." Moeller is correct to insist on the importance of rendering the Bürgerrecht the normal legal status of clergymen. But the fact that the modifications in the articles for the clergy follow tradition demonstrates the Rat's traditional motives, the fact that its program was independent of the evangelical preachers'.

47. A. Baum, p. 55, p. 64-65. Virck, Pol. Corr. I, p. 93, n. 2, details rumors of clerical conspiracies against Strasbourg. The Rat itself lists the Emperor, the Kammergericht, and both Landvogten of Alsace as authorities to whom the chapters have appealed. AST 47-I/8.

48. See above, p. 42 ff.

49. Zell, Christeliche Verantwortung, s3v ff.

50. Zell does not overtly deny that he has attacked clerical immunities, and the Fiscal's articles directly alleged that he did.

51. See above, pp. 86-87.

52. Bucer DS I, p. 297, ll. 25-35. See also DS I, p. 298, ll. 4-10.

53. The Rat approved the articles for priests taking the Bürgerrecht on June 13 (Moeller, "Kleriker als Bürger", p. 212). Bucer presented his defense to the Rat on June 20, responding to the Bishop's complaint to the Rat of June 16 (Bucer, DS I, p. 293).

54. Chrisman sketches Capito's career, pp. 88-91.

55. Wolffgang Capito, An den Hochwürdigen fürsten und herren Wilhelmen Bischoffen zu Straßburg/ unnd Lantgraven zu Elsas. Entschuldigung. (Straßburg, 1523), AAr.

56. Chrisman gives a confusing account of how Capito happened to interview Zell (p. 108-109). The Entschuldigung makes no mention of Capito acting in any official capacity, and it is difficult to imagine how the Provost of St. Thomas could have had official responsibility to oversee the episcopal Penitentiarius or the pastor of St. Laurentz, benefices controlled respectively by the Bishop and the Lower Chapter of the Cathedral. We know of no evidence that Capito's "examination" bore any relation whatever to alleged disturbances resulting from Karsthans' stay in Strasbourg, which had ended nine months earlier. Zell was accused of associating with Karsthans in the Fiscal's twenty-four articles (Zell, CV K4 ff), a matter already before ecclesiastical courts, and of which Capito makes no mention. Capito himself describes his admonition to Zell as part of a private, self-appointed project to reconcile the warring parties in Strasbourg (Entschuldigung, BB3v). That he acted in some manner as a partisan of the Bishop emerges from his first statement after the narration of Zell's tirade concludes: he concluded that he could no longer support the Bishop in this matter,

since he could not oppose God (Entschuldigung, CC3r). It would seem possible that Capito had hoped that the removal of an irritant, Zell, would permit him to woo the Bishop to his own concept of evangelical reform.

57. A. Baum, p. 204.

58. Capito asserts in November that the chief causes were his conviction that the clergy should not employ their immunities against the common good, the fear of an anticlerical civil war which citizenship might allay, and that he thought it possible to obey both Rat and Bishop. He then says that he might have waited, had not (unspecified) occurrences in the Chapter moved him to act immediately. Entschuldigung BB1r.

59. Capito, Entschuldigung AA4v.

60. Capito, Entschuldigung AA4v-BB1r.

61. Capito, Entschuldigung, FF3v-FF4r.

62. Capito, Entschuldigung FF4r-GG1r. This long historical survey of the way in which humanly created religious law and even the misapplication of Scripture may be justified on grounds of brotherly love, that is, for the sake of peace and unity, highlights the survival of Capito's earlier conviction that the Holy Spirit's office in the church is above all to make peace, in contrast to Zell's firm association of the Spirit with the divine Word which destroys all contrary human institutions. Capito writes that he had explicitly criticized Zell on these grounds at their interview. Zell was responsible for the "scandal and defection from the Gospel that would certainly stem from such a clumsy riot, and yet his office was to inculcate the peace-making spirit with the words of Christ. Such indignation, envy, and hatred as was then before our eyes was no fruit of the spirit, but an evil, repulsive to all respectability.... I would not excuse him on the grounds that he spoke the Word of God for [the Word] had to serve the same end as the Spirit of God--a spirit of wisdom and understanding, a spirit of counsel and of might, a spirit of the knowledge and the fear of the Lord, who also always brings us to good order, who drives [us] to peace, friendship, and love." But what Zell has done has not only overturned good order, but caused hate, envy, and desires to attack the peace-loving and innocent. "It is the characteristic of a Christian to live with the community, not to seek separate ways." Entschuldigung BB3v-BB 4r. The true minister is he who serves the Spirit, service marked by the peace he brings to the community. Capito then claimed that he had been driven from this position by Zell's fierce assertion of the absolute divine power of the Word, yet there are obvious survivals of it in his ecclesiology. No doubt his experience in ecclesiastical diplomacy rendered him sensitive to the fragility of the concrete institutional structure of the Church.

63. Capito, Entschuldigung GG1v-2r.

64. Bucer and Zell required obedience of church laws which did not immediately jeopardize the soul, but in the form of passive submission to tyranny, not obedience of legitimate law. Their rejection of the ecclesiastical hierarchy, as we have elsewhere observed, created a power vacuum which only secular government had the mandate to fill

(note Capito's own affirmation of the magistrate's Scriptural license). The concept of the religious role of secular government which they developed (under Capito's influence?) rapidly took on the characteristics of a religious government by human legal administration, leading to charges that they were creating a "new papacy."

65. By the time Capito wrote his pamphlet, Das die Pfafheit schuldig sey Burgerlichen Eyd zuthun/ On verletzung irer Eeren (Strasbourg, December, 1524), his attempt to preserve religious government through the hierarchy had vanished, although the hierarchy's laws, if not contrary to God's, must still be obeyed by true Christians who are willing to suffer tyranny. This latter treatise also demonstrates the use to which the preachers were able to put the old modifications in the Bürgerrecht for clerics. While Capito makes no fuss about actually swearing the oath of citizenship, he uses the permission granted for clergy to pay others to accomplish its citizens' tasks to show that there is no legitimate reason for the clergy's immunity, since nothing need divert a pastor from his duties (a2v). It is well to remember that Bucer did not consider that he was dissolving the clerical estate as the first estate of Christendom, providing service which excelled all others', but rather only purifying the estate (Das Ym Selbs, DS I, pp. 51-53).

66. Bucer's request in mid-November, 1523, (DS I, pp. 302-303) was rejected by the Rat, and not accepted until September 22, 1524. Zell obtained the Bürgerrecht November 26, 1523. See A. Baum, p. 56.

67. It was so regarded by the Bishop and the chapters, who included it prominently in their list of grievances forwarded to the Reichsregiment in the summer of 1524, and by the Reichsregiment itself in its letters to the Rat (Pol. Corr. I, pp. 94-96). It is no accident that the Rat included Capito's Das die Pfafheit schuldig sey Burgerlichen Eyd zuthun with its official reply to the Reichsregiment in January, 1525, along with Bucer's defense of liturgical changes. See below, p. 180.

68. See below, p. 166 ff.

69. A. Baum, p. 65.

70. See Pol. Corr. I, p. 93, n. 2.

71. A. Baum, pp. 65-66, 81-82. Chrisman (p. 142) fails to distinguish between this flight and the mass exodus in December, 1524; also failing to date the Treger riots correctly and to distinguish them from the demonstrations of the parishioners of Young St. Peter, her narration of the canons' self-exile is confused.

72. See below, p. 172 ff.

73. Because A. Baum was not aware of the existence of this document, the Rat's order is missing from his narration of events (p. 66).

74. AST 87/14. The last clause would seem to be an attempt to prevent the continued removal of treasures from the city. Chrisman reads this incorrectly as an order to the preachers to take the Bürgerrecht, since henceforth they will be under the city's jurisdiction (p. 115).

75. A. Baum, p. 66.

76. A. Baum, p. 66. The chapters offered to pay 40 gulden per chapter (against the Rat's demand of 40 pfund pfennig, about double in value)

and a scale of from one to four gulden per member (against the Rat's demand of a scale with a top tax of 36 Pfund).

77. See below, pp. 178-179.

78. Cited A. Baum, pp. 67-68.

79. A. Baum, p. 68.

80. A. Baum, pp. 68-69.

81. A. Baum, pp. 70-73.

82. Daniel Specklin, who towards the end of the sixteenth century wrote a chronicle of the history of Strasbourg from a highly polemical Protestant vantage point, recounts several occasions during the Middle Ages on which the clergy left the city, either as a whole, due to an interdict, or as individual cloisters, as a rebuke. See Daniel Specklin, Les Collectanées, Fragments recueillis par Rudolphe Reuss. Fragments des anciennes chroniques d'Alsace, Bulletin de la Societé pour la conservation des monuments historiques d'Alsace, 14, 1889, pp. 105-119 (970-1002); p. 132-135 (#1048-1065); p. 367 (#1804).

83. The canons' flight from the city, of course, did not end all relations with the Rat. Using their exile as a visible token of their oppression by the Rat, they were successful in awaking extremely influential allies: several cities, the Reichsregiment at Esslingen, and later Archduke Ferdinand and the Landvogt of Lower Alsace, after their need to conciliate Strasbourg during the Peasants' War had ended. On the other hand, the Rat regarded the treasures removed by the canons' as the property not of the canons but of the chapter foundations, organically part of the city. That a large part of the chapters' incomes should flow out of the city to the canons scattered in other towns was intolerable. After protracted negotiations, the canons agreed to return to the city if allowed to govern their own internal affairs, but in all other respects conforming to the Rat's requirements. The agreement was signed January 21, 1529, not long before the Mass was prohibited in the chapters. It is obvious that economic and external political considerations, not religious or internal political ones, pushed the Rat to seek the canons' return. See A. Baum, pp. 130-146.

84. One of the perennial problems of historians of the Strasbourg Reformation is to account for this ambiguity. Chrisman vigorously argues that the majority of Ratsherren did not side with the Reform until 1528, since it was not until then that the ambiguities disappeared. She disparages the judgments of A. Baum (Magistrat und Reformation, p. 97), Wendel (L'Eglise de Strasbourg, p. 26), and H. Strohl (Le Protestantisme en Alsace, p. 18) that the city and the Rat supported the evangelical movement by 1524 (Chrisman, p. 161, note 10). We think her correct in arguing that the Reformation was not imposed upon the city by a cabal of Ratsherren and preachers (p. 96), and that on later issues, such as the abolition of the Mass in the chapters, the Rat even acted as a brake (pp. 175-176). Yet her analysis fails to account for the Rat's protection of the preachers, for its eventual support of every step the preachers took between 1523 and 1525, and for the clear elements of evangelical ideology that found their way into both words and content of the Rat's decisions, climaxing in the Rat's public defense of the ecclesiastical "innovations" of the preachers before the

Reichsregiment in early 1525.

85. Cited by A. Baum, p. 17, n. 1. In contrast to the vigorous suppression of the new ideas by the Rat of Ober Ehenheim a year later (Bucer, DS I, p. 348 ff), the Strasbourg Rat gave the "Gospel" a relatively friendly home.

86. Zwingli, Werke, Corpus Reformatorum, vol. 8, pp. 81-82. It should be noted that Bucer had only recently arrived from Wissembourg, where the local Rat's irresolute attitude ended in his exile. Bucer wrote to Zwingli not long after the Zürich Rat had set up a public disputation so that Zwingli could not fail to defeat his opposition. (Moeller, "Zwinglis Disputationen: Studien zu den Anfängen der Kirchenbildung und des Synodalwesens in Protestantismus," Zeitschrift der Savigny-Stiftung für Rechtsgeschichte 56 (1970), pp. 275-324). Bucer could hardly have helped comparing the Zürich Rat's embrace of Zwingli's Gospel with his own frosty reception.

87. Chroniques de Wencker, Fragments recueillis par l'Abbe L. Dacheux, Fragments des anciennes chroniques d'Alsace, Bulletin de la Société pour la conservation des monuments historiques d'Alsace, IIe serie, 15, 1892, p. 149, #3013.

88. AST 87/1. See J. Adam, pp. 38-30.

89. I am indebted to M. Jean Rott for this information.

90. Annales II, p. 257, #4408. See Chrisman, p. 100.

91. Annales II, p. 258, No. 4409. After the publication of two books bearing the name Karsthans (Karsthans, published in Flugschriften aus den ersten Jahren der Reformation, vol. 4, ed. O. Clemen; Gesprechbiechlin neüw Karsthans, DS I, p. 406 ff.), the name was adopted as a general literary figure in Protestant pamphlets, the pious peasant who is persuaded by the Gospel. In this 1522 collision, however, "Karsthans" is consistently used as a proper name for this peasant preacher. After he himself apparently gave it as his name, it appeared as such in the Rat's minutes, in the formal charges against Zell, and in Zell's response, in each case as the man's proper name.

92. Annales II, p. 260, no. 4411.

93. Annales, II, p. 259-260, no. 4410.

94. Annales II, p. 261, no. 4413.

95. The Rat's past intrusions into the preaching office had consistently depended both on the religious convictions of the Ratsherren and on their duty to preserve the internal peace of the city. For example, in 1510 the Rat put a stop to Dominican sermons against the Immaculate Conception, while warning the Franciscans not to taunt the other order about its brothers, executed at Bern in reference to this matter a few years before; "Item, Herr Böcklin and others should go to the Dominican Fathers and [say] that they should leave the Mother of God alone from the pulpit. The lords reported that they had spoken with the Dominicans about the Conception of the Virgin Mary: that they not do it any more, for the common man was displeased about it and might...inflict something unseemly upon them one day. To which the Dominicans answered that they did not wish to preach further, that they would desist from it, but the Franciscans were taunting them and saying they had a vein of

one of the heretics burned at Bern. Unfortunately, it is true. Thus it is announced that the aforementioned lords should request the Franciscans not to taunt the Dominicans in regard to their honor; but what they preach to the praise and honor of the Mother of God, that is welcome." 1510, Annales I, p. 229, no. 3385. The Ratsherren moved on the basis of both danger to the city's order and the general population's religious feelings, which they warmly shared.

96. A. Baum, pp. 16-17. Baum prints the texts of the two placards, p. 191.

97. "[The Rat wills] daß ire bürger, auch geistliche und weltliche inwoner by und mit einander fridlich bliben und leben mögen. Diwil dann meister Mathis der Lütpriester, noch bitzhar nichts anderst, dann wie man verhofft, das Gottswort und die h. Geschrift gepredigt, und darby sich vielmol erbotten, wie jemants vermeint dass er anders sag, woll er sich eins solchen uß der h. Geschrifft, und mit dem Gotteswort underwisen." Annales II, p. 263, no. 4417.

98. The deputies should tell Zell that he "das wort Gottes on forcht sinen kirchenspielkindern und andern, so sin predigt hören, sagen mag, dann ein Rhat des willens in bey dem wort Gottes und der warheit zu schützen und zu schirmen und do by zu handhaben. Dargegen auch by im verfiegen daß er sich anderer unnützen theding und stempeneien nicht underziehen soll." Annales II, p. 263, no. 4417. The Rat's request that non-parishioners be continued to be admitted to his sermons echoes Zell's own argument that Christians are under no absolute obligation to hear sermons only in their own parish (Zell, CV D2v; See above, chapter 1, p. 35. A year later, Zell himself placed great weight on what the Rat's delegation had told him: "The government of this praiseworthy city Strasbourg, through four well-regarded men from this same government, told him [Anton Firn], me, and all preachers of this city that we should from then on preach the Gospel and the holy biblical writings purely, clearly, and without admixture of human fables, examples, and the like. In that regard they would take care of us, as was right." Zell, Ein Collation auff die einfuerung M. Anthonii Pfarherrs zu S. Thomans... (Strasbourg, 1523), D2v. Zell no doubt embroiders on the message, making it rather more explicitly evangelical than the Rat had intended.

99. Annales II, p. 263, no. 4417.

100. Annales II, p. 263, no. 4418.

101. A. Baum, p. 17, n. 1, 2.

102. See above, pp. 140-141.

103. See above, p. 144.

104. Indeed, by asserting in its January 4 decision that Zell had often offered to demonstrate the Scriptural foundation of his sermons, the Rat suggests that it was not unopposed to giving him an opportunity to defend his views before the religious government. See above, p. 146.

105. A. Baum, pp. 17-19. The Bishop's letter to the Rat sketching his case against Zell (March 10, 1523; AST 47 - II/6), is in part misread by Chrisman (p. 106). There is absolutely no mention made of any failure by Zell to say Mass. The Bishop hardly implies that priests need not preach; he merely objects to the content of Zell's attacks on

the "entire order of the Christian church," and insists that Zell's duties as *penitentiarius* be properly carried out. Chrisman also ignores the indication that Zell was currently engaged in presenting a defense to the Vicar (see Appendix). We read that paragraph as a reproach to the Rat. The Bishop is asserting that, although the threat of unrest cited by the Rat may be real, the way in which Zell's supporters have been acting during Zell's defense is contrary to (the Rat's responsibilities under) the *Rachtung* of Speyer (*Speyrischen vertrage*): "Das man gewyßlich in der Stat Straßburg einer beschwerlichen uffrure unnd empüre/ gegen unnser priesterschafft warttend sein musst/ Wiewol wir uns dann solchs gegen euch und einer gehorsamen gemeynde gar nit versehen/ So bewegen wir doch/ das gemelter Meyster Mathis ime selbs/ ein solchen grossen anhang macht; der ime trutzlicher weyß one widerrede/ *In der Rechtferttigung/ darzun er yizt gegen unserm Fiscal steet/* [emphasis mine] mit vilerley bösen freveln hochmutigen unerbern wortten und geperden bystand thut/ Welcher anhang nit allein der antwurt so unnsern Räten uff jungst anbringen der Lutherischen Irrungen/ von euch begegnet/ Sunder auch dem uffgerichten angenomenen besigelten Speyrischen vertrage/ zu wider ist."

106. *Annales* II, p. 264, no. 4418.

107. See above, pp. 67-68.

108. *Pol. Corr.* I, p. 63 ff.

109. Bucer, *DS* I, p. 293 ff. A. Baum (p. 32) notes that the Bishop's letter expressly stated that he expected his request, that the Rat reconsider its grant of protection to Bucer, to be rejected, thus making it clear that he thought the Rat was determined to protect partisans of the new Gospel.

110. Bucer, *DS* I, pp. 345-347.

111. See above, p. 141.

112. A. Baum, p. 33; Chrisman, p. 132 ff.

113. A. Baum, pp. 33-34. Capito, as Provost of the chapter, initially temporized, citing fear of riot to justify delay in dismissing Firn. Not until Zell formally celebrated Firn's marriage on November 9, leaving no ambiguities, did the chapter act. The chapter was caught in a power struggle between the Dean, Nikolaus Wurmser, around whom the anti-evangelical majority of the canons gathered, and the Provost, Capito, whose position was relatively new and thus weak, but who had certain canons siding with him. In a similar fashion, though more effectively, the Cathedral chapter was neutralized by its Provost, Sigismund von Hohenlohe, who sided with the evangelicals and used his position to protect Zell. In Strasbourg, conversions in the upper hierarchy served chiefly to weaken ecclesiastical institutions, giving the movement more room to grow. See Charles Schmidt, *Histoire du Chapitre de St. Thomas* (Strasbourg, 1860).

114. A. Baum, p. 34, n. 3. This is an example of how *Ratsherren* acting as individuals and through their families and *freundschaften* could lend the prestige of their office and the influence of their social position to the movement, even when the Rat as a whole could or would not.

115. A. Baum, pp. 34-35; Adam, p. 57 ff. Firn refused to accept the chapter's letter of dismissal, and the embarrassed chapter delegation was finally forced to leave it with his new "wife."

116. A. Baum, pp. 35-36.

117. A. Baum, p. 38. Schultheiß had married on the twenty-third of November; a long chain of clerical marriages followed in January. Capito, however, did not marry until summer. Bucer performed Zell's ceremony, giving him and his bride, Katharina Schütz, the Eucharist in both species. Adam, p. 61 ff.

118. This is proved by the title given by Peter Butz to the document: "Instruction zu Epo der priester halb so Ewiber nemen/ ouch der Ewigen Zins/ des almusen und des Schirms halb." AST 47-II/9. The text itself does not refer to the latter three issues; AST 47-I/6, a separate sheet of paper filed elsewhere in the archives, contains the Rat's instructions for these issues. That the issues were presented together by the delegation is indicated by the Bishop in his letter of response, AST 47-II/10. The Rat's delegation was sent in response to a letter from the Bishop, written Nov. 27, complaining of Wolfgang Schultheiß' marriage (AST 47-II/8, Bishop to Rat, Freitag noch Katharina (=November 27), 1523). This is the letter which Baum argues must exist (p. 38). The letter expresses the Bishop's outrage not only at the crime itself, which, he implies, was understood as a basic attack on the order of the church, but also at the flagrant disregard for seemly clerical conduct: "We are furthermore informed that a monk among you named Wolff Schutheis last Monday openly celebrated a marriage earlier contracted with a citizen's daughter by going to church and thereafter with public drinking and dancing in a public inn."

119. This document, AST 47-II/9, written in the hand of Peter Butz, was prepared for by an earlier draft in the hand of Dr. Caspar Baldung, the city's legal consultant (AST 87/6). The chief difference in the earlier draft is a more strongly stated profession of the desire not to interfere in the Bishop's jurisdiction. The crossouts in Butz' version indicate a process of elimination of most professions of obedience to the Bishop and also of several unguardedly evangelical statements, leaving the objections to the Bishop's proposed action in higher relief. Butz' final text is the one quoted, with one of the "evangelical" crossouts reproduced in brackets: "Es trugt Ein Rat solcher nuwerungen und anderer der geistlichen unordenlichen und ergerlichem wesen das sich vil zit har hie for in der Stat Straßburg gebrucht und gehalten hett und noch nit wenig sonder groß beswerd und mißfallens. Ein Rat mecht auch wol lyden das sin f. gen. als den oberkeit solchs zu straffen zustanden mit recht gegen den selbigen zu allen theden handelt und gotlich und recht ist daran man sin f. g. nit verhindern werd.

Aber do neben sin furstlich gnad dienstlich zu erinnern Nach dem das gemein volck allenthalben in stat und land durch die manigveltigen druck so etliche Ior har fur augen komen dar zu durch die predicanten der massen der gotlichen ouch menschlichen satzung erfaren und erinnertt werden wither dan in langen Ioren under der gemein nie gesin/ Wu man domit straffen des geistlichen rechts wider die priester so (nach dem geheis gottes wie sy offenlich an den cantzlen furgeben) zu der Ee griffen strenglichen furfaren und darneben anderer priester und geistlichen so offenbar und ergerlich leben zu wider gotlicher und menschlicher satzung und aller erbarkeit zu bosem Exempel handelen [?] furgon und gegen den selbigen nit mit glichformiger stroff die in dem Vermag der geistlichen rechten uffgelegt furfaren solt. Was deshalb by gemeinen man und by menglichen so den Eren geneigt erachtet und geredt werden mocht. Zwar nichts anderst dan das man einen der sich nach zulossung gottliches geschrifft elichen verwibt ouch erlich begert zu leben-siner pfrund aller friheiten und pristerlichen ampts berauben vertriben und ußschliessen, Und ein andern der in offenbarer uppikeit laster und schanden seß die gots goben und empter zu niessen und gebruchen, gedulden und pliben ließ/ Dan sin f. gen. unverborgen ouch clor vor augen wie wol der standt der heiligen Ee von got neimans sonder allein villicht uß guter meynung von den vettern der kirchen den priestern und ordens lut verbotten/ und daruber ein geistlich strefflich gasatz verordent das do solich gesatz nit allein sonder ouch das M ? Key[e] gesatz allen geistlichen so zu der E griffen oder sonst in Ergerlichen wesen concubinen und mit ? lichtvertigen frawen wonen/ glichformig pene und straffe ernant and ußgedruckt. [Begin crossout:] So dan ein lange zit har zu wider gotlicher verordnungen auch menschlicher satzung vil der geistlichen Iren uppigen schaden und ergerlicher wolust rublich zu gebruchen unverhindert pliben und so man Itz nach dem geheiß gottes handelt die selbig understund zu vertriben. [End crossout.] Also wu do selb glichformige stroff nach Inhalt der racht an beiden orten nit gebrucht und furgenemen das daruß under der gemein mer widerwillens und zwitracht erwachssen wurden das dan sin. f. g. uß ange ? Erberkeit by ir selbs zu ermessen hatt.

Deshalb an sin f. g. Eins Rats dienstlich bit solchen uberboswerlichen last so nit allein das zitlich sonder ouch das ewig und der selen heill belangen ist in gnediger rechtung und der massen ein gedenckens zu haben, ob zu verhietung einer solchen entbotung [?] uff itz angesatzten richstag by Bepstlicher heiligkeit Keyr M[t] und gemeinen stenden so ein vetterlichs gnedigs und cristlichs insehen furzunemen wer uff das solche zwitracht hingelegt und einen gotgefellige cristliche einigkeit furgenommen word.

Item sin/ f/g/ ouch betten und ansuchen das sin f. g. nachmals verstendige gelerte fromme menner der heiligen geschrifft verordneten den [?] so uff die predigern acht nemen und, wu sy anderst predigten dan was der gotlichen geschrifft gemes und das sy uß der heiligen geschrifft nit bewisen mochten, abwisen, damit der ley und das gemein volck nit also in irsal und zu verderbens irer selen gefurt werden."

120. The preachers repeatedly witnessed to the slowness with which opinion changes concerning this central mark of the medieval clerical estate. Bucer's marriage to a nun, of course, was sharply attacked (*DS* I, pp. 166-169, 173-174, 295-299). Zell mentions resistance to marriage repeatedly (*CV* 14r-v; *Collation* A2v). The married priests also refer to such resistance in their appeal from their excommunication (*Appelation der Eelichen Priester/ von der vermeinten Excommunication des hochwirdigen Fursten hern Wilhelmen Bischoffen zu Straßbourg* (Strasbourg, 1524), A2v-A3r. The reluctance of many *Ratsherren* to countenance clerical marriage clearly reflected the attitude of the population at large, as did the gradual osmosis of the new ideas.

121. Zell, *Collation*, D1v-D4r. In contrast to the Rat, Zell's sermon at Firn's wedding had attacked the suggestion that the priests delay

their marriages until a council had reformed the law. Councils had no other power than to buttress or clarify Scripture, Zell said, and on the subject of marriage Scripture was entirely clear. Human law could not resist the soul's urgent need.

122. Rapp, Institutions ecclésiastiques, livre 5, p. 70 ff.; Francis Rapp, "L'Eveque de Strasbourg, Guillaume de Honstein, et la Réformation," Revue d'histoire et de philosophie réligieuses (Strasbourg, 1974), no. 1, p. 86.

123. See below, p. 161. If those with concubines were to be punished equally with the married under the Nürnberg Mandate, that would escalate the penalty for cohabitation from a cash fine to loss of benefice, an additional factor causing great awkwardness for the Bishop.

124. The appeal for a council was not only a tactic for causing a delay in the enforcement of a problematic law. It offered those who valued legal compliance and political security their only means of achieving religious change. A free council might undertake reforms, or at least grant permission for each local government to make its own decisions; there could be change without paying the price of disobedience. During the first four months of 1524, the Rat's diplomats struggled to bring such a meeting about. See Pol. Corr. I, pp. 86-91.

125. See above, chapter 1, pp. 22 ff.

126. Printed in Röhrich, Geschichte der Reformation in Elsass (Strasbourg, 1830), I, p. 455.

127. The Rat's version of this clause of the Nürnberg Mandate, which had read that the Gospel was to be preached "nach Auslegung der von der christlichen Kirche gutgeheissenen und angenommenen Schrifften" (Adam, p. 57), was the following paragraph: "Daß Ihr und alle die so sich Predigens in unsrer Stadt und Oberkeit unterziehen und gebrauchen, auff allen Canzlen nichts anders, dann das heylig Evangelium und die Lehr Gottes frey offentlich und was zu Mehrung der Lieb Gottes und des Nächsten reicht, dem gemeinen christlichen Volk verkünden wöllt, und andre Stempeneyen dem heiligen christlichen Glauben ungemäß, auch alle Reitz und Schmähewort, darzu alles des den gemeinen Mann in Aergernuß oder Zweifel führen, oder zu einer Empörung und Ungehorsame gegen seine Oberkeit, sy sey Geistlich oder Weltlich reitzen oder bewegen möcht, euch gänzlich enthalt, entziehet und nit hören laßt." Rorich, Geschichte, I, p. 455. The order against seditious talk against the religious as well as secular government is wholly consistent with the Rat's posture of legal regularity.

128. AST 47-II/10, Bishop to Rat, Montags noch Lucie (=December 14), 1524.

129. Adam, p. 60 ff.

130. A. Baum, p. 36.

131. Adam, p. 61.

132. See Chrisman, pp. 24-26. Consulting the Schöffen was a frequently used means of galvanizing popular support for a controversial policy.

133. AST 87/10, the conclusions of the special commission, and AST 47-I/7, Butz' text for the presentation to the Schöffen (full of crossouts and redrafts), are parallel. The latter document spells out the threat

of Imperial Acht and Bann more clearly, and warns citizens more bluntly to let the priests manage their own quarrels.

134. AST 87/10. Chrisman (p. 135) misreads A. Baum (p. 37); there is no mention either in his text nor in any of the documents he cites of having the Schöffen "place Firn under the ban."

135. A. Baum, p. 37, asserts that he had found no evidence that the presentation had ever been made; Chrisman, referring to Baum, states that "in January 1524, before any meeting of the Schöffen had been called, five more clerics took wives." (p. 135). The title of Butz' worksheet, however, which Baum did not know existed, is "Was man den schoffeln furgehalten uff ___ [date illegible]." The use of the participle renders it at least possible that the Schöffen were in fact consulted. It is difficult to go further and speculate that the response of the Schöffen was the cause of the Rat's December 19 decision to protect Firn, however, since the chroniclers would surely have seized upon such a conspicuously pro-Reform action. If the meeting took place, it was certainly later than December 14, since the instructions for the presentation mention the Bishops' reply to the Rat on that date, and it almost certainly preceded the decision to protect Firn on the nineteenth, which would have rendered the compromise suggested to the chapter senseless.

136. Cited in Bucer, DS I, p. 345-346; Pol. Corr. I, p. 87-88. Chrisman misinterprets the instructions. The Rat did not "aver that [concubinage and clerical marriage] went against the teaching of ancient councils and were thus illegal." (p. 135). It rather provided its delegates with an answer if someone else should so aver.

137. A. Baum, pp. 42-43; Chrisman, pp. 135-136. The Rat mentions the preachers' request for the opportunity fully to defend their actions in AST 47-II/14.

138. AST 47-II/14. cf. A. Baum, p. 43, contra Chrisman, p. 136. Chrisman considers it the Rat's intention to use the married clergy as a bargaining point to achieve the discipline of all the clergy (p. 137). We consider it quite possible that such a motive was at work in at least a minority of Ratsherren. Yet she is inattentive to the thrust of the text. The Rat does not "reaffirm its essential agreement with the Bishop's policy"; nowhere in this document does the Rat recommend that the married priests "be firmly dealt with." It tells the Bishop that his policies are going to cause a riot, and it begs him to put off the prosecution until all the estates can resolve the difficult question at the coming Reichstag. So that the reader may judge for himself, we provide the relevant portions of the text (the first paragraph outlines the preachers' petition): "Und wie wol nun ein Rat nie des willen gesein und noch nit ist sein fen. gn. an irer ordenlichen zu geburende Iurisdiction zu verhindern, So hat doch Ein E. Rat uff furgenomen handlung auch in bedocht schwebender lauff und diser sorgkveltiger Zit by im selbs als der Ie gern friden erhalten und empörung verhieten wolt erwegen. Wo also gegen den gedachten priestern so zu dem Sacrament der heiligen Ehe gegryffen. uber ire hievor vilveltig und nach töglich offentlich anruffen und begeren sy irer ler und handlung halb zu verhör lossen zu kommen/...daruber unverhort strenglich furgefaren und darneben anderer so innen glich und höhere Empter in der Stat und dem Byschump Strasßburg haben und

tragen so vil jar und nach mit jren lichtvertigen frauwen und bosem Exempell zu ergernuẞs des nechsten und wider verbot gotes geistlicher und weltlicher satzungen gewont [?] verschonen [?] und die selbigen nit mit glichformiger furforderung und peen zustraffen auch irer Wurd und Empter entsetzen und berouben solten [?] als dan noch vermog der rechten wie sein fen. gen. des wissens tregt billich beschicht. Das harus by der genein so des worts gots und der heyligen geschryfft mer erfaren und geeupt dan in vor langen Jaren Je beschehen ein grosser ungwyll erweckt und zu gesorgen nichts anders dan irrung zwytracht und emporung sich zutragen und begeben wurden. [There follows a paraphrase of the Bishop's letter of December 14]....Deschalb an sein f. gen. Eins E. Rats dienstlich und fruntlich byt gelegenheit der Zyt und swere der sach harin genediclichen zu bedencken und Eim Rat zu Eren und gefallen zweyung und uffrur zwischen geistlichen und weltlichen zu verhieten die Citation uffzusch ___?___ tzen und bitz zu volstreckung und End des Ietzigen Richstags zu prorogieren. do dan an E. Rat der endtlichen zuversichtlichen hoffnung ist. Dwyl solche schweren und wichtige hendel nit allein in disem Bishump sonder auch in vyl andren furstentumben lendren und stetten sich zugetragen. Es werd durch gemein Cristlich stend des heligen Romischen Richs Ietz uff dem Richstag zu Nüremberg so ein vätterlichs gnedigs und geburlichs insehen furgenomen damit solcher last auch die Zwispeltigenn meynungen hingelegt und ein Cristlicher gotgefelliger fryd uffgericht werd." The document closes with another paragraph of requests for the Bishop to reconsider his action.

139. A. Baum, p. 45.

140. AST 47-II/16. Wilhelm clearly meant to preserve the ethical distinction between estates; he asserted that his objectives were "animarum salutem et publicam decentiam honestatemque clericalem." That there was a clerical "honestas" to be distinguished from that proper to a layman, of course, was a major target of the evangelical preachers' polemics.

141. A. Baum, p. 47.

142. Appelation der Eelichen Priester...(Strasbourg, 1524), under the names of Zell, Firn, Lucas Bathodius (Hackfurt), Wolf. Sculteti (Schultheiss), Conrad Spatzinger, Alexander [?], and Johannes Nibling.

143. A. Baum, p. 48-49: "Wir erfahren in der Folgezeit nichts Besonderes mehr in der Sache der verheirateten Prädikanten. Der Magistrat schültzte sie."

144. Cf. the attitude of Agnes Trenß in the summer of 1524, a common citizen's widow who judged that the climate was ripe for her to marry her daughter to Caspar Hedio, the evangelical cathedral preacher. See below, pp. 215 ff. The total effect of the Rat's actions was to protect clerical marriage in Strasbourg, to help render it respectable.

145. For the progress of innovations in the cult, see Adam, p. 70 ff., A. Baum, pp. 84-85.

146. AST 87/8.

147. A. Baum, p. 84.

148. Rapp, Institutions écclésiastiques, livre 5, p. 90 ff., provides a brilliant discussion of economic grievances against the chapters.

149. It is essential to understand that this system was to a large extent ethically justified according to normal medieval values. The diversion of money through pluralism to scholars and officials made the medieval educational and administrative systems possible. For parish tithes to go to support the cycle of prayer and the broad spectrum of ecclesiastical interests nourished by chapter benefices was wholly proper; the parish participated in a much richer liturgical life than would have been possible without incorporation, and the valuable prayer of the clerical estate was sustained. The poor might resent financial exactions in lean years, and some might begin to view the clergy as idle exploiters of the sweat of others. Those who remained integrated in the medieval sacral system, however, might have wished to reform the chapters, but not to abolish them or their financial bases. Only when canons' "work" was discredited could that begin.

150. A. Baum, pp. 78-79; Chrisman, pp. 113-114; Adam, p. 67 ff.

151. In the summer of 1523, Bucer had distinguished between having a benefice and being renumerated for preaching or lecturing before a group which volunteered to pay him out of their own pockets. Since the Mandate only mentioned privation of benefices and of clerical freedoms as the penalty for marriage, he hoped to continue to function. The St. Aurelien parishioners' first request conformed to these standards; they were willing to pay Bucer themselves. The April request that Bucer be named pastor, however, did in fact provide him with a benefice.

152. See the Rat's instructions to the delegation to the Nürnberg Reichstag, Bucer, DS I, pp. 346-347, where the delegates are told how to explain how the Rat has never supported Bucer's activity. See also above, p. 47 ff.

153. A. Baum, pp. 79-80; Chrisman, p. 114.

154. A. Baum, pp. 81-82; Adam, pp. 79-80. For the date of Capito's entry, see the petition of the parishioners of St. Aurelien (Bucer, DS I, p. 368, l. 31).

155. Printed Bucer, DS I, pp. 366-368. The introduction to this edition incorrectly asserts that the election was made "ohne Rücksicht auf die Rechte des Thomasstiftes [p. 366]", considering that the petition twice states that it was done with the eventual permission of the chapter (p. 367, ll. 31-35; p. 368, ll. 5-6). This permission may have been the work of Capito, or simply a shrewd way for the chapter to shift the blame to the Rat for the violation of the Nürnberg Mandate.

156. A. Baum, p. 78, n. 2.

157. The parishioners did assert that the "worthy Doctors and preachers" of the city had said Bucer was best qualified (DS I, p. 368, ll. 4-6), and Capito was a doctor of theology; further, the chapter's permission may well have been Capito's work.

158. One may note that it was on the grounds of avoiding seditious organizations that the Rat originally refused Bucer permission to preach. See above, p. 141.

159. See Philippe Dollinger, "Un Aspect de la Guerre des Paysans en Alsace: L'organization du soulèvement," in *Paysans d'Alsace*, *Publications de la Societé Savante d'Alsace et des Regions de l'Est*, vol. 7,

Strasbourg, 1959, pp. 69-79; and Rapp, Institutions écclésiastiques, livre 5, pp. 23-32.

160. Printed Bucer DS I, pp. 369-372.

161. A. Baum, pp. 81-86. The Rat itself had ordered on April 16 that all cloisters' possessions be inventoried, and that their contracts providing annuities and rents be filed with the Rat. A. Baum, pp. 106-107.

162. A. Baum, p. 86.

163. See above, p. 109.

164. AST 47-II/24; Baum, p. 125. The Bishop explained the appeal to the Rat in a letter on September 12, 1524 (AST 47-II/26).

165. See Pol. Corr. I, p. 93.

166. See above, pp. 134-135 and Chrisman, p. 142. Chrisman confuses the chronology, placing the canons' self-exile shortly after a petition by certain Franciscans on November 9, 1523, which had led to a series of riots, (which she fails to connect to the Treger affair). See below, p. 178 ff. Yet her observation that popular opinion linked the canons' self-exile with the flight of the nobles in 1420, is very probable.

167. The entire Treger affair is well and clearly narrated by Johannes Müller, Bucer, DS II, pp. 17-33.

168. AST 87/13. A. Baum did not know of this source, and so could not fully understand the context of the preachers' petition on August 31 (A. Baum, pp. 86-87). See below, p. 175 ff.

169. The Rat's position is expressed in two documents. AST 87/14, the one used by Chrisman (p. 115) is a brief order that a commission draw up a presentation to the Schöffen on the issue. It is not an "edict." Its final paragraph outlines the way the remaining Stiftherren are to be treated; they (not the preachers) are to be questioned about their intentions, and then ordered to take the Bürgerrecht and to pay the tax on wine and customs duties. See above. The second document, AST 47-I/8, is in fact the edict resulting from the decision of the Rat and the Schöffen. Since it does mention that the Rat's intention to support the Gospel, and implies that the matter of appointing preachers involves the salvation of souls, Chrisman's analysis of the "omissions" in the Rat's decision is without foundation (p. 115-116).

170. The projected reassembly of the Nürnberg Reichstag in Speier during the fall of 1524, eventually forbidden by the Emperor. Pol. Corr. I, p. 92, n. 3.

171. "...Thus, if anyone in this honorable free city Strasbourg...is dispossessed of his long-held property by force, it would not only be to the loss of good name and the injury of the common city, but against its articles and to the destruction of the brotherly peace which previously [ruled] in this city.... [The Rat has decided] that since such support [underhaltung] of the pastors is only a temporal good and does not regard the salvation of souls, that, for the sake of the furtherance and support of the Holy Gospel and the maintenance of a god-pleasing peace, it wills to maintain [erhalten] the pastors of the four Pflegereien [i.e. the parishes in which the Rat already controlled the appointment of the pastor] until the end of the coming Reichstag, and

none the less to negotiate with the chapters as intensively as possible to bring them to put them in the Rat's hands...." AST 47-I/8.

172. AST 87/14.

173. See Jean-Robert Zimmermann, Les compagnons de métiers à Strasbourg, Publications de la Société savante d'Alsace et des Régions de l'Est, Collection "Recherches et Documents", tome x, Strasbourg, 1971, for the Rat's dealings with the brotherhoods of journeymen; for the artisan class in general, see Jean Rott, "Artisanat et mouvements sociaux à Strasbourg," in Artisans et Ouvriers d'Alsace, Publications de la Société savante d'Alsace et des Régions de l'Est, 9, Strasbourg, 1965.

174. See Chrisman's analyses of the composition of the first three parishes to request evangelical preachers, pp. 139-140, 303-305.

175. AST 87/21 printed, Bucer, DS I, pp. 373-376.

176. A. Baum, pp. 82, 87-88.

177. Bucer, DS II, pp. 25-27.

178. See the admirably clear treatment by Johannes Müller, Bucer, DS II, pp. 17-33, from which the subsequent discussion is drawn.

179. A. Baum, p. 94.

180. Annales I, p. 246, no. 3484, recording a decision of the XV, the Rat's standing committee for internal affairs.

181. AST 47-I/11. The Rat does not appear as the enemy of its Catholic citizens, however; it orders those on both sides to behave like Christians ought.

182. Pol. Corr. I, pp. 94-95, no. 177. A new Rat took office January 10. A. Baum, p. 126.

183. Pol. Corr. I, p. 95, no. 178. The Rat asserted that it had acted "in no other manner than as we possessed and still possess good right, means, and power from divine law." Its other claim, that it had acted out of the most pressing urgency, does not disguise the implication that divine law provided the Rat with the right to break or at least to bend human customs and statutes.

184. Pol. Corr. I, pp. 95-96, no. 179.

185. A. Baum, pp. 133-137. These documents were delivered by the Rat's delegation on February 15. We regard this as wholly conclusive evidence that the Rat's majority subscribed to the changes which had been undertaken in Strasbourg's religious life. It does not, of course, mean that the Ratsherren promised to subscribe to every one of the preachers' future demands.

186. Chrisman, p. 150; Bucer, DS II, p. 425. All masses had been abolished except the Fronmessen of the four great churches.

187. Elements of the Rat's old policy of insulating the town from direct episcopal action appear as late as December, 1523, when the Rat suggested that the Bishop create an administration to examine sermons. Yet a year earlier, the Bishop had moved against Zell through the administra-

tion guaranteed by the Rachtung of Speier, the Vicar and Fiscal; it was that administration which the Rat ultimately frustrated.

Chapter 4

1. Two Ratsherren were consistent opponents of the new religion: Konrad von Duntzenheim and Martin Betscholt. See Johannes Ficker and Otto Winckelmann, Handschriftproben des sechzehnten Jahrhunderts nach Strassburger Originalen, (Strassburg, 1905), vol. 1, pp. 2-3. That they were not alone is clear from the Rat's decree of January 1, 1525 (AST 47-I/11), which told the partisans on both sides to behave. In assembling evidence for majority adherence to the Gospel, A. Baum cites evidence of the continued existence of a substantial minority (p. 96, n. 4).

2. A. Baum, pp. 96-97.

3. That is to say that the Rat's requirements themselves only loosely prescribed what style of life clerics might adopt. Given the Rat's concessions, the requirement of citizenship did not prescribe the degree of engagement with urban lay life that a cleric had to adopt. One might well be a citizen and a wholly cloistered monk, if only the strict legal conditions are considered. The Rat's protection of marriage did not in itself prohibit celibacy.

4. Clemens Ziegler, a peasant resident in Strasbourg, was criticized for his presumption in writing a book in 1524. See below, p. 225.

5. See Chrisman, pp. 235-237; A. Baum, pp. 99-124.

6. Rapp, Institutions écclésiastiques, livre 5, pp. 166-168.

7. See Bernd Moeller, "Piety in Germany around 1500," in The Reformation in Medieval Perspective, ed. Steven Ozment, Chicago, 1971; Rapp, Institutions écclésiastiques, livre 5, p. 166 ff.

8. Rapp, Institutions écclésiastiques, livre 5, pp. 12-19; in 1519 a Ratsherr heard one man assert that if he had all the money between Strasbourg and Colmar, he would not buy an indulgence (Annales I, p. 239, no. 3442). See also Annales I, p. 241, no. 3448.

9. AST 87/1.

10. Rapp, Institutions écclésiastiques, livre 5, p. 168; Jean-Robert Zimmermann, Les Compagnons de Métiers à Strasbourg, Publications de la Société savante d'Alsace et des Régions de l'Est, Collection "Recherches et Documents", tome x, (Strasbourg, 1971).

11. See Charles Schmidt, Histoire litteraire, passim; Chrisman, pp. 45-78. We find "humanism" far too vague a description for the conservative, scholasticism-oriented, pious cluster of scholars in Alsace.

12. Rapp, (Institutions écclésiastiques, livre 5, p. 141 ff.) argues that the impossibly bright ideal of clerical character and the exaggeratedly grim criticism of actual practice preached by the learned reformists was itself a major contribution to anticlericalism, fostering the hatreds which eventually erupted in the Reformation. Yet the clergy was not singled out for criticism by the reformists. They criticized all estates vigorously; the attacks on the clergy were different not in kind, but in degree, and that only moderately. The conservative

ideological influence of the reformists should not be underestimated. The ambivalence of reformist circles is illustrated by their role in the Reformation. To succeed, Reformation ideology was required not merely to capitalize on popular discontent with the clergy's failures, but to alienate the population from the very standards upon which the reformists based their criticism.

13. See Rapp, Institutions écclésiastiques, livre 5, pp. 2-55. Rapp regards the Rat's program not only as the expression of anticlerical feeling, but as a calculated attempt to exploit it: "Disons-le nettement: dans l'âme populaire couvait une sorte de haine à l'encontre des prêtres et des moines et, de ces sentiments, les politiques, même s'ils en mesuraient l'exagération, croyaient expédient de tirer parti." (p. 55).

14. Rapp, Institutions écclésiastiques, livre 5, pp. 23-32, 90-104.

15. Eckhard zum Treübel [Drübel], Ain dumietige ermanung an ain gantz gemayne Christenheit (Strasbourg, 1523).

16. Röhrich, Mittheilungen, III, p. 25 ff.

17. Eckhart, Ain dümietige ermanung, A2r.

18. Eckhart, Ain dümietige ermanung, A2r-v.

19. Eckhart, Ain dümietige ermanung, A2v.

20. Eckhart, Ain dümietige ermanung, A2v-A3v.

21. Eckhart, Ain dümietige ermanung, A3v.

22. Put into strict theological language, Eckhart's arguments are reduced to the claim that commerce in the sacraments destroys their secondary, ex opere operantis effects; since he does not discuss the primary, "objective" ex opere operato effects, however, one cannot accuse him of Donatism. Yet he does not make the distinction himself, and his rhetoric is very negative.

23. Eckhart, Ain dümietige ermanung, A3r.

24. For the association of "gremplerei" with "wucherei", see the entry of the former word in Jacob Grimm and Wilhelmm Grimm, Deutsches Wörterbuch, (Leipzig, 1935), Band 4, Abt. I, Teil 6, Col. 111.

25. Röhrich, Mittheilungen, III, p. 6 ff.

26. Annales II, p. 260, no. 4410.

27. See above, pp. 12-13.

28. Röhrich, Mittheilungen, III, p. 25 ff.

29. Ibid.

30. Zell, CV, z2v ff., L1 ff; Bucer, Summary, DS I, p. 128 ff; Otto Brunfels, Vom dem Evangelischen Anstoß (Strasbourg, 1523); Brunfels, Von dem Pfaffen Zehenden (Strasbourg, 1524).

31. Capito, Entschuldigung, AA3r-BB4v.

32. See above, p. 177 ff.

33. Thomas Brady, of the Department of History at the University of Oregon, informs me that Nikolaus Kniebis, a prominent evangelical Ratsherr, purchased extensive ecclesiastical lands during the movement. See also Joseph Fuchs, "Les Prechter de Strasbourg, une famille de négotiants banquiers du XVI siècle," Revue d'Alsace, 95, 1956.

34. Rudolphe Peter, "Le Jardinier Clement Ziegler, l'homme et son oeuvre," Unpublished thèse de baccalaureate en théologie, l'Université de Strasbourg, 1954, pp. 82-83.

35. Annales I, p. 248, no. 3493.

36. AST 80/1 (1523?).

37. Bucer, DS I, pp. 366-368; see above, p. 168 ff.

38. Chrisman, p. 139, pp. 303-304.

39. Bucer, DS I, p. 368.

40. A. Baum, p. 79.

41. Bucer, DS I, p. 366, l. 3 - p. 367, l. 2.

42. Bucer, DS I, p. 367, ll. 12-19.

43. This theme is repeated several times in the course of the petition.

44. See above, p. 83 ff.

45. It is conventional wisdom that in medieval tracts written to guide laymen in the pious life, the imitatio Christi tended to be conceived as an imitatio monachorum. Voluntary asceticism and contemplation permitted even laymen to live like monks, though outside the walls of the cloister. For those who were influenced by such models, the laymen suffered a competitive disadvantage over against the consecrated clergy. Since his life was directed at the secular world in his vocation, marriage, etc., it could not be exclusively directed at the next world. Of course, there were other means of being pious. In the process of obtaining merit through good works, however, the poor man suffered a handicap in comparison to the rich. If the pauper was often thought to be intrinsically less subject to temptation, he still could not buy masses, etc., and was thus forced to the fringes of the sacral system. Evangelical ideology eliminated in principle any religious 'buying power.'

46. Bucer, DS I, p. 368, ll. 1-4. It is precisely in this light that Bucer presents himself in the Verantwortung an den Rat in June of 1523. See above, chapter 3, p. 168.

47. Bucer, DS I, p. 368, ll. 14-23. The Scripture, not the laws of Rat or Empire, define the powers of the congregation. This quasi-legal principle had already been asserted by the parishioners of St. Thomas in defense of Firn. See above, pp. 161-162.

48. See the beautifully documented study by Jean Rott, "Artisanat et mouvements sociaux à Strasbourg," in Artisans et ouvriers d'Alsace, Publications de la Societé savante d'Alsace et des régions de l'Est, 9, Strasbourg, 1965. Rott concludes that salaries did not improve in the face of stiff inflation, and that the elimination of feastdays subtracted a good deal of workers' leisure time without compensation. Yet there were none of the threatening movements that had characterized

the preceding generation and the following one.

49. Zell, CV, z2v ff., L1 ff.

50. See above, pp. 177-178.

51. Bucer, DS I, pp. 366-368.

52. A. Baum, p. 78.

53. AST 69/2.

54. AST 69/2.

55. AST 69/2.

56. AST 69/3. The petition is also signed by Dr. Michael Rott.

57. Rapp, Institutions écclésiastiques, livre 5,

58. AST 69/4.

59. AST 69/4.

60. See Bucer's parallel argument, contrasting monastic disobedience to authority and irresponsibility in the face of human need with the Gospel's commands of subjection and love of neighbor. See above, p. 86.

61. Both religious government through the magistrate and the preachers' authoritarian articulation of divine law in Scripture, reinforced with Roman law, were attacked as new versions of the Papacy. See Chrisman, pp. 204-232, and Francois Wendel, L'Eglise de Strasbourg, sa constitution et son organization, 1532-1535, Études d'histoire et de philosophie réligeuses publies par la Faculté de Théologie protestante de l'Université de Strasbourg, 38, Paris, 1942.

62. AST 69/5.

63. It would seem unlikely, however, that the addition of ministers to the pool of marriage prospects went very far to compensate Strasbourg families for the loss of their ability to concentrate their resources by sending children to the monastery.

64. AST 69/6 (June 4, 1524).

65. AST 69/6.

66. AST 69/6. The coherence of individuals in social groups such as the family or the freundtschafft helped to cushion the social and psychological stress of "innovative" actions. Once the new norms were accepted by the group, the individual gained support for his values. It would seem exaggerated, however, to locate the appeal of Reformation ideology in an offer to fulfill a popular nostalgia for "community." It is clear that both preachers and townsmen were aware that the Word, being prior to all human institutions, had the "right" to divide society and all social groups. Hedio's readiness to refuse a magisterial order to leave his wife is typical. We consider the evangelicals' rhetoric of unity and their redirection of blame for the prevalent disunity to have been means of dealing with the conflicts, both internal and external, involved in accepting a changed framework of values, rather than a cause of their original acceptance of the new ideas (contra Moeller, Reichsstadt und Reformation).

67. Pol. Corr. I, p. 93, n. 2.

68. See above, p. 172.

69. AST 87/13 (August 22/23, 1524), signed "die pfarkinder zu S. Laurentzen, zum Jüngen S. Peter, zu S. Martin, zu S. Aurelien, zu S. Stephan." Two other parish names are crossed out, one, S. Andres, remaining legible. The difference in tone of the petition sent by the preachers in their own names a few days later, written in a smoother style with much clearer theological argumentation and more extensive demands, seems to us to indicate that laymen composed this petition, although it may well have been edited by a preacher. See above, p. 173 ff.

70. "Third, gracious sirs, many of us are obedient citizens of your Honors who seek our sustenance in crafts and work in the fields, tired from the whole week, would gladly relax and have some peace on holy days. However, through the bad order of churchly pomp and pointless choir chant, that is denied us. [Thus] we request [you] graciously to consider our situation, and to obtain that on holy days, after the preaching and godly Christian offices are finished, we might leave the temple singers. For we do not otherwise want their goods or their work, but seek only peace, unity, citizenly tranquility, quiet, obedience, and divine honor." AST 87/13. That this could well have represented widespread lay opinion is clear from the near-riot which erupted at the church of the Dominicans on February 21, 1523, when the choir began to sing as Bucer was preaching (A Baum, p. 83).

71. This was a prominent argument of the evangelicals in every step of change, most conspicuously in the final abolition of the Mass in 1529. See Chrisman, pp. 155-176.

72. See above, p. 177 ff.

73. Chrisman, p. 235 ff., A. Baum, p. 99 ff.

74. Mathias Wurm von Geudersheim wrote two pamphlets in 1523 concerning his struggle to get his sister to leave the convent of St. Nicolaus in undis, including the Trost Clostergefangener, dedicated to Eckhart zum Treübel, a friend and fellow knight. His sister resisted, and on January 28, 1524, he and his brothe Peter petitioned the Rat to order that they be permitted to talk with her. The petition was granted, but their sister would not leave. Röhrich, Mittheilung, 3, p. 10 ff. See also the Strasbourg chronicle of Trausch, vol. 4 of the Fragements récueillis, no. 3889.

75. A. Baum, p. 118 ff.

76. AST 69/15.

77. See A. Baum, p. 119. AST 87/20, AST 69/13-14 are examples of such petitions.

78. For this development, see Robert Stupperich's introduction to Bucer's treatise Grund und Ursach, DS I, pp. 187-188, and J. Adam, p. 65 ff.

79. AST 47-II/34.

80. AST 47-II/35, 36, 37, 38, 39, 40, 41.

81. See above, p. 65 ff.

82. Chrisman, pp. 155-176.

83. Annales I, p. 261, no. 3512.

84. See above, p. 90 ff.

85. See above, p. 77 ff.

86. Peter, Clement Ziegler, passim.

87. Clemens Ziegler, Ein fast schon büchlin in welche yederman findet ein hellen und claren verstandt von dem leib und blut Christi. (Strasbourg, 1525), A2r.

88. Ein fast schon Büchlin, A2v-A4r. Ziegler does not include overt attacks on individual preachers, however. Rather, he praises the power of the Spirit in Luther, the same Spirit which he claims for himself (Glv). He also writes that he does not mean his polemic to imply that all preaching or writing is bad, but only that which does not "grasp" the Gospel's light. We do not claim that Ziegler attacks the activity of preaching or writing as means by which the Holy Spirit makes his will known. It is the establishment of an exclusive class of religious professionals which his broad diffusion of the Spirit-given duty to preach threatens.

89. Ein fast schon büchlin, D2r.

90. Ein fast schon büchlin, E3r.

91. Ein fast schon büchlin, D2v ff.

92. See above, p. 61, n. 37.

93. Ein fast schon büchlin, B4v-Clr.

94. Large sections of this pamphlet are to be found in a French translation in Peter, Clement Ziegler, pp. 85-87, in which he renders the title as the "Bien belle exégèse du Notre Père" (Ein fast schöne uszlegung und betrachtung des Christlichen gebetts, Strassburg, 1525). It is from Peter's translation that we have worked, since the only surviving German copy was unavailable to us.

95. Peter, Clement Ziegler, p. 85 ff.

96. Ziegler attacks clerical 'fiscalism' repeatedly, e.g. Ein fast schon büchlin, Blr.

97. Strasbourg residents did not, by and large, support the peasants' violence (Chrisman, pp. 151-152), voting almost unanimously (through the guilds) to support the Rat's neutrality during the War. Yet that is not to say that the economic interpretation of renewed, Scripture-directed society did not find roots within Strasbourg walls.

98. Typical of the preachers' economic passivity was the response made to a letter sent to Bucer by Friedrich Meyger, complaining that some of the conspicuously pious members of the Rat were eating the poor's substance through usury. (Manfred Krebs and Hans Bott, Quellen zur Geschichte der Taüfer, Elsass I, vol. 7, Gutersloh, 1959, no. 172). A few days later, Bucer and the other preachers added usury to a long list of other evils which they wanted the Rat to correct. (Krebs and Rott, no. 178), but there is no evidence that they went any further.

BIBLIOGRAPHY

Adam, Jean. *Inventaire des archives du chapitre de St. Thomas de Strasbourg*. Strasbourg, 1937.

Adam, Johann. *Evangelische Kirchengeschichte der Stadt Strassburg*. Strassburg, 1922.

Andreas, Willy. *Deutschland vor der Reformation*. Stuttgart, 1932.

________. *Strassburg an der Wende vom Mittelalter zur Neuzeit*. Leipzig, 1940.

Anrich, Gustav. *Martin Bucer*. Strassburg, 1914.

Appelation der Eelichen Priester/ von der vermeinten Excommunication des hochwirdigen Fürsten hern Wilhelmen Bischoffen zu Strassburg. Strasbourg, 1524.

Archives de St. Thomas. Series of manuscript sources deposited in the Archives Municipaux, Strasbourg, France.

Baum, Adolf. *Magistrat und Reformation in Strassburg bis 1529*. Strassburg, 1887.

Baum, Johann Wilhelm. *Capito und Butzer*. Elberfeld, 1860.

Berger, Peter L. *The Sacred Canopy*. New York, 1967.

________, and Luckmann, Thomas. *The Social Construction of Reality*. New York, 1967.

Bizer, Ernst. *Studien zur Geschichte des Abendmahlstreits im 16. Jahrhundert*. Gütersloh, 1940.

Boon, R. "De Eerste Drie Geschriften de Straatburgse Reformator Martin Bucer: Het Begin van de Ontwikkeling zijner Theologie." *Nederlands Archief voor Kerkgeschiedenis*, vol. 39, 1952-1953.

Bornkamm, Heinrich. *Martin Bucers Bedeutung für die europäische Reformationsgeschichte*. *Schriften des Vereins für Reformationsgeschichte*, 169, Jahrgang 58, Heft 2, Gütersloh, 1952.

Bosch, J. W. "Bucer over de verholding van kerkelijk Ambt en zielsorg." *Gereformeerd Theologisch Tijdschrift* 37. 1936. Pp. 397-407.

Brunfels, Otto. *Von dem Evangelischen Anstoss*. Strasbourg, 1523.

________. *Von dem Pfaffen Zehenden Hundert unnd zwen und fyertzig Schlussreden*. Strassburg, 1524.

Bucer, Martin. *Instruction in Christian Love, 1523.* Translated by Paul Traugott Fuhrman. Richmond, Virginia, 1952.

________. *Martin Bucers Deutsche Schriften.* Edited by Robert Stupperich. 4 vols. Gütersloh, 1960-62.

Capito, Wolfgang. *Das die Pfafheit schuldig sey Burgerlichen Eyd zuthun....* Strasbourg, 1524.

________. *Entschuldigung an den hochwürdigen Fürsten unsern Herren Wilhelmen Bischoffen zu Strassburg.* Augsburg, 1524.

Chrisman, Miriam U. *Strasbourg and the Reform.* New Haven, 1967.

Courvoisier, Jaques. *La Notion d'église chez Bucer. Etudes d'histoire et de la philosophie réligieuse de la Faculté de Théologie de l'Université de Strasbourg*, 28. Paris, 1933.

Crämer, Ulrich. *Die Verfassung und Verwaltung Strasburgs von der Reformationszeit bis zum Fall der Reichstadt (1521-1681). Schriften des Wissenschaftlichen Instituts der Elsass-Lothringen im Reich an der Universität Frankfurt.* Frankfurt am Main, 1931.

Dankbaar, Willem Frederik. *Martin Bucers Beziehungen zu den Niederlanden.* Den Haag, 1961.

Dollinger, Philippe. "Un Aspect de la Guerre des Paysans en Alsace: L'organization du soulèvement," in *Paysans d'Alsace. Publications de la Société Savante d'Alsace et des Régions de l'Est*, vol. 7. Strasbourg, 1959.

________. "Patriciat noble et patriciat bourgeois à Strasbourg au XIVe siècle," in *Revue d'Alsace*, 94. 1955.

Douglass, E. Jane Dempsey. *Justification in Late Medieval Preaching; A Study of John Geiler of Keisersberg.* Leiden, 1966.

Eckhart zum Treübel. *Ain dümietige ermanung an ain gantz gemayne Christenheit.* Strasbourg, 1923.

Eells, Hastings. *Martin Bucer.* New Haven, 1931.

Ficker, Johannes. *Thesaurus Baumianus, Verzeichnis der Briefe und Aktenstücke.* Strassburg, 1905.

________, and Winckelmann, Otto. *Handschriftproben des sechzehnten Jahrhunderts nach Strassburger Originalen*, 2 vols. Strassburg, 1905.

Fragements des anciennes chroniques d'Alsace. Vol. 1: *La Chronique Strasbourgeoise de Sebald Büheler*; Vol. 2: *Les Collectanées de Daniel Specklin*; Vols. 3 and 4: *Annales de Brant* [divided between Vol. 3 and Vol. 4, cited as *Annales* I or II] *La Chronique de Jaques Trausch* and *La Chronique de Jean Wencker.* Strassburg, 1892-1901.

Fuchs, Joseph. "Le Droit de bourgeoisie à Strasbourg," in *Revue d'Alsace*, 101. 1962.

________. "Les Prechter de Strasbourg, une famille de négotiants banquiers du XVI siècle," in *Revue d'Alsace*, 95. 1956.

________. "Richesse et faillite des Ingold, négotiants et financiers Strasbourgeois du XVI siècle," in *La Bourgeoisie Alsacienne. Publications de la Société Savante d'Alsace et des Régions de l'Est.* Strasbourg, 1954.

Gerbert, Camill. *Geschichte der Strassburger Sectenbewegung zur Zeit der Reformation, 1524-1534.* Strassburg, 1889.

Grabner, Adolph. *Zur Geschichte des Zweiten Nürnberger Reichsregimentes 1521-1523. Historische Studien* XLI. Berlin, 1903.

Grimm, Jacob and Grimm, Wilhelm. *Deutsches Wörterbuch.* Leipzig, 1935.

Hatt, Jacques. *Liste des membres du Grand Sénat de Strasbourg, des stettmeistres, des ammeistres, des conseils des XXI, XIII et des XV du XIIIe siècle à 1789.* Strasbourg, 1963.

________. "Les Métiers Strasbourgeois du XIIIe au XVIIIe siècles," in *Revue d'Alsace*, 101. 1962.

________. *Une ville du XVe siècle: Strasbourg.* Strasbourg, 1929.

Hedio, Caspar. *Von dem zehenden zwo trefflicher predig Beschehen im Münster zu Strassburg.* Strassburg, 1924.

Hofmann, Konrad. *Die Engere Immunität in Deutschen Bischofsstädten im Mittelalter.* Inaugural-Dissertation, University of Tübingen. Paderborn, 1914.

Knobloch von, J. Kindler. *Das Goldene Buch von Strassburg.* Wien, 1886.

Knod, Gustav C. *Die Stiftsherren von St. Thomas zu Strassburg, 1518-1548.* Strassburg, 1892.

Koch, Karl. *Studium Pietatis; Martin Bucer als Ethiker.* Neukirchen-Vluyn, 1962.

Kohler, Walther. *Zwingli und Luther, ihr Streit über das Abendmahl nach seinen politischen und religiösen Beziehungen*, 2 vols. *Quellen und Forschungen zur Reformationsgeschichte* 6-7. Leipzig, 1924-53.

Kohls, Ernst-Wilhelm. *Die Schule bei Martin Bucer in ihrem Verhältnis zu Kirche und Obrigkeit. Pädagogische Forschungen. Veröffentlichungen des Comenius-Instituts*, 22. Heidelberg, 1963.

Krebs, Manfred and Rott, Hans Georg. *Quellen zur Geschichte der Taüfer 7, Elsass I, Stadt Strassburg 1522-1532.* Gütersloh, 1959.

Krüger, Friedheim. *Bucer und Erasmus: Eine Untersuchung z. Einfluss d. Erasmus auf die Theologie Martin Bucers. Veröffentlichung des Instituts für Europäische Geschichte, Abt. Abendländische Religionsgeschichte*, Bd. 57. Wiesbaden, 1970.

Landmann, Florenz. "Thomas Murner als Prediger." *Archiv für Elsässische Kirchengeschichte*, 10. 1935.

________. "Zur Charakteristik Thomas Murners." *Archiv für Elsässische Kirchengeschichte*, 15. 1941-42.

Lang, August. *Der Evangelienkommentar Martin Butzers und die Grundzüge seiner Theologie. Studien zur Geschichte der Theologie und der Kirche*, Zweite Band, Heft 2. Leipzig, 1900.

Langsdorff von, Karl Georg Wilhelm. *Die deutsche-protestantische Politik Jacob Sturms von Strassburg.* Inaugural-Dissertation, University of Heidelberg. Leipzig, 1904.

Lévy-Mertz, Georges. "Le Commerce Strasbourgeois au XVe siècle," in *Revue d'Alsace*, 97. 1958.

Luther, Martin. *Werke. Kritische Gesamtausgabe.* Weimar, 1883.

Mann, Julius. *Die Kirchenpolitik der Stadt Strassburg am Ausgang des Mittelalters.* Inaugural-Dissertation, Kaiser-Wilhelms Universität. Strassburg, 1914.

Mieg, Philippe. "Note sur les négociants Strasbourgeois Muege au XVe siècle," in *Revue d'Alsace*, 98. 1959.

Mitchell, Charles B. "Martin Bucer and Sectarian Dissent." Unpublished Ph.d. thesis, Yale University. New Haven, Connecticut, 1960.

Moeller, Bernd. "Die deutschen Humanisten und die Anfänge der Reformation." *Zeitschrift für Kirchengeschichte*, 70. 1959.

________. "Kleriker als Bürger" in *Festschrift für Hermann Heimpel zum 70. Geburtstag* II. Göttingen, 1972.

________. *Pfarrer als Bürger. Göttinger Universitätsreden*, 56. Göttingen, 1972.

________. "Piety in Germany around 1500," in *The Reformation in Medieval Perspective.* Edited by Steven Ozment. Chicago, 1971.

________. *Reichsstadt und Reformation. Schriften des Vereins für Reformationsgeschichte*, 180, Jahrgang 69, Gütersloh, 1962.

Moeller, Bernd. "Zwinglis Disputationen: Studien zu den Anfängen der Kirchenbildung und des Synodalwesens in Protestantismus." *Zeitschrift der Savigny-Stiftung für Rechtsgeschichte* 56. 1970.

Müller, Johannes. *Martin Bucers Hermeneutik.* Gütersloh, 1965.

Murner, Thomas. *Der Schelmenzunft. Deutsche Schriften*, vol. III, 1925.

Oberman, Heiko. *Forerunners of the Reformation: the Shape of Late Medieval Thought.* New York, 1966.

Ozment, Steven. *Homo Spiritualis.* Leiden, 1969.

_______. "Marriage and the Ministry in the Protestant Churches." *Concilium* 8, 1972.

_______. *Mysticism and Dissent.* New Haven, 1973.

Pauck, Wilhelm. *Das Reich Gottes auf Erden: Utopie und Wirklichkeit.* Berlin and Leipzig, 1928.

Pelikan, Jaroslav. *Spirit versus Structure: Luther and the Institutions of the Church.* New York, 1968.

Peter, Rodolphe. "Le Jardinier Clement Ziegler, L'homme et son oeuvre." Unpublished thèse de baccalaureate en théologie. University of Strasbourg, 1954.

Pfleger, Luzian. *Kirchengeschichte der Stadt Strassburg in Mittelalter. Forschungen zur Kirchengeschichte des Elsass*, 6. Colmar, 1941.

Pollet, J.v., ed. *Martin Bucer, études sur la correspondance*, 2 vols. Paris, 1959-62.

Rapp, Francis. "Ce qu'il en coutait d'argent et de démarches pour obtenir de Rome la confirmation d'une élection épiscopale. Le cas de Guillaume de Honstein, évêque de Strasbourg en 1506," in *Revue d'Alsace*, 101. 1962.

_______. *Institutions écclésiastiques et gens d'église: Abus et réformes dans le diocèse de Strasbourg 1450-1525.* Unpublished thèse de Doctorat d'Etat. University of Strasbourg, 1972.

_______. "L'Eveque de Strasbourg, Guillaume de Honstein, et la Réformation." *Revue d'histoire et de philosophie réligieuses.* Strasbourg, 1974.

_______. "Recherches sur l'histoire sociale de l'Eglise; Haut et bas clergé dans le diocese de Strasbourg à la veille de la Réform," in *Revue d'Alsace*, 103. 1965.

Reuss, Rodolphe. *Histoire d'Alsace.* Paris, 1920.

_______. *Histoire de Strasbourg.* Paris, 1922.

Ritter, Francois. *Catalogue des incunables et livres du XVIe siècle de la Bibliothèque municipale de Strasbourg.* Strasbourg, 1948.

________. *Catalogue des livres du XVIe siècle ne figurant pas à la Bibliothèque nationale universitaire de Strasbourg.* Strasbourg, 1960.

________. *Répertoire bibliographique des livres imprimés en Alsace au 16me siècle de la Bibliothèque nationale et universitaire de Strasbourg*, 3 parts. Strasbourg, 1932-45.

Röhrich, Timotheus Wilhelm. *Geschichte der Reformation im Elsass und besonders in Strassburg*, 3 vols. Strassburg, 1830-32.

________. *Mittheilungen aus der Geschichte der Evangelischen Kirche des Elsasses*, 3 vols. Strassburg, 1855.

Rott, Jean. "Artisanat et mouvements sociaux à Strasbourg," in *Artisans et ouvriers d'Alsace. Publications de la Société savante d'Alsace et des Régions de l'Est*, 9. Strasbourg, 1965.

________. "L'Humaniste Strasbourgeois Nicholas Gerbel et son diaire (1522-1529)," Extrait du *Bulletin Philologique et Historique* (jusqu'à 1715), 1946-47. Paris, 1950.

Schimpf, Anselme. "Les tailleurs de pierre Strasbourgeois" in *Artisans et ouvriers d'Alsace. Publications de la Société savante d'Alsace et des Régions de l'Est*, 9. Strasbourg, 1965.

Schmidt, Charles. *Histoire du chapitre de Saint Thomas de Strasbourg pendant le moyen age.* Strasbourg, 1860.

________. *Histoire littéraire de l'Alsace*, 2 vols. Paris, 1879.

Schmidt, Gerhart. *Martin Bucer als Protestantischer Politiker.* Borsdorf-Leipzig, 1936.

Schmoller, Gustav. *Strassburg zur Zeit der Zunftkämpfe und die Reform seiner Verfassung und Verwaltung. Quellen und Forschungen zur Sprach- und Kulturgeschichte der Germanische Völker*, 11. Strassburg, 1875.

Schultz, Rudolf. *Martin Butzers Anschauung von der christlichen Oberkeit.* Inaugural-Dissertation. University of Freiburg, 1932.

Sigmund von Hohenlohe. *Kreuzbüchlein.* Edited by Johannes Ficker, *Quellen und Forschungen zur Kirchen und Kulturgeschichte von Elsass und Lothringen*, 1. Strassburg, 1913.

Sittler, Lucien. "Les associations artisanales en Alsace au moyen age et sous l'ancien régime," in *Revue d'Alsace*, 97. 1958.

Sittler, Lucien. "Les Mouvements sociaux à Colmar du XIVe au XVIe siècle," in *Revue d'Alsace*, 95. 1956.

Skalwalt, Stephan. *Reich und Reformation.* Berlin, 1967.

Spijker, W. van 't. *De ambten bij Martin Bucer.* Kampen, Kok, 1970.

Stenzel, Karl. *Die Politik der Stadt Strassburg am Ausgang der Mittelalters.* Inaugural-Dissertation. Strassburg, 1914.

Stephens, W. Peter. *The Holy Spirit in the Theology of Martin Bucer.* London, 1970.

Strauss, Gerald, ed. *Manifestations of Discontent in Germany on the Eve of the Reformation.* Bloomington, Indiana, 1971.

Strohl, Henri. *Bucer, humaniste chrétien. Cahiers de la Revue d'histoire et de philosophie religieuses*, 29. Paris, 1939.

________. "Bucer interprète de Luther," in *Revue d'histoire et de philosophie religieuses XIX.* 1939.

________. "La Notion d'église chez Bucer dans son développement historique," in *Revue d'histoire et de philosophie religieuses*, 13. 1933.

________. "La Théorie et la pratique de quatre ministères à Strasbourg avant l'arivée de Calvin," in *Bulletin de la Société de l'histoire du protestantisme français*, 84. 1935.

________. "Traité de l'Amour du Prochain," in *Cahiers de la Revue d'histoire et de philosophie religieuses*, no. 32. 1949.

Stupperich, Robert. *Bibliographia Bucerana. Schriften des Vereins für Reformationsgeschichte*, 169, Jahrgang 58, Heft 2, Gütersloh, 1952.

________. "Brüderdienst und Nächstenhilfe in der deutschen Reformation," in *Das Diakonische Amt der Kirche.* Stuttgart, 1953.

________. "Bucers Anschauungen von der Kirche." *Zeitschrift für systematische Theologie*, 17. 1940.

________. "Die Kirche in M. Bucers theologischer Entwicklung." *Archiv für Reformationsgeschichte*, 58. 1938.

Virck, Hans. *Politische Correspondenz der Stadt Strassburg im Zeitalter der Reformation. Urkunden und Akten der Stadt Strassburg*, vol. 1. Strassburg, 1882-98.

Wendel, Francois. *Calvin, sources et évolution de sa pensée religieuse.* Paris, 1950.

Wendel, Francois. *L'Eglise de Strasbourg, sa constitution et son organization, 1532-1535. Etudes d'histoire et de philosophie religieuses publiés par la Faculté de Théologie protestante de l'Université de Strasbourg*, 38. Paris, 1942.

________. *Le Mariage à Strasbourg à l'époque de la Réforme, 1520-1692. Collection d'études sur l'histoire du droit et des institutions de l'Alsace*, 4. Strasbourg, 1928.

Williams, George H. *The Radical Reformation*. London, 1962.

Winckelmann, Otto. *Das Fürsorgewesen der Stadt Strassburg vor und nach der Reformation bis zum Ausgang der sechzehnten Jahrhunderts. Quellen und Forschungen zur Reformationsgeschichte*, 5. Leipzig, 1922.

________. "Strassburgs Verfassung und Verwaltung in 16ten Jahrhundert." *Zeitschrift für die Geschichte des Oberrheins*, N.F. 18. 1903.

Wingren, Gustav. *Luther on Vocation*. Translated by Carl. C. Rasmussen. Philadelphia, 1957.

Wittmer, Charles and Meyer, J. Charles. *Le Livre de bourgeoisie de la ville de Strasbourg, 1440-1530*, 3 vols. Strasbourg, 1948-61.

Zell, Mathis. *Christeliche Verantwortung*. Strassburg, 1523.

________. *Ein Collation auff die einfuerung M. Anthonii Pfarherrs zu S. Thomans zu Strassburg/ unnd Katherine seines eelichen gemahels/ von Mattheo Zeel von Keyserssbergk Pfarrherrn im hohen stifft da selbst/ do auch dise einfürung beschehen ist*. Strasbourg, 1523.

Ziegler, Clemens. *Ein fast schon büchlin in welche vederman findet ein hellen und claren verstandt von dem leib und blut Christi*. Strasbourg, 1525.

Zimmermann, Jean-Robert. *Les compagnons de métiers à Strasbourg. Publications de la Société Savante d'Alsace et des Régions de l'Est. Collection "Recherches et Documents,"* tome x. Strasbourg, 1971.

Zwingli, Ulrich. *Werke*. *Corpus Reformatorum*, 8. Leipzig, 1914.